Poetry & Money

Poetry & ...

Series Editors

Ralph Pite *University of Bristol*
Deryn Rees-Jones *University of Liverpool*

Series Board

Peter Barry *Aberystwyth University*
Neil Corcoran *University of Liverpool*
James Longenbach *University of Rochester, USA*
Jan Montefiore *University of Kent*
Barbara Page *Vassar College, USA*
Marjorie Perloff *Stanford University, USA*
Adam Piette *University of Sheffield*
Stan Smith *Nottingham Trent University*

Also in this series

Poetry & Money

A Speculation

Peter Robinson

LIVERPOOL UNIVERSITY PRESS

First published 2020 by
Liverpool University Press
4 Cambridge Street
Liverpool
L69 7ZU

British Library Cataloguing-in-Publication data
A British Library CIP record is available

ISBN 978 1 78962 253 9 cased

Typeset by Carnegie Book Production, Lancaster
Printed and bound by CPI Group (UK) Ltd, Croydon CR0 4YY

for Ornella, Matilde & Giulia

Contents

Preface

Thinking towards *Poetry & Money: A Speculation* began when I discovered that the special topic for a paper being taught at Cambridge during the early 1980s would be 'Literature and Money', and I was invited by Adrian Poole to give two lectures in a series he was organizing. The first, on Victorian and Decadent poetry, was called 'Speculative Diction and Jingling Rhymes', and the second, on modern poems, 'Contracts and Prophets'. Soon after, I gave a paper focused on contemporary poets and money to a graduate seminar – after which Christopher Ricks contacted me about the topic, strongly urging that I continue with it. We met and he suggested I get in touch with an academic publisher who specialized in short intensive studies of unusual subjects. But I didn't have a book. What I had was the idea that I was writing a book on the subject of poetry and money, which has been carried around for over forty years – and in that time my relations to both have, understandably enough, unpredictably evolved.

Life, and other projects, got in the way. Still, as a temporary lecturer at Aberystwyth, I gave another version of the 'Poetry and Money' research paper. The part related to Adrian Stokes's 'Weathering' had been developed for an essay first published in *PN Review* in 1981. About a decade later, asked to contribute to the magazine *Poetica*, edited from Tokyo, I dusted off and revised the second of those Cambridge lectures. Many years later, some passages from the first, 'Speculative Diction and Jingling Rhymes', were developed for parts of a chapter in *The Oxford Handbook of Victorian Poetry* (2013), which addressed poetry about prostitution, while the passage about Bernard Spencer's 'The Behaviour of Money' in the *Poetica* essay was extended for my introduction to *The Complete Poetry, Translations & Selected Prose* of Bernard Spencer (2011). Some of these published writings and other materials have been drawn upon, revised, and adapted here.

Back in the early 1990s, Kevin Jackson contacted me about including a poem of mine called 'Plain Money', its title from the writings of John Ruskin on this subject, in *The Oxford Book of Money* (1995). This eventually provided an opportunity to acquaint myself with its editor's extraordinary gathering of poetry and prose. Though his book is not the textual source for which *Poetry & Money* might be a commentary, it would not have been the same without the hints, guesses, and insights provided by his labours of love and money. A few years before this anthology appeared, life had once again intervened, in the form of a serious health problem and a change in my affective life. Neither of these lessened my interest in the topic, but they removed the occasion to research it – or better, the impulse passed into poetry, where poems being written and published continued to be shadowed with reflections on the intersection of these two symbolic structures and forms of life.

Returning to live and work in England in 2007, we were in time first to put down a mortgage on a home, and then to experience at first hand the Credit Crunch of 2008–09. What followed, in the form of austerity, though there are many who have experienced it as impoverishment, reminded me of much learned back in childhood and youth, as well as returning me to poems by a host of writers concerning money that over so many years had kept coming to my attention. Since the idea of this book first germinated in the early 1980s, there has emerged the so-called New Economic Criticism, and I have done my best to take account of its various writers, publications, and findings, as can be tracked in footnotes to the chapters and the bibliography.

There are as many reasons why poets might be interested in money as there are for anybody else; those reasons, though, naturally divide between why they are interested as any of us might be, for reasons of continuance and survival, security and self-esteem, and why they might be interested in it strictly *as poets*. This latter itself can be a question that admits of different explanations, for there are particular historical reasons why poets, in relation to their identities as writers of poems, have been interested in money for their survival (in the sense that different human vocations and occupations attract different amounts of remuneration), and why they might, as poets in the act of composing or thinking about poetry, be especially interested in money. What follows is a sequence of chapters on the metaphors, paradoxes, contradictions, and mysteries which link but also divide these two very old ways of attributing value to, or deriving it from, human life.

Among key distinctions will be the difference between money as an actual unit of exchange in an economy, including instances of material tokens for such exchange, coins and notes, on the one hand, and on the other, money as a form of mental attention, a way of accessing material objects and the material world not merely in actual exchanges where currency is offered for goods, but in the more abstract circumstances where envy, for instance, can motivate the desire for something which is necessarily calculated not only in the terms of the object desired that another possesses, but also the economic power that would be necessary to achieve that state of imagined improvement: so that money is not only a means for facilitating exchange, but everywhere to be discerned in states of mind and motivations for action – and also, matter for poetic and literary thought and work. A further set of preliminary discriminations, which will resonate throughout, are those between conditions of barter, precious metals, coinage, paper money, cheques, credit cards, transfer mandates – in other words, the scale of 'currencies' from near brute through to the most rarefied of institutional facts, which now include electronic communications of data. The importance of these distinctions for thinking about poetry and money becomes clearer in discussions of attributed value in appreciation (whether, for instance, poems, too, are institutional facts), and in the history of themes and metaphors that have populated poems down the centuries.

The ten chapters of *Poetry & Money* have emerged with the following shape: the first three are introductory and approach the theme from their related angles; the central four are arranged more or less chronologically from the later sixteenth to the twentieth centuries and beyond, with topics emerging from economic conditions and poetic responses to them; the final three draw the book to a conclusion by focusing on the conditions of trust that may be active in both poetry and money. The book touches on the following issues: the difficulties that poets (like innumerable other people at one time or another) have faced as regards having enough money to keep going; the difficult relations that poetry has almost always had with the marketplace, and why that should be, with illustration of a characteristic case in the publishing history of a particular volume, as well as some happily less usual ones; the use of metaphors from gold, money, wealth, and poverty in poetry; the analogies between the nature and behaviour of money and of poetry, poetic form, and language, including ways in which the movement and value of poetry may or may not resist that of money; the efforts made by some poets and writers on poetry to reserve and preserve the value of poetry from its being tainted by exchange value, with how and why this may misfire in practice, suggesting that, despite the evident differences between the realms of money and of poetry, there is much to learn, and reconcile ourselves to, by considering their interrelations.

The core aim of the book is, then, to explore two very different, but inextricably interrelated, human instruments for the attribution of value to the world. Both of them are so old as to have origins before recorded history, and both are now in, or taken to be in, states of near-perpetual crisis. So this book will also be a contribution to discussions about value in art and its relation to what is called instrumental value in a scientific and seemingly thoroughly market-driven culture. It will therefore, by the by, be a defence of poetry as a form of life, and a defence of money as a medium of exchange at the service of human communities and cultures. It will also be an exploration of metaphor in poetry and in the structuring of rituals and institutions.

Both poetry and money illustrate, often starkly, a necessarily doubled attribution of value: when in use they both give value to objects and actions in life, and they both need, for this to be effective, to have belief in their value sustained. Furthermore, while this value requires the active presence of an institutional framework in which value can be asserted, to formulate it in this way is to underplay both the necessity of active belief in the functioning and value of those institutions, and the requirement that this active belief be transactional, and have co-active uptake from engaged and informed others. Economic crises are situations in which the working of finance and money is made visible precisely when it shows signs of breaking down. The poetry of economic crisis similarly draws attention to the ordinary functioning of language, and to poetic language, because they are suddenly seen to be under the threat of no longer working.

Thus, though these two means of recognizing and attributing value in and to the world show homologies consistent with their both being and involving human practices, as this book will show and illustrate, the struggles between them have revealed conflicting values in their evaluating actions. The book offers examples of poetry engaged in the attributing and granting of counter-values, in circumstances where economic forces appear to endanger the survival of such values; examples of poetry scarred by being in such direct conflict with unhappy conditions; and poems in which the desire to avoid contamination with 'exchange value' can damage the exchange values of its own human activity. Poetry, if it is to exist and continue to exist (for it is not unimaginable that a state of society could develop in which it had died out), has to adapt itself to whatever economic conditions befall. In the concluding sections of the book, I look at how, despite its dependence upon material and labour costs, upon 'consumer' confidence and market conditions, poetry has benefitted from its minimal material base and consequent smallness of up-front economic investment. It will thus be an account of how this particular cultural activity has resisted, as best it can, the necessity of money and attempted to survive despite countervailing, or amidst unsympathetic, market and monetizing forces.

So the inextricability of money from all aspects of life appears as both a problem and, perhaps, an opportunity. It is a practical problem too, because there is so much poetry related to money, and so much writing on poets that inevitably touches on their financial situations, that there is no beginning or end of it. What I have done is to spin a thread to follow through a labyrinth. The examples chosen cannot be exhaustive, as neither can the argument developed; nor do those examples, strictly speaking, illustrate the thread of argument, because in most cases it was encountering them that suggested there was something to be said. The argument has emerged from its illustrations. And I have, understandably enough given my position in life, been obliged to find out about the workings of money at the same time as learning about the making and reading of poetry. Nor is there any getting to the end of either.

This book is, then, by no means a definitive account of the relationship proposed by its title, and its footnotes aim not only to attribute sources and suggest further reading, but also to indicate other poems not discussed and to point towards roads that could not be taken. I regret not being able to spend more time on poems not written in English, but there wasn't space enough even to discuss all of those in my own first language. As already suggested, the ubiquity of the money theme is effected not least by means of metaphor, the understanding of one thing in terms of another, and this doesn't seem accidental either, for it is as if money were itself a form of figuration, an intermediary allowing us to understand one thing as another, whether it be relations between the work we do and the things we can afford to buy, getting and spending, or between what we have to put on the market and what we can then go out and purchase, buying and selling. A final point about what the book is not: it does not and cannot pretend to be an economic history, or a history of coinage, or of the workings of money, and only touches upon these, in the light of others' writings on them, if and when they intersect with the reading and understanding of the poems about money chosen for attention here. In this sense the title of the book, with its collocating ampersand, indicates the single entity it addresses; and while I have some history of writing, and writing about, the former element, I can make no special claim to understand the latter, and in this assume myself not unlike many, perhaps most, of my readers.

So this book might be thought the repayment of a debt incurred with myself. I have tried to keep its style and mode as personal as possible, and not only for that reason. After all, if one of money's powers is to interpose itself between persons, and to turn even this attempt of mine to communicate with you into a transaction which can only be facilitated by your financially inflected access to one or other forms of its dissemination, then the best I can do to counteract that interposition is to make what I have to say as personal a gift of myself as this literary critical genre, with its editorial principles and ideas of marketability, will allow.

Attempting to follow a thread through poetry related to money from the late Middle Ages to the present day might be considered a quixotic project, and I thank the many colleagues who have provided aid on the way. For advice with regard to poetry from the medieval and early modern periods, I am particularly grateful to Aisling Byrne, Mary Morrissey, and Helen Hackett. Much of *Poetry & Money* was written while employed by the University of Reading, and I was aided in completing it by a term of research leave in early 2019, for which I was and am most grateful, and particularly indebted to Gail Marshall, Michelle O'Callaghan, Peter Stoneley, Steven Matthews, and David Brauner. Many others have contributed to the evolution of this book, including an unnamed financial advisor or two, as well as some people working in the 'financial industry' that have experienced the mixed fortunes of having me and mine, that's to say Ornella Trevisan, my wife, and our daughters Matilde and Giulia, to whom I have dedicated this book, as clients. Christopher Ricks's early encouragement has already been mentioned, and the example of J. H. Prynne's poetry and conversation coincided with that help. I would also like to mention the encouragement and stimulus of spending some years as the sponsor for post-doctoral research conducted by Natalie Pollard and Matthew Sperling at the University of Reading, the former working on lyric economies and the later on the economics of small-press publishing.

Why, you might be wondering, did I not simply make the book available through what is now called open access? One answer would be that, aside from the support of my employing institution noted above, I have received no grants or other external support for its writing from any funding body. Open access in the humanities, as I am not the first to note, may be a further way in which the cultural value of what we do can be sold down the river. Nobody would get far suggesting to scientists that they give away their patented discoveries, even if their cutting-edge-today-dated-tomorrow research papers are, for the most part, as durable as mayflies. In the humanities our writings are the thing itself, not announcements of evidence that discoveries have occurred. So you see, I'm just the same as anyone else when it comes to wanting to monetize my activity, though only too aware that the man-hours which have gone into it, and the value which I hope others may derive from it, do not have an appropriate monetary value. So if you have bought your own copy of this book, my thanks go out to you, and if you are reading a library copy, then don't forget someone has ordered and purchased it to facilitate its value, and not only for money, in your life and studies. *Poetry & Money* is on many counts, as its subtitle indicates, *A Speculation*; and I'll be forever in your debt if you'll trust it to give benefit, and to deserve credit where credit is due.

PR   *30 November 2019*

CHAPTER ONE

Introductory issues

1. Co-operative activity, credit, and trust

Some while ago I was teaching a creative writing class, attempting to interest the assembled students in an exemplary show-don't-tell short story. The class was not going especially well – for I was hearing too much of my own voice. So I asked them: 'What do you think of it then?' 'I wouldn't pay money to read it,' muttered one of the students. 'You're paying nine-thousand pounds a year to read it,' came back another. Rather than a laugh, this lightning-quick and witty truth was met all round with a grimly ironic, an almost stoical silence from the room. And I was silenced too. For what would I dare to say, given that they were also paying their tuition fees for the next words that would come from my mouth? Foregrounding the cash value of tertiary education in future earning power had meant that having access to my accumulated knowledge, wisdom, and pedagogical skills needed to be worth not only the fees and loans for rent and living expenses, but also the 6% interest charged on the debt.[1]

To exemplify such problems of cost-benefit analysis, I might have referred them to John Maynard Keynes's 1927 essay 'Are Books Too Dear?'[2] Raising its issues could have led to a discussion about the history of the book, and how the publishing trade manages its debit and credit columns, taking on and spreading risk in new volumes. I could have invited reflection on what it had cost, as far back as our show-don't-tell author composing his story onto a 1920s typewriter, to bring that story before their eyes – and to reflect upon the economic exchanges that had taken place to make our

---

[1] My younger daughter, completing a degree at the time, assumed (in both senses) a debt of some £50,000 so as to become employable at a level that will facilitate its repayment.

[2] Donald Moggridge (ed.), *The Collected Writings of John Maynard Keynes,* vol. 19, *Activities 1922–1929: The Return to Gold and Industrial Policy* (London: Macmillan, 1981), vol. 2, 664–70.

reading and discussing possible long before they entered my room, got out their laptops or smartphones, and settled down to engage or not.[3]

Alternatively, I might have pulled down a copy of Wallace Stevens's *Necessary Angel*, and read out this passage from 'Imagination as Value':

> To me, the accumulation of lives at a university has seemed to be a subject that might disclose something extraordinary. What is the residual effect of the years we spend at a university, the years of imaginative life, if ever in our lives there are such years, on the social form of our own future and on the social form of the future of the world of which we are part, when compared with the effects of our later economic and political years?[4]

Writing in 1948, Stevens is able to imagine university life, however costly in fees and expenses, as a space independent from, or prior to, 'economic and political' activities. Yet this is precisely what those contemporary students had been obliged to doubt, because the effect of 'imaginative life' on the 'social form of our own future' or 'the future of the world' has become too luxuriously abstract a value to be priced into the monetary investment, an investment evaluated in so far as it maximizes those students' 'later economic' contributions, whether to themselves, or to their nation's GDP.

Equally I might have invited them to reflect on how, as Bernard Williams reminds us, a 'necessary condition of co-operative activity is trust, where this involves the willingness of one party to rely on another to act in certain ways', and the philosopher notes the connection that this trusting and trustworthy behaviour has to motivation in economic theory: 'A may trust B to do something because A knows that B expects punishment if he fails to do it. In this case B's motives for co-operating are crudely and immediately egoistic', but they may be less so, as when 'B may have an interest in long-term co-operative activities with A and may believe that if he defaults on this occasion, A will not trust him again. This is the motivation that Adam Smith famously found reassuring in his baker.'[5] But,

---

3   For reflections on 'The Political Economy of Reading', see William St Clair, *The Reading Nation in the Romantic Period* (Cambridge: Cambridge University Press, 2004), 433–51.

4   Wallace Stevens, 'Imagination as Value', in *Collected Poetry and Prose,* ed. Frank Kermode and Joan Richardson (New York: Library of America, 1997), 733.

5   Bernard Williams, *Truth and Truthfulness: An Essay in Genealogy* (Princeton: Princeton University Press, 2002), 88. He alludes to Adam Smith, *The Wealth of Nations* Book 1, Chapter 1, paragraph 2: 'It is not from the benevolence of the butcher, the brewer, or the baker that we expect our dinner, but from their regard to their own interest.' See also Simon Jarvis, *Wordsworth's Philosophic Song* (Cambridge: Cambridge University Press, 2009), 99.

alas, the students were in the last teaching term of their final year. Both monitory and future-collaborative motivations were weakening fast.

Williams further notes that 'Trustworthiness as a *particular* type of disposition comes in against a more settled background, in which patterns of co-operation are established, and people are standardly trusted to do their part in a venture in which, for instance, they make their contribution after the other parties have made theirs.'[6] It was in such a 'settled background' that a co-operative response had been requested, a request disturbed by two of the forms in which trust enables human social processes coming into nullifying conflict. For if the conversational exchanges that make up such an educational occasion require mutually trusting expectations to be fulfilled, so too do the economic exchanges with their monetary instruments which enabled our being there to have the conversation. The currency itself – the money they would or wouldn't pay to read the story – is also a 'settled background' of promise, trust, and credit, which reinforces our belonging to an economy by confirming its symbolic representations – including the portraits of writers such as William Shakespeare and Jane Austen that have graced them.[7]

Yet when Alexander Pope asks in 'The Fourth Satire of Dr. John Donne, Versified' who 'makes a *Trust*, or *Charity*, a Job, / And gets an Act of Parliament to rob?',[8] the word '*Trust*' figures ambivalently on both sides of these accounts. Mary Poovey has asserted that, not long after Pope wrote his couplet, by the 1740s writers were denying that literary and literal writing about money, or as money, had equal traction, and

> this denial began to take the form of generic distinctions (novels as opposed to financial commentary, political economic systems as opposed to romances), which were increasingly equated with – or used to define – the distinction between fact and fiction. Left suspended by these disavowals were specific words – like *credit* and *value* – that retained a place in the lexicons of both sets of genres and that remained as switchpoints or sites of overlap between them, even as these concepts became central to the function of various kinds of money.[9]

---

6 Williams, *Truth and Truthfulness*, 89.
7 A great many countries have images of poets on their currency. Bosnia and Herzegovina, for instance, has, since its independence in 1998, chosen to have only poets, eight of them, plus one Nobel-Prize-winning short-story writer, on its convertible Marka.
8 Alexander Pope, Imitations of Horace *with* An Epistle to Dr Arbuthnot *and* The Epilogue to the Satires, ed. John Butt, Twickenham Edition, vol. 4 (London: Methuen, 1939), 37.
9 Mary Poovey, *Genres of the Credit Economy: Mediating Value in Eighteenth-Century and Nineteenth-Century Britain* (Chicago: Chicago University Press, 2008), 17.

The word 'trust', through its ambivalence, serves as a key switch-point or site of overlap linking together the formal institutional fact of money, as John Searle defined it, with the informal ones that are poems.[10] It is so deployed here because it can signify social bindings that differently characterize any collaborative activity, virtuous or vicious – and the word's uses range from indicating a strictly faith-requiring trust in God, through the tested behaviour of said-to-be-trustworthy persons, to the financial arrangements that are trust funds, and by metaphorical extension even to the name for a group of public intellectuals: a Brains Trust.[11]

Still, at that moment in my seminar it appeared that the monetary value of educational investment could only be seen as valuable in monetary terms. It was as if the national government had converted many of its young citizens into a speculative project, expecting a return on its investment for the lifetime of the debt, that the wisdom of its credit facility could be directly calculated in the length of time required to repay the interest-bearing sum, which, in turn, would depend upon the level of earning power leveraged in the employment market by the graduate of this or that university. This, in turn, had monetised higher education not in terms of the appropriate provision for any particular individual, but as a means to a monetarily calculated aspirational end. The recognized risk in this government speculation is that future national economic performance will not employ its investments at a sufficient level to repay the debt, turning them into future non-performing assets – a toxic debt-book such as had recently destroyed banks. At that moment in the seminar with which I began, the metaphorical power of money beneficially to evaluate and enable other phenomena, such as that collaboratively educational 'social form' of a mutual benefit to future life indicated by Stevens, had, at least momentarily, faltered.

One difficulty with a monetary value is that this evaluation itself only has a value if convertible into a different non-monetary value. This is how money functions to enable the exchange of materially incommensurate goods. It is a reason why profits made on the stock market tend to be converted into property or other material wealth in order to precipitate out, as conspicuous consumption, for instance, from the mere and endless fluctuations of abstract capital expressed in rapidly shifting numbers. But if the incurring of student debt is valued in relation to the promise of future

---

[10]   See John Searle, *The Construction of Social Reality* (New York: Free Press, 1995), 87–8. The distinction is applied to the understanding of poetry's social performativity in my *Poetry, Poets, Readers: Making Things Happen* (Oxford: Oxford University Press, 2002), 2–5.

[11]   See *OED* meanings 1–6 for positive senses related to reliability, meaning 7 being the first economic sense synonymous with 'credit' from 1509, and meaning 8 from 1825 being a group of companies organized to reduce competition and the like.

salary, tax-paying, and GDP, then you are evaluating a present number in the terms of a future number, and nothing of any other value seems added into or precipitated out of the justificatory equation. No ethical judgment is being made about what the future employees will do to repay the debt. Nor is 'added value' being calculated either in their individual lives or in communal contributions. At best, it is taken for granted from the lack of a measure for such added value. At worst, it is overlooked because thought irrelevant. But not only do supposedly value-free economic calculations undervalue other standards of worth, they effectively suck any such worth out of the activities that they monetarily calculate.

Now the thought that monetary exchanges should insist on themselves as the dominant, the dominating, and indeed the only idea in social transactions is by no means new.[12] A poem written in an earlier decade by a student poet not much older than those in that creative writing seminar, 'An Episode for Sarah' by John Wilkinson, moves with a vertiginous pace mimicking its scepticism about the basis of money in a society – 1970s Britain – which had recently abandoned the Bretton Woods Agreement that stabilized money in the aftermath of World War II. This resulted in a weakening of the currency both through trading on financial markets and inflation at home.[13] In this domestic interior poem from the first half of that decade, the lyric voice asserts 'I'll stay'

> so passive that money speaks, my being no more than
> unemployed for the season, teaches me my shortcoming
>
> my guarantee; I promise to pay the bearer on demand
>
> those fields of evidence the government taps for us
> of revenue, up to the hilt, we're the credit society
>
> now[14]

---

[12] Colin Nicholson not only has shown how the creation of specious credit drives the fourth book of Pope's *The Dunciad*, but finds its concerns close to Marx's in his writings from a century later. See *Writing and the Rise of Finance: Capital Satires of the Early Eighteenth Century* (Cambridge: Cambridge University Press, 1994), 195.

[13] Martin Amis, who blames it on OPEC, remembers that in 'the Sixties you could live on ten shillings a week' but then 'abruptly, a *bus fare* cost ten shillings'; *The War against Cliché: Essays and Reviews, 1971–2000* (London: Jonathan Cape, 2001), xii. In his novel *Money: A Suicide Note* (1984) John Self's parents give him a bill for his upbringing and education. See Nicky Marsh, *Money, Speculation and Finance in Contemporary British Fiction* (London: Continuum, 2007), 48–53.

[14] John Wilkinson, *Useful Reforms* (Richmond, Surrey: Arnica Press, 1975), unpaginated [25].

The poem deploys flexibly self-attentive line endings and eccentric punctuation in a series of attempts to slow down a rapidly inflationary circulation, one where the value of the currency is declining sharply, no longer guaranteed either by gold or a fixed rate of exchange. Such line endings are the overt signs of poetry's, and poetry about money's, great claim – which is to give a meaningful shape in rhythmical numbers to its numerical themes. Wilkinson's poem was composed at about the moment when, with a memorable adjustment in the meanings of words, sterling, unbacked by bullion, was described as 'floating downwards' on the money markets.[15] In 'An Episode for Sarah', the currency is looking around for what collateral it can find, while the young couple in the poem's interior are intent on finding some support, and the speaker is perhaps expected to go and do something, like get a job, rather than sit smoking in a chair, but 'we're the credit society / now' and it's the money speaks, promising 'to pay the bearer', the form of words for the promise to honour the currency's value in precious metal.

Wilkinson's early poem thus implies an almost universally held assumption that the history of money shows a development from material bases in either goods or precious metals to ever more abstract forms of symbolic representation, an assumption exemplified by a writer on art and money referring to the 'processes of abstraction that have become synonymous with modern finance, as wealth circulates through representations that become increasingly independent of their material origins'.[16] Others have argued, though, that, as exemplified by financial transactions in Mesopotamia from 2500 BCE, the need to abstract and symbolize (to calculate tax due on agricultural produce, for instance) precedes and enables the emergence of currency.[17] This, in turn, suggests that the human need for sociality to organize survival, and the concomitant power relations ensuing (indicated in Williams's discussion of trust, and his allusion to Adam Smith) were not produced by the calculating of debt and credit in money terms, but rather emerge from collaborative sociality as a means to its wider operation. Yet, as so often in human history, the tail wags the dog and the medium of exchange comes to impede exchange, as in that faltering of the seminar with which I began.

[15] Harold Wilson's devaluation of sterling by 14.3% on 18 November 1967 had occurred when the currency was still on what survived of the Bretton Woods system, meaning that it traded at a fixed exchange rate supported by Bank of England interventions in the market. It was the severe reduction of assets to this end that required the devaluation.

[16] Nicky Marsh, 'Debt and Credit', in *Show Me the Money: The Image of Finance, 1700 to the Present,* ed. Paul Crosthwaite, Peter Knight, and Nicky Marsh (Manchester: Manchester University Press, 2014), 8.

[17] See Matthew Rawlinson, *Real Money and Romanticism* (Cambridge: Cambridge University Press, 2010), 7–13.

In the mid-1970s, Wilkinson's poem implies, the getting and spending of money had become newly slippery, hard to hold onto or trust in, and though these lyric reflections momentarily come to rest at a line end, or in the poet's pocket, still the poem and the currency hurries on, its reader mimetically deceived by enjambments that promise some pause, but, like money too, won't stop long enough to redeem their promises, for the money is 'neither here nor there', again illustrating that 'we're the credit society'

now, I mustn't breathe at the neither here nor there

it is neither
here nor there, my lungs disturb you by rule of, of

nature, of nature, the funny careful rhetoric that

burns a hole in my trouser pocket slung on the chair.[18]

Caught up in the circulatory difficulties that it vocalizes as diagnosis, breath in his lungs being also poetic afflatus, the poem's haste and stammer alights on 'nature' as a grounding, as if ventriloquizing the sound of money speaking; thus it appears descriptive of the 'credit society' towards which it ironically glances. Because unable to slow the poem, the syntax and lineation affirm that its words are like promissory notes, in the words of Thomas Love Peacock (whom we shall encounter in later chapters), whose 'promise shall always be a payment, and the payment shall always be a promise.'[19] Yet though this poem, like its poet, has temporarily nothing to live on, it has been heading, all along, to a concealed – but conclusive-sounding – rhyme on the repeated 'there' and the final 'chair', with its sound affinity between an object in space and an intangible absence. This rhyme appears to be part of that 'funny careful rhetoric', which might include poetic technique, staging a tacit counterclaim of value in its straitened circumstances.

[18] Wilkinson, *Useful Reforms*, unpaginated [25]. The poem is indebted to such phrases as 'payment an edge of rhetoric' and 'cash as a principle of nature' in J. H. Prynne, 'A New Tax on the Counter-Earth', *Brass* (Lewes: Ferry Press, 1971), 34–5.

[19] Thomas Love Peacock, *Paper Money Lyrics and Other Poems* (London: C. and W. Reynell, 1837) in H. F. B. Brett-Smith and C. E. Jones (eds.), *The Works of Thomas Love Peacock*, vol. 7 (London: Constable, 1931), 100. Alan Jenkins borrowed Peacock's title for his *Paper-Money Lyrics* (London: Grey Suit Editions, 2014).

2. *Value for money*

In a situation such as that seminar, the assumed value of doing a thing for its own sake, for reasons that can also be described in terms of ethically weighed benefits to individuals and societies, had been stripped away to reveal the monetary cost, including the future indebtedness to specific individuals, of having access to these same cultural values.[20] Those students' words further revealed that such a stripping away had already been brought about elsewhere and in places of greater power – for the students were only reflecting the economy in which they found themselves obliged to gamble their present studies on the promise of more lucrative future employment. It is unsurprising, then, that when the higher arguments about cultural value are losing, or have lost, traction, the only value those students felt inclined to reach for was a monetary one. What my silence might also have represented, then, was the dawning realization that in such a situation when a money value is used to bottom out a precipitous slide, rather than finding secure ground in that money value, since it is one of exchange, I found myself tumbling further because unable to discover a way of evaluating that value other than by another monetary calculation – such as the cost in unemployment benefits or loss of GDP that might result from failing to educate appropriately these same young people.

My momentary silence may be related to the assumed power relations in the seminar, the sudden reversal by which my *raison-d'être* and the cultural sanction it received had been reversed by the producer-consumer relationship in our more thoroughly market-driven economy. I was selling my wares of literary skill and sensitivity towards a modern classic text, and they were buying into it, or not. As is regularly asked: were the students and taxpayer getting value for money from our universities? The universities, in turn, might ask whether taxpayers are provided with a suitable accounting model for evaluating whether as a sector they are producing an appropriate level of returns on investment; they may ask whether they are getting value for money from the politicians who have seemed set on improving 'standards' by monetizing everything, right down to the next sentence I would eventually utter to those creative writing students.

A fuller account of that moment in my room would need to explain how it was I came to be sitting there in front of those fifteen students, surrounded by hundreds and hundreds of poetry books in a variety of languages, including shelves full of volumes, magazines, and anthologies containing poems I had written myself; and how it was on the basis, somehow, of

---

[20] For a discussion of doing something 'For its Own Sake', as her chapter is entitled, also in relation to teaching in universities, see Helen Small, *The Value of the Humanities* (Oxford: Oxford University Press, 2013), 151–73.

the cultural capital, to recall Pierre Bourdieu's term, through which my parents had been able to 'invest in people', as celebratory institutional plaques boast, and the objectified cultural capital that I had accumulated through my efforts over the years, that the university was paying some of its economic capital in salary, so the sector's pension provider could have funds to invest for keeping my wife and me going through the potential decades of a twenty-first-century retirement. What's more, as we faced each other – those students and I – it would be more than possible that the young people, reminded of the debts with which they would be burdened on graduating and attempting to find work and so pay it back in taxes, might feel generational resentment towards the lucky man in front of them, someone who was being well enough paid to sit with them and discuss the value, or not, of that show-don't-tell short story.

Nevertheless, as I might have wondered then, and am wondering now, would the first student's comment ('I wouldn't pay money to read it') have been the same had I offered them an example of how to write a show-don't-tell *poem*? One reason why it might not is that fiction retains the social expectation that you will go online, or drop into an airport bookshop, for instance, to buy some to pass the time on a long flight, or when wishing to escape from the pressures of what you usually do to earn a living. Still, the common assumption nowadays would probably not be to indicate the badness of a poem by saying that you wouldn't go out and pay money to read it. Commentators would edit out the financial aspect and go straight to the idea that it's boring or sentimental, or it's *poetry* – so they can't understand and don't like it. Young people are, of course, capable of turning up their noses at poetry. They 'too, dislike it', for 'there are things that are important beyond all this fiddle', while, like Marianne Moore, the author of those phrases, they are able when reading 'with a perfect contempt for it' to discover in it 'after all, a place for the genuine.'[21] Yet they, too, may assume that poetry remains exempt from the value-for-money calculation – either because it's priceless ('the genuine') or because it's worthlessly unable to be monetized, and therefore fully deserving, whatever its cost, of that 'perfect contempt'.

3. Fixed price and immeasurable worth

This contrast between poetry's culturally precarious yet stubbornly resilient status and its conventional denigration is by no means unrelated to its connections with money, as has been noted regarding the being and value of Wordsworth's philosophic song:

---

[21] 'Poetry', in Marianne Moore, *New Collected Poems,* ed. Heather Cass White (New York: Farrar, Straus & Giroux, 2017), 27–8.

> Poems are themselves a kind of fetish or idol. They are historical
> objects which often claim a more than historical truth; particular
> objects which often claim a universal meaning; they are things
> which almost claim the dignity of persons, things which claim to
> have not just a fixed price but an unmeasurable worth.[22]

This passage, appropriately enough, exemplifies the condition it identifies. One way that poems may function as 'a kind of fetish or idol' in literary criticism is by the anthropomorphic attribution to the works themselves of an agency located elsewhere in human persons bracketed out.[23] In this prose it is the poems that 'claim' a 'more than historical truth', or a 'universal meaning', or almost the 'dignity of persons'. But they can do no such thing, although these claims can be made for them, as the critic does by reiterating them here. The fate of poems for which no such claims have been made – effective oblivion – might be a permanent reminder of their powerlessness as regards making such claims on their own behalf. What is true about Jarvis's observation, aside from its exemplifying the treatment of poems, residually, as 'fetish or idol', is their ability, despite everything, to figure in cultures as occasions for intensive debates over questions of value. Yet the formula is oddly inaccurate. Since nothing in our economy has a permanently 'fixed price', and some things, like airline tickets and hotel rooms being booked online, are adjustable in that very instant according to the electronically recognized supply and demand occurring, the contrast between 'fixed price' and 'unmeasurable worth' may not be appropriate to the conditions in which we buy volumes of poetry and read them.

W. S. Graham touches on a nexus of such relations when, in the penultimate section of 'A Private Poem to Norman Macleod', he too draws back the veil on the monetary grounds upon which its relation with the named interlocutor are based:

> But this, my boy, is the poem
> You paid me five pounds for.
> The idea of me making
> Those words fly together
> In seemingly a private
> Letter is just me choosing
> An attitude to make a poem.[24]

[22] Simon Jarvis, *Wordsworth's Philosophic Song*, 53.

[23] See my *The Sound Sense of Poetry* (Cambridge: Cambridge University Press, 2018), 75–8.

[24] W. S. Graham, *New Collected Poems*, ed. Matthew Francis (London: Faber & Faber, 2004), 227. For Graham's letters and his finances, see my 'Dependence in

These verses are directed both to the poem's named addressee and to the editor of the magazine where it first appeared, for Macleod (1906–85) was one and the same person. As a result, Graham's poem may uneasily straddle not only the space of private epistolary communication and published availability, but also that between giftlike community-affirming utterance and the needs-must of a poet with no other visible means of support than patronage charity and the miniscule market price of his writings. If these considerations indicate one end of poetry's fetish-idol status, the other is dramatized by the movement around the first line end, where the implicit claim in 'this ... is the poem' drops flatly down to 'You paid me five pounds for', or, in reverse, by how the section rises to conclude by reasserting the poet's agency, his 'choosing / An attitude to make a poem', where the stressed words 'make' and 'poem' affirm an independent status claim.

Poetry books have a cover price when new, but, unless caught up in the rare editions market, where other forms of fetish value come into play, you can find them in online second-hand sites for the price of the postage plus one penny. Thus our experience of poems in life is, rather, to find them of shifting and uncertain price, value, and worth. The larger the print run of a poetry book the more likely, when its bubble bursts, that copies will be found littering the neglected shelves of charity shops. At the same time, particular poems, John Keats's 'Ode on a Grecian Urn' for instance, whose value in the minds of readers depends upon its material existence in innumerable copies, including very cheap ones and online access, is not dependent on the survival of any one of these, and may now have a global 'worth' that cannot be measured, not least because there is no exchange value to measure it by. This worth, though, has to be kept up by the teaching and reading of Keats's poem wherever poetry is still appreciated and promulgated as contributing to a well-stocked mind.

I bought W. S. Graham's *Implements in their Places*, where 'A Private Poem to Norman Macleod' was first collected, around the time it was published in 1977. The book contained twenty-six titles and, at the rate Macleod paid for his poem, Graham ought to have been paid at least £130 for the right to publish the book at all (and probably more because the title poem is distinctly longer). The publisher would have needed to charge an appropriate price to cover printing costs, warehousing, and distribution, and the booksellers would need to deduct a third (as was standard then) for their profit margin. The publishers would have to make sufficient profit on the exercise to contribute proportionately to their overheads. The poet too could expect to be paid a percentage of the profit on the marketing of his work, over and above the price per poem – which is, in any case,

the Poetry of W. S. Graham', in *Twentieth Century Poetry: Selves and Situations* (Oxford University Press, 2005), 70–1.

usually offered as an advance against royalties from sales. The publisher, Faber & Faber, does not make its records available for public scrutiny.[25] The 1970s, though, was a difficult time for poetry publishing, and we can glimpse some of the travails through which it went by looking at what happened in one instance of that most precarious publishing venture, the issuing of a volume containing poems rendered from a different language.

Translations from the Night: Selected Poems of Jean-Joseph Rabearivelo (1901–37),[26] edited with English translations by John Reed and Clive Wake, appeared as African Writers Series 167 from Heinemann Educational Books in 1975. The series, which was inaugurated in 1962, had been edited for its first ten years by Chinua Achebe; among its greatest successes was the first publication, a reissue of Achebe's 1958 *Things Fall Apart*, a novel initially published in an edition of 2,000 copies which went on to sell many millions worldwide.[27] Such volumes as Achebe's are featured in histories of publishing houses because they support the directors' and editors' artistic taste, their cultural significance in the processes by which solitary persons composing works in obscurity are transformed into Nobel Prize Winners, and, last but – for commercial publishers – by no means least, their decisions are rewarded with substantial profits. In such cases, cultural and economic capital may coincide, acting as emblematic justifications for entire publishing enterprises. The opposite might be the case for the book whose publication I discuss here. In such cases, the interests of cultural and economic capital divide. The publishers are presented with dilemmas, and, in responding to them, they show their mettle.

Translations from the Night is a bilingual *en face* paperback of 73 text pages and 22 pages of preliminary matter, including an eight-page introduction and a two-page bibliography. The Print and Binding Order for the book, to Dawson and Goodall, reveals a total print quantity of 5,050 copies of the 96-page paperback in Metric Crown 8vo. It was eventually published worldwide in a print-run of 5,000 copies, at a unit price of 90p and 70p for other editions. The unit cost appears to have been 20.54 pence, the total production cost being £1,027. An advance of £160 was paid. Copyright fees were deducted from royalties. The royalty rate was 8% worldwide, divided as follows: 50% to the owner of the rights, Solofo Rabéarivelo, and 25%

[25] Toby Faber, *Faber & Faber: The Untold Story* (London: Faber & Faber, 2019), gives an account of the firm's history by editing together correspondence and other materials from their archive. The chapter on 1971–79 is called 'A reasonable hope of survival' and briefly summarizes the 'economic outlook' as 'grim' (319).

[26] The poet's name is presented without acute accent on the first 'e' in the Heinemann volume, but usually has an accent in French publications. Except when quoting others' writings, I follow the French convention and give his name as 'Jean-Joseph Rabéarivelo'.

[27] Alan Hill, *In Pursuit of Publishing* (London: John Murray, 1988), 120–1.

each to the translators Dr Wake and Professor Reed.[28] The first (and only) print run for the book appears, in today's terms, remarkably high, and is three-fifths more than that for Achebe's *Things Fall Apart*. This is a tribute to the success of the African Writers Series, to Heinemann's distribution structure, and to their regional offices. The title page has, underneath the HEB windmill logo, 'LONDON / HEINEMANN / NAIROBI IBADAN LUSAKA'. The archive folder of papers related to the publication of *Translations from the Night* doesn't contain sales figures, royalties paid, or copies of reviews.

The editor handling the book at Heinemann was James Currey, who had come from Oxford University Press to manage the African Writers Series in 1967, working at Heinemann for eighteen years.[29] On 23 November 1973, he wrote to Clive Wake (at Darwin College, The University, Canterbury, Kent) to say he was preparing a contract, adding: 'I calculate that you will need to cut the length by four poems (8 pages). In addition you will want to substitute the Malagary [*sic*] poem for a further poem.' Wake replied seven days later, on 30 November 1973:

> I have removed four poems with translations (one a longish one which would have gone over onto a second page).
>
> If necessary, a further two pages could be saved by printing the poems 'Naissance du Jour', 'Autre naissance du jour' and 'Une autre' one after the other on the same page (the first two would probably fit nicely onto one page).
>
> Since they are variations on a theme, they could be treated as a single poem in this way. The eight sonnets at the beginning should be printed two to a page.
>
> I shall let you have the translation of the Malagasy poem as soon as possible.

Sadly, this would not be the end of the culling. Reed and Wake were attempting to publish their collection of Rabéarivelo's work during one of the worst economic crises in British post-war history, running from the steep climb in oil prices with the Yom Kippur War (6 to 25 October 1973) to the three-day week (1 January to 7 March 1974) and the defeat of Ted Heath's Conservative government in the general election of 28 February 1974. In the official history of the Heinemann publishing house, the chapter on the 1970s reports that the company effectively survived the period, despite pressures upon their profits produced by rapid inflation

---

[28] Details are from the Heinemann file of correspondence, unused typescripts, and commercial documents related to this publication, held at the University of Reading, Special Collections, call number HEB 11/14, published with permission.

[29] Alan Hill, *In Pursuit of Publishing*, 143.

and increasing prices for materials and printing costs. The folder of papers in Special Collections at the University of Reading illustrates these pressures, showing their impact on editorial decisions, the final shape of the published volume, its representation of the poet's work, and diffusion among readers.

On 23 July 1974, Currey wrote again to Wake noting that the translator of the Malagasy poem to be included, Reverend Alan Rogers, could be paid a fee of £10.00 for his work 'which will, I'm afraid, have to be deducted from royalties.' He then adds:

> We are being absolutely frightened rigid by present printing prices and our first look at the estimate has suggested a price of about £1.00, but we are trying other printers. We'd expect to put it out on one of our printing days in 1975. The first one is in February.

By midsummer, however, the situation had become even graver. Currey's candid and informative letter to Wake for 2 August 1974 spells it out in full:

> I warned you that the price situation of Rabby was difficult. We have had it costed three ways, and the cheapest estimates we have been able to get are:
>
>> (a) 160 pages (that is including all the matter – 128 pages of poetry in English and French and some 24 pages of preliminary matter. I had hoped to have each poem starting on a new page. Unfortunately we have had to rule this out) 95p (UK only £1.20).
>> (b) 128 pages (that is running on the pages as in <u>French African Verse</u>) 80p (UK only £1.20).
>> (c) 96 pages (that is cutting about 16 pages of verse and 10 of translation) 70p (UK only 85p).
>
> We discussed this at length yesterday at our weekly meeting and everybody strongly favoured the reduction. I know this is a terrible nuisance for you but I know you were pretty horrified, as we were, by the price we had to put on <u>French African Verse</u>. Could you possibly rapidly let me have a list of twelve pages of French poems to be cut in priority order. We shall work out the lay-out of the manuscript before setting and it may well not be necessary to cut as many as ten pages of French poetry and their English translations.
>
> I am so sorry about this but there is no doubt that there is a strong inclination among people to buy the earlier titles in the series

because they are so much cheaper. So we are having to shorten books if possible either using a smaller typeface and smaller margins, or by reducing the length of collections of poetry or stories.

For this series, sales of units are closely related to pricing policy. The way to keep sales up (and profit margins stable) is to reduce the quality of the product. This can be achieved by reducing the quality of both the design and the printing. We see Currey (and the editorial committee) ruling out the 'new page for each new poem' option, and mentioning reductions of point size and page margins. The official history of the house suggests that this policy was successful. The chapter on the 1970s is entitled 'A Prosperous Decade Despite the Recession'.[30] However, difficulties with the Rabéarivelo volume point towards the decline this series experienced over some fifteen years.

Wake replied to Currey's letter on 5 August 1974, with the response of the weaker party in an unequal collaboration:

> It is disappointing that this volume will have to be cut, but we fully understand the difficulties. We had hoped to be able to publish the whole of the Traduit de la Nuit collection, but this will not now be possible. I am attaching a list of poems that could be excluded, in order of priority. I hope they cover the right number of pages, and with a bit of luck a couple could be saved. Please do your best!
>
> I have suggested that the first thing to go could be the Malagasy version of the last poem, since most readers will not be able to use it anyway and it is perhaps a dispensable luxury.
>
> Since some of the Traduit de la Nuit poems have been omitted, I suggest the remainder should not be numbered at all, but that the transition from poem to poem be indicated typographically.
>
> One page of the introduction will have to be altered, so I enclose a Xerox copy of the altered original for you to substitute for your copy. I stupidly did not number my copy of the typescript, but it is the sixth page of the text of the introduction.
>
> I did consider the possibility of cutting the introduction, but it is already fairly short and it would really have to be rewritten if it were to be shortened any further. I think it would be best to leave it as it is.

Then follows the list of suggested cuts 'in order of priority; the poems at the bottom of the list are those we would most prefer to keep'. Ten

---

[30] John St John, *William Heinemann: A Century of Publishing 1890–1990* (London: Heinemann, 1990), 566–8.

sections of 'Traduit de la Nuit' are at the foot of the list, with six separate poems at the top. None of the poems on the list survive in the published volume, dismembering the title sequence being a particularly damaging consequence. Among the papers preserved in the archive is an envelope containing the French and English texts cut on 8 August 1974. The folder also includes a sheaf of photocopied Malagasy woodcuts offered as possible material for the book cover. These too were not used. Here, then, is the briefest account of how an international publisher only a few years after sterling was floated on the money markets finds itself obliged to relegate to archival near-oblivion poems by a respected francophone poet such as his emblematically entitled 'Ton Oeuvre' (Your Works).[31]

4. Poetry being used

Among reasons the 'fetish or idol' idea of a poem might not be wholly helpful is that it imagines the value of such totemic works as magically or superstitiously attached to the object, whereas, more accurately, this value is to be found in the use to which these objects are and have been put in individual lives. The difference of value between some of Shakespeare's sonnets and almost all of Edmund Spenser's, for instance, resides in the much greater and wider uses to which the former have been put, increasingly in recent centuries, by innumerable readers in different times and places. Spenser's *Amoretti* are certainly valued by lovers of poetry, and by scholars of Elizabethan verse, and these imply uses that need not be underestimated. But beyond such heights of current evaluation, which doubtless includes an element of fetish or idol, there are innumerable poems and poets' oeuvres that are forever finding themselves, as it were, devalued by neglect and in need of revaluation, so as to achieve the kinds of minimal attention from some readers that would allow them to have value in the circulating systems of our lives. An outline of such a predicament, and a way out of it, perhaps, may be found in the reflections of a poet, writing a poem, on the edge of a writing block which in later interview he explained thus: 'when I first realised about 1965 that anyone was reading me at all it stopped me writing for four or five years.'[32]

[31] For more on publishing constraints and opportunities, see 'Introduction: The Limits and Openness of the Contemporary', in *The Oxford Handbook of Contemporary British and Irish Poetry*, ed. Peter Robinson (Oxford: Oxford University Press, 2013), 7–12.

[32] See Roy Fisher, *Interviews through Time*, ed. Tony Frazer (Bristol: Shearsman Books, 2013), 23 and 45. For Simon Jarvis's interpretation, see 'A Burning Monochrome: Fisher's Block', in *The Thing about Roy Fisher: Critical Studies*, ed. John Kerrigan and Peter Robinson (Liverpool: Liverpool University Press, 2000), 173–92.

Roy Fisher's lyric 'Suppose –', written over two days on 30 April and 1 May 1967, explores how poems may still be used, and how value may thus accrue to them. It suggests thoughts about poetry's use by deploying two of the past participle's usages, as in an object that 'used to' do something, and in something that is 'used', second-hand, or even used up. To this it adds a verb colloquially employed by poets or readers discussing a poem's techniques and asking if or how the poem 'works':[33]

> Suppose that once in a while
> It still works, just as it used to.
>
> Somebody unwraps it among the teacups,
> Curtained from street flashes
> By afternoon clatter,
> A crowd of faces and feet,
> That sort of thing;
>
> Opens it, finds a poem –
> The old flat arrangement,
> Dry track of half a voice –
> And lets it drift on his own thoughts,
> Like a simile.

Fisher's strategy is to close-focus on a process and to separate out its parts, keeping the subject mysterious at the opening by reducing the topic focus of its exploration to the pronoun 'It' until the end of line 7. Thus it describes this 'it' as like a solid object that has been purchased, an object therefore having, in that particular transaction, what was called a 'fixed' exchange value. It has then been brought home, where, like a new car driven off the forecourt, it may suffer a dramatic loss of value, first in not being enjoyed sufficiently, and then in resale price. Fisher lets the more restricted associations and reflections that may arise from a reader not knowing what is being talked about develop until 'it' is perhaps unexpectedly revealed to be 'a poem'.

Crucial to Fisher's deceptively casual lyric is the staging of an exchange, an interaction, of the 'Somebody' in line 3 letting the poem 'drift on his own thoughts', evoking the different kind of exchange which may take place when two attentions are involved in the reading of composed words:

---

[33] For poetry's 'use' or its 'utility' and how 'Poetry may "work", but can it / Be seen or shown to work?', see F. T. Prince, 'Not a *Paris Review* Interview', *Collected Poems 1935–1992* (Manchester: Carcanet Press, 1993), 250 and 253. See also my 'Truth in Style', in *Reading F. T. Prince,* ed. Will May (Liverpool: Liverpool University Press, 2017), 69–72.

As a mirror, held to face another,
Deepens it with recessions
This used idea, abandoned
And pinched up into caricature,
Monitors and shakes the new.

'This used idea' is 'used' in the sense of an old poem which contains materials that have historical marks on them, but also one now being 'used' by this fresh reader, who, reading it for the first time, is producing a uniquely new amalgam of the two tracks of thought, poet's and reader's, represented by the two mirrors in which 'reflection' can deepen 'with recessions'. 'This used idea' is the work of the composing poet, which has been 'abandoned', rather as Paul Valéry said he left poems, and is then 'pinched up into caricature' by readers who make of it what they can.[34]

The poem now takes a number of ambitious, if hedged-round, directions – exemplifying how 'the new' may be monitored and shaken by the act of reading, with its unique interplay of two thought processes:

Between them, a guttering freedom,
Just enough light to ask questions by:

Why Alexandr Blok, the beautiful,
Dealt out humbug,
Still made sense —[35]

The final five lines with their remnant syntax (neither a full sentence, the first couplet a gestural assertion, the second three-line group a fragmentary answer to an implicit question) both puzzle and intrigue. The pages of the notebook in which the poet did his work reveal how difficult it was to find this wording, the final handwritten version in the notebook not quite achieving the form of the printed text. Fisher's first draft moves towards an attempted conclusion thus:

~~Turns up the intelligence~~
~~of a guttering freedom~~
Enough at least
~~It~~ does enough to display
– well – a guttering freedom

~~Does enough at any rate~~

34 See Paul Valéry, 'Concerning *Le Cimetière marin*', in *The Art of Poetry*, trans. Denis Folliot (Princeton: Princeton University Press, 1958), 144.
35 Roy Fisher, *Matrix* (London: Fulcrum Press, 1971), 11.

The poet has been 'given' or he has found that original phrase 'a guttering freedom' and is searching for a syntactical structure that will introduce and establish it. The 'does enough' tactic is worked at and abandoned in the deletion of the entire line that ends this first attempt. Fisher keeps his phrase and attempts to set it working with a different approach:

> Even if no more than this;
> The exposure of a guttering freedom,
> Of the possibility of asking
> ~~Certain~~ Questions: ~~for example,~~ for example
> ~~Why~~ How Alexandr Blok, the beautiful,
> ~~Had to deal so much humbug~~
> ~~To reach so much sense.~~
> ~~Should have~~
> ~~With all that sense.~~
> ~~Approached such sense deviously~~
> ~~By way of such humbug.~~
> Came by such humbug to such sense.[36]

There are six further attempts at this conclusion, the last of which is the closest the handwritten drafts get to the definitive version:

> Between them, a guttering freedom,
> ~~And~~ Just enough light to ask questions by:
>
> Why Aleksandr Blok, the beautiful, for example –
> Well; ~~why~~ how he ~~dealt so much~~ could deal all that humbug
> And still made ~~so much~~ sense.[37]

These brief transcriptions from the poet's workbook exemplify the qualities of form and shape produced by efforts of discovery and correction, where, in happy instances, the attention to detail contributes to the eventual value of the thing done. They are reminders of the labour that goes into making poems, something their existence as completed, printed commodities to be unwrapped 'among the teacups' might, like the art that conceals art, haplessly allow us to overlook.

Yet it is Fisher's reflexively critical effort that achieves the less-is-more close to his poem, making the asking of the question appear as a quick dart to a 'telling' point – and not as a laboriously articulated thought in which the noise of opinionated prose writing, the crossed-out phrase 'at

---

[36] Roy Fisher, No. 25 Workbook 11/xi/66–12/i/69, 17–19. Roy Fisher Archive, University of Sheffield.
[37] Ibid. 23.

any rate' for instance, dissipates the insight in its accommodating gestures ('for example') or added emphases ('so much' crossed out twice in the final draft above). This work of compression and cutting, to offer the idea without insisting on it, its phrase present from the first draft, to have it come out sharply and directly, is effected close to that writing block Fisher reported on some years later. At the top of page 4 in this workbook he had written, perhaps at a later date, in pencil: 'BLOCKED', and in the margin alongside some note taking dated '3rd Jan Tues. [1967]' he has added 'sterile'. It is only right, then, that this generous interpretation of Blok's symbolist 'humbug' should allow Fisher to start finding a way out of his block by imagining a reader's work in the exchanges of poetry's making and reception.

The possibility of finding 'the new' by reading a poem is identified with freedom, but an endangered, a 'guttering' freedom like a candle at risk of being blown out, which takes the poem back to its opening, its sense that only 'once in a while' the poem, or the process of reading a poem, 'still works' as it did. This 'guttering' freedom is what, I suspect, brings in the allusion to Alexandr Blok, the largely pre-revolutionary Russian poet and symbolist, whose sequence about the 1917 Revolution, 'The Twelve', expresses a prophetic ambivalence about the coming times. Fisher is probably referring to the Russian poet's symbolist poetry and doctrine with its various idealisations and cults of beautiful ladies as 'humbug', but he adds that his poems 'still made sense' – rather as a reader might use a 'Gyres' theory of history, or of voices from the Beyond, in W. B. Yeats's work to access the continuing cultural value and significance of his poems.[38]

What Fisher's 'Suppose –' tacitly underlines is that because the reading of a poem is an interaction with a space for freedom in which 'to ask questions', it follows that the outcome of this interaction cannot be predicted. So the poem cannot be gone to as a tool that serves to perform a predetermined task. But this should not lead us to suppose that it is therefore not being 'used' in some ungrounded and unmotivated act of what is called disinterested contemplation. 'Disinterest' is another misleading word, derived from the aesthetics of Immanuel Kant: the poet who writes and the engaged reader reactivating the work in that 'dry track of half a voice' are intensely interested, in precisely the sense that their interests are being sustained and advanced by engaging with this object in careful reading, and its promoting with admiration or praise.

---

[38] For his 'mystic summer' and 'Verses about the Most Beautiful Lady', see Avril Pyman, *The Life of Alexandr Blok*, vol. 1, *The Distant Thunder 1880–1908* (Oxford: Oxford University Press, 1979), 84–8, and for 'The Twelve', see vol. 2, *The Release of Harmony 1908–1921* (Oxford: Oxford University Press, 1980), 284–91.

Though unwrapping 'Suppose –' many times over more than thirty years, I have never quite employed it as now to illustrate how poems can be used. I too have allowed the poem to 'drift on' my 'thoughts' and written those thoughts out for my argument. Yet such a use, which is occasioned by Fisher's own questioning of the poem's implement-hood, exemplifies a current characteristic of poetry's place in the world, and a thinking about that place; for the poem would truly be used as an 'implement' if – as I very frequently do – we went to it and read it without reflecting upon how or what we might be using it for. To speak thus of 'Suppose –' is an activity that resembles a carpenter considering a hammer 'disinterestedly' when it no longer functions to knock in a nail, only to find that it isn't broken and still works.

5. The outermost reaches of the responsible

What I didn't reflect on during that moment of seminar crisis with which this chapter began, that brief educational freeze-up and silence, was how lucky I could count myself for having been able to convert an interest in poetry into a salary. But then, if I were to boast of this too loudly, someone would surely point out how it isn't the poetry that has been paying the salary, but the teaching of it. Despite qualifications connected with the symbolic capital accumulated by publishing poetry over many years, on the back of the capital that contributed to being in a position to be inspired by it in teenage, and then cultivate an interest in it through secondary and tertiary education, they would be right.

Roy Fisher turned to related questions in 'The Making of the Book', the very next and only other poem he completed in 1967, composing it on the 20 May. Four years later, when putting together *Matrix*, he placed 'Suppose –' as the opening poem and 'The Making of the Book' as its envoi. The relation of this work to its immediate predecessor is that it further explores two matters only touched on in the earlier poem. Into that picture it adds some of the many ancillary actions and activities which prepare the way for someone to unwrap the poem 'among the teacups' – pointing thus to what is involved in turning the work in the notebook transcribed above into a purchaseable object which can be unwrapped, once bought; and it explores what the parameters of its still working 'just as it used to' might include. With a certain sardonic and faintly disgusted irony, Fisher recommends caution and skill in adjusting the supportive prose to locate the book within the poetic marketplace, placing his entire poem between inverted commas to distance the voicing: 'Let the Blurb be strong, / modest and true. / Build it to take a belting; / they'll pick on that.' Here, poetry and money snuggle up to each other, for the blurb is the sales-pitch for the book, and the reviews, if nasty ('they'll pick on that') may sink it without trace. Four more quatrains describe and mildly deride considerations of marketplace and literary-world presentation, at which point the poem offers a grandly consequentialist, though half incredulous, argument for its own good in the world:

> For poetry, we have to take it, is essential,
> though menial; its purpose
> constantly to set up little enmities.
>
> Faction makes a reciprocal
> to-and-fro of the simplest sort – and characterless
> but for an 'aesthetic' variable,
> inaudible to all but the players.
>
> And this little mindless motion,
> that nobody but the selfless and Schooled-
> for-Service would ever stoop to,
> drives the Society.

Picking up a hint from 'Suppose –', then taking it out of the confines of that single interior and one reading mind, 'The Making of the Book' turns its 'mirror, held to face another', which 'Monitors and shakes the new', into this 'reciprocal / to-and-fro' that the poet then goes on to describe as a 'miniscule dialectic, / tick-tacking away, not more than notional, / in obscure columns'. Nevertheless, poetry

> at length transmits itself
> mysteriously through Education –
> which pays off the poets too,
> one way and another –
>
> out past Government,
> past Control and Commodity
> even to the hollowness
> of the seventeenth percentile, the outermost
> reaches of the responsible.[39]

Fisher's tongue may be firmly in his cheek, but that's because, however implausible, he has noticed that – despite the managerial instrumentality of our societies, something not to be confused with the 'use' to which we can put something even so superficially flimsy and insignificant as a poem – still, poetry is able to reach beyond even that monetized shibboleth 'the

---

[39] Fisher, *Matrix*, 64.

seventeenth percentile, the outermost / reaches of the responsible' to keep us alive, for, as he adds: 'If the reviewers fall idle, everybody drops dead: / it's as simple as that.' Thus, while the idea of going and buying some poetry and unwrapping it 'among the teacups, / Curtained from street flashes / By afternoon clatter, / A crowd of faces and feet' may be far from many people's thoughts, teaching the appreciation of poetry remains an activity considered among the reasons why tertiary educational institutions would pay an appropriately qualified person a salary.

If Fisher's 'The Making of the Book' treats the high calling of poetry in a society with a sardonically comic inflection, he nevertheless touches on much that will emerge in this book. 'Suppose –' offers an account of how responding to a poem, or any work of art for that matter, involves neither the identification and taking on of its intrinsic qualities nor the projection onto it of a reader's wishes and desires. Rather, it involves using the shaped and tempered energy of the latter to activate and direct to a purpose those parts of the former that it can identify. It offers a transactional or exchange model of artistic process whose contribution is to help bring into existence 'the new', and by so doing to sustain a perpetually threatened 'freedom' in which free inquiry and critique can occur. The second poem takes this use-based, but neither intrinsic nor utilitarian, idea of poetic value, and puts it back into the marketplace, into the competition for attention, and its implicit transactions with price and money. It does this to assert, against the grain of its own scepticism, how amongst all this getting and spending even poetry may come to help perform its own 'essential, / though menial' work.

CHAPTER TWO

Money is a kind of poetry

1. *Payments and metaphors*

On 21 August 2012 at 12:05 pm, the American poet Charles Simic posted a short piece on *The New York Review of Books*' NYRDaily, a response called 'Poets and Money'. He was taking up the concluding remark of an essay from the same venue posted seven days and just over an hour earlier by the novelist Tim Parks called 'Does Copyright Matter?' There this expatriate English writer ended by asserting: 'If people only read poetry, which you can never stop poets producing even when you pay them nothing at all, then the law of copyright would disappear in a trice.'[1] To set a mood for Simic's response, at the top of the page his editor placed a reproduction of Edvard Munch's *Melancholy* (1894). In it a gloomy-looking young man sits beside the sea with his chin resting on one hand while in the distance, around the curve of strand, a lovers' tryst between a man in black and a woman in white is taking place. Though the young foreground figure is brooding on his tortured love life, its use above Simic's article suggests we are looking at a financially embarrassed poet.

'Wonderful! I said to myself after I read this' – is how Simic begins: 'The world is going to hell, but we poets have something to look forward to. We never got rich in the past and won't see a dime in the future.'[2] Despite copyright laws, he notes, our poems are easily available on the internet, and even if attention spans have fallen to the point where only short lyrics have a chance of notice, still people will be reaching for their phones to find a few words to read at a wedding or a funeral – something that, he almost gloats, they wouldn't be doing with a chapter from a novel or short

---

[1] http://www.nybooks.com/daily/2012/08/14/does-copyright-matter/. Accessed 21 December 2017.

[2] http://www.nybooks.com/daily/2012/08/21/poets-and-money/. Accessed 21 December 2017.

story. Displaying only a superficial *Schadenfreude* at the expense of novelists and other prose writers with an eye on the marketplace, Simic performs a characteristically poetic trick in that – like the Cinderella of the arts it is – poetry looks doomed to be condemned to the ashes by an ugly sister or two, but then through an unlikely trans-valuation ends up living happily ever after with the handsome prince.

This second chapter of mine takes its title from Wallace Stevens's aphorism in *Adagia* and explores further what is suggested, but also concealed, by the ampersand in the title *Poetry & Money*. Stevens's aphorism sets the relationships between these two in the terms of a metaphorical comparison, for his 'Money is a kind of poetry'[3] is structured as a slightly muffled (through the 'kind of') 'A is B' metaphor.[4] Because they are not tautologies ('a rose is a rose') or syllogisms of the 'Socrates is a man' variety, where the A term is one in the set of B, metaphorical elucidations point towards affinities across a portion of the spectrum of possible relations between the two terms. Thus metaphors eventually break down in that the terms being compared only go so far until irreconcilable differences emerge – such as that you can't take a poem to the shops and expect to buy something with it, as Geoffrey Hill might be insinuating when he wryly notes: 'Whether poetry is unreal is best tested by using it to settle a hotel bill.'[5] And because currency 'is used to exchange equivalents in wealth – in any place, in any time, of any kind', it is described by Marc Shell as 'the great metaphor'.[6]

A curiosity of human speech and understanding is that syllogisms and tautologies are not only of nearly no use in poetry, they have little role to play (because, as with Socrates being a man, banally true) in daily life either. It is one of the reasons why 'eggs are eggs' formulas should set rhetorical persuasion barometers twitching. *Poetry & Money* notices the ubiquity of metaphors derived from money and economic activity in this art, and asks what role metaphor has in the developing criticisms or acceptances of the financial and social constraints explored throughout. This second chapter includes reflections on the nature of metaphor, for monetary metaphors in poetry don't seek only to connect through associative thinking, but also to mark a separation between these areas of human activity and meaning – it

[3] Wallace Stevens, *Collected Poetry and Prose,* ed. Frank Kermode and Joan Richardson (New York: Library of America, 1997), 905.
[4] For William Empson on metaphor and the 'A is B' assertion, see Chapters 18 and 19 of *The Structure of Complex Words* (1951; London: Penguin Books, 1995 edn.), 331–74.
[5] Geoffrey Hill, *The Book of Baruch by the Gnostic Justin* (Oxford: Oxford University Press, 2019), 136.
[6] Marc Shell, *The Economy of Literature* (Baltimore: Johns Hopkins University Press, 1978), 137.

being in the nature of metaphor, and simile, to depend upon a more than background unlikeness between the objects or ideas conjoined.

A senior academic has described 'poetic language' as 'essentially metaphorical', explaining that 'metaphors express relationships, sometimes in surprising ways and therefore stimulate new perceptions.'[7] He adduces the associated benefit of open-endedness in literary thinking: 'A characteristic feature of literature may be that propositions are exploratory and multifaceted, seeking suggestive correlation rather than resolution.'[8] This characteristic, one not open to tautologies and syllogisms, depends upon the fundamental 'unlikeness' inherent in metaphorical comparisons (for in metaphors, A must not be the same as or a part of B), which then requires tact in their deployment and interpretation so as not to extend them to where they will 'break down' somewhere beyond sense.

This required tact and judgment in the use of metaphors suggests, in turn, that the age-old contrast between reason and imagination is false if strictly adhered to, because the imaginativeness of a metaphor depends upon its being used within the bounds of its applicability, and to apply tact and judgment appropriately requires rationality and 'wit' in an older sense of that word. The challenge, then, of Stevens's 'Money is a kind of poetry' appears both in its suggestively illuminating expression of a relationship, and its assumption of fundamental differences. That a metaphor is capable of confusing us, if not appropriately appreciated for what it does and does not reveal, while it can also illuminate if interpreted within awareness of its necessarily double nature, goes to the heart of the quarrel between poets and philosophers such as Plato – and, in turn, bids to resolve it in the necessarily combined action of both imagination and reason in the understanding of any metaphor, metaphor being the grounds for our capacity to say things which may be usefully interpretive and not merely tautologically self-evident.

Simic's comment piece performs only a mock melancholy, if melancholy at all, for he then revels in a time-and-motion contrast between writing poems and novels:

> To write a six-hundred-page novel takes years. You go and work at your desk every day the way a miner goes to his mine and you feel as drained afterwards. Of course, that kind of work should be amply rewarded. A poet stands by the window watching the rain fall, or looks at the lock of hair of his old sweetheart, scribbles something down on a piece of paper and is through for the day. The most outrageous thing about poetry is that poems composed

---

[7] Rick Rylance, *Literature and the Public Good* (Oxford: Oxford University Press, 2016), 74.
[8] Ibid. 79.

in such a lackadaisical manner end up in anthologies your kids are supposed to study in school. Not only that, but they may fall in love with them, memorize them, and try to imitate them.

Adam Smith thought that 'some both of the gravest and most important, and some of the most frivolous professions' were performers of unproductive labour, and, doubtless aware of his own inclusion in their ranks, counted among them 'men of letters of all kinds'.[9] By contrast, Marc Shell reminds us that Ruskin argued for the 'concept of the poet as a laborer who is or who produces some kind of economic value', which in *The Political Economy of Art* was associated with the labour of the goldsmith.[10] Dispensing above with a labour theory of poetic value, Simic also abandons one of Sir Philip Sidney's supports for a defence of poetry in his treatise.[11]

The American poet too – like Fisher in the previous chapter – sees poetry performing its social function through the conduit of education; still, to flavour his irony, he underplays not only the contribution to the productive economy in the making and selling of poetry books (the poet's work a necessary if not sufficient requirement), but also the laborious and long-term commitments required to scribble 'something down on a piece of paper' that is worth reading. As a poet, he suggests, you can be done with your inspiration before most people have got to work. If time is money, then the restricted amount of it a poem might need won't require much remuneration. Yet poets too will be reminded of Whistler's reply in his court case against Ruskin when asked how long it had taken him to produce what the British art critic described as the impudence of asking 'two hundred guineas for flinging a pot of paint in the public's face'. Rather, that sum was for what Whistler described to the court as 'knowledge I have gained in the work of a lifetime.'[12] His reply cuts the 'time is money' copula, because it isn't possible to charge, or expect to be paid, the cost of a lifetime's devotion for every haiku you compose while looking out at the rainfall.[13]

---

[9]   Adam Smith, *The Wealth of Nations,* ed. Edwin Cannan (New York: Modern Library, 2000), 361.

[10] Marc Shell, *The Economy of Literature* (Baltimore: Johns Hopkins University Press, 1978), 132.

[11] See Philip Sidney, *A Defence of Poetry,* ed. J. A. Van Dorsten (Oxford: Oxford University Press, 1966), 22–3. For an economic reading, see Catherine Bates, *On Not Defending Poetry: Defence and Indefensibility in Sidney's Defence of Poesy* (Oxford: Oxford University Press, 2017).

[12] Cited in Daniel E. Sutherland, *Whistler: A Life for Art's Sake* (New Haven and London: Yale University Press, 2014), 158.

[13] See Linda Merrill, *A Pot of Paint: Aesthetics on Trial in Whistler v Ruskin* (Washington and London: Smithsonian Institute Press, 1992), and especially 'The

Such a disconnecting of the copula linking time and money reinforces other disconnections too. If you can't monetize your activity, then it's difficult for those who control cultural access in a society to set up institutional portals through which the poets have to move in order to be acknowledged as worthy of payment. Simic underlines this social exclusion by comparing the unrewarded state of the poetic vocation in a capitalist country with the enforced exclusion of poets from official acceptance in an old-time communist one:

> In a country that now regards money as the highest good, doing something for the love of it is not just odd, but downright perverse. Imagine the horror and anger felt by parents of a son or daughter who was destined for the Harvard Business School and a career in finance but discovered an interest in poetry instead. Imagine their enticing descriptions of the future riches and power awaiting their child while trying to make him or her reconsider the decision. 'Who has recognized you as a poet? Who has enrolled you in the ranks of poets?' the trial judge shouted at the Russian poet Josef Brodsky, before sentencing him to five years of hard labor. 'No one,' Brodsky replied. He could have been speaking for all the sons and daughters who had to face their parents' wrath.

But it is not quite no one that recognizes you as a poet if those people with short attention spans are reaching for their phones to find appropriate words for a wedding or funeral and happen to alight upon yours. They acknowledge you with the gift of their attention. The analogy with Brodsky's plight when condemned for antisocial activity is applicable to all those poets, especially when setting out, who have as good as no reward in either money or attention.

Yet some poets have taken that as their best claim to higher value, a claim also subject to ironies of history and changing circumstances. The very existence of Emily Dickinson's poems, now viably published in many editions, underlines the potential marketability of values which are even directly opposed to being sold, as in 'Publication – is the Auction / Of the Mind of Man –' where the poet refuses to 'sell / The Royal Air –

> In the Parcel – be the Merchant
> Of the Heavenly Grace –
> But reduce no Human Spirit
> To Disgrace of Price –[14]

Value of a Nocturne', 217–28, including whether 'a fixed relation did exist between a picture's price and its intrinsic value', 219.
[14] Christanne Miller (ed.), *Emily Dickinson's Poems: As She Preserved Them* (Cambridge,

Perhaps the irony of the future commercial marketability of this poem had been built into Emily Dickinson's practice as a poet, for Virginia Jackson has noted apropos of 'The Merchant of the Picturesque / A Counter has and sales' that 'if Emily Dickinson does not live and breathe in her writing, she *did* live and breathe print culture'. This is emblematically represented by 'The Merchant of the Picturesque' being written around 1867 'on the verso of an advertising flier for "Orr's Boneset Bitters and Lavender Cordials"', which, Jackson adds, is 'at the very least suggestive, at least at the distance of over a century':[15]

> To Children he is small in price
> And large in courtesy –
> It suits him better than a check
> Their artless currency – [16]

'The Merchant of the Picturesque' is probably unfinished, and only exists in the draft on the advert, while its economic analogies suggest a more equivocal relation to the marketplace than in 'Publication – is the auction'. Poets can resist the monetizing of their compositions and, in so doing, prepare the way for others to make a handsome profit out of them, as when the British government's refusal to allow copyright protection on Shelley's *Queen Mab*, with its panegyric against commerce, created the pirate's charter that allowed the poem to be circulated cheaply and read by extraordinary numbers of people.[17]

Simic's article on 'Poets and Money' is fluent in being paid on both sides, to recall Auden's early title, by deploying the fundamental paradoxes in relations between these two forms of value. The contrasts Simic makes between poets and novelists or other writers of marketable prose has the benefit of underlining why the two terms in my title, *Poetry & Money*, make unusual sense together – because the cultural conditions for popular fiction writers, biographers, celebrity memoirists, popular historians, and staged playwrights are distinctly different from those of poets, different in that for all of these writers success can reasonably be measured in sales figures and

---

MA, and London: Harvard University Press, 2016), 386–7. It was written onto sheet 5 of fascicle 37 in late 1863.

[15] Virginia Jackson, *Dickinson's Misery: A Theory of Lyric Reading* (Princeton and Oxford: Princeton University Press, 2005), 198.

[16] Miller (ed.), *Emily Dickinson's Poems: As She Preserved Them'*, 538–9. Miller's note on 776 reads: 'there is no evidence of a drafted final line, although there is room for at least one more line on the advertising flyer on which ED wrote the poem; syntax, meter, and rhyme suggest the poem is unfinished.'

[17] See William St Clair, *The Reading Nation in the Romantic Period* (Cambridge: Cambridge University Press, 2004), 317–22.

royalty statements, while critical recognition is related to the leveraging of these rewards. For poets, though, there is, to all intents and purposes, little or no connection. And that is the reason why bringing them together in this title by means of that ampersand is, paradoxically, a source of significance and meaning, for it has the air of a paradox or riddle, and promises that writing about such a topic will unpick it or solve the puzzle.

2. Poets' obsession with money

"'If I am obsessed with money, as a poet shouldn't be, there's a reason for it," was what Humboldt had told me.'[18] Von Humboldt Fleisher, or his creator Saul Bellow, sees things in a related but different light from their compatriot Stevens, author of the adage 'Money is a kind of poetry'. When Humboldt goes on to explain why he is obsessed, his reason is – some might think – faintly provincial, for this poet (said to be based on Delmore Schwartz) explains:

> 'The reason is that we're Americans after all. What kind of American would I be if I were innocent about money. I ask you? Things have to be combined as Wallace Stevens combined them. Who says "Money is the root of evils"? Isn't it the Pardoner? Well the Pardoner is the most evil man in Chaucer. No, I go along with Horace Walpole. Walpole said it was natural for free men to think about money. Why? Because money is freedom, that's why.'[19]

Not only is obsession with money found in places other than the United States, the idea that money buys freedom doesn't stand up to full investigation, for the freedom you buy will depend on your entanglement with the price of its cost, which will likely reduce freedom; and nor is it meant to in Bellow's fiction, for Humboldt is being himself in such talk, and his reason, as the narrative makes plain, is the familiar one. It is often assumed thus that there was, or ought to have been, a sort of *cordon sanitaire* isolating Stevens's professional and his poetic life, as is implied when Humboldt concedes that 'a poet shouldn't be' at all 'obsessed with money'; but the assertion that 'Money is a kind of poetry' and Stevens's two articles on the insurance business suggest otherwise.

Humboldt has attempted, in admirable yet foolhardy and time-discredited romantic fashion, to live the life of the poet as such, to be someone who has bet everything on the writing of poetry, and to pass this off,

[18] Saul Bellow, *Humboldt's Gift* (New York: Viking Press, 1975), 159.
[19] Ibid. 159.

win or lose the bet, as his single social identity. Basil Bunting's 'What the Chairman Told Tom' voices the world's view of such a presumption. 'Poetry? It's a hobby', it begins, and then notes Ruskin-fashion that 'you've got a nerve' to ask for 'twelve pounds a week' to write it. In 1965, when this joke satire was composed, the ventriloquized speaker gets 'three thousand a year and expenses', explaining 'but I'm an accountant.'[20] The consequence for Humboldt, as it was for Schwartz, and, differently for the Tom Pickard of Bunting's title, was to be involved in a lifelong struggle to have his continuance funded through positions in an academy whose restrictive practices he found hard to accept, or be hustling sponsorship from those with money to spare and a desire to use it for accruing cultural kudos – or in other ancillary ways that poets have been obliged to accept, such as begging and borrowing from friends, friends like Bellow's narrator and partial alter ego, Charlie Citrine. Delmore Schwartz was not the only mid-twentieth-century poet without a trust fund to attempt this performance. W. S. Graham, as we saw, was another.

But why ever should Humboldt tell Charlie Citrine that a poet shouldn't be obsessed with money? After all, poets would naturally have more than one reason to be so obsessed, and among their sets of reasons might be ones particular to them as poets. We all, including the poets among us, have our reasons to be compelled to think about it, whether because we don't have enough to get by, or we have so much we have to employ others to look after it (and can we trust them?) – or other reasons connected with any of the innumerable stages between these conditions of excess and lack. Most poets these days are unable to earn a living as, strictly speaking, poets, so will be obliged to think about money in relation to their day jobs; and in some cases – those of the banker-poet Samuel Rogers, the East India Company employee Thomas Love Peacock, the bank clerk T. S. Eliot, and Wallace Stevens the insurance man – their professions would require them to think about money, perhaps on a daily basis.[21]

Humboldt's assertion pinpoints the other side of this bohemian attempt to be a poet and nothing but a poet, even when there is little or no family money to sustain you through the long stretches on minimal earning that inevitably come with writing poetry. This is the romantic notion that writing it is an activity, and requires a form of attention, too pure to be sullied with thoughts of mere money. It is as if poets, like priests, were not supposed to be of this world, because poetry offers values that are at odds

---

[20] Don Share (ed.), *The Poem of Basil Bunting* (London: Faber & Faber, 2016), 126.

[21] See Martin Blocksidge, *The Banker Poet: The Rise and Fall of Samuel Rogers* (Brighton, Chicago, and Toronto: Sussex Academic Press, 2013). For Rogers's recording of conversations and his independent means, see Christopher Ricks's introduction to Samuel Rogers, *Table-Talk & Recollections* (London: Notting Hill Editions, 2011), viii.

with it, and they can therefore have nothing to do with it. Hence, perhaps, comes the slight puzzlement that has existed about how Stevens could have combined being a poet with working for an insurance company in policy evaluation and damage claims, or how the author of *The Waste Land* could have spent his days working in an office underneath the pavement in the City of London calculating the repayments for pre-war debts after the Great War had upset the entire structure of international financing. This latter thought can be picked up fully formed in Ezra Pound's quixotic *Bel Esprit* attempt to raise funds that would free his ally from the bank and allow him to write more poetry, an intervention Eliot was embarrassed by and rejected. Though Eliot's scruple suggests his prudent sensitivity to a British milieu recently abandoned by Pound, Lawrence Rainey sees the scheme's failure as the moment when the latter's political impulses shifted from 'reasoned assent or conditional trust' to 'faith'.[22]

Some poets, D. H. Lawrence and Ezra Pound prominent among them, would sustain the belief that the practice of an art and trafficking in money were near incompatible – and in the case of Pound his monetary writings can be traced back to his thoughts about the problem of how artists may be supported to make their cultural contributions when their art form, or their particular practice of it, fails to be marketable during their lifetimes.[23] The example of Pound brings up a further set of reasons why poets might be especially obsessed with money: because their experience as poets leads them to find not so much that they are suffering an obsession with it, but that they are intensely interested in this ubiquitous medium of exchange that so dominates the world in which they must also live, and which their culture's inherited ideas and assumptions has obliged them to be and to see themselves as at odds with it, however it too compromises them.

3. The meaning of a metaphor

'Money is a kind of poetry' neatly combines the terms of my book's title; but unfortunately, it being an aphorism, the writer didn't stop to explain what he meant.[24] Puzzled by what Stevens might have signified by his aphorism, others have stepped in, ones such as Dana Gioia, who takes Stevens's

---

[22] Lawrence Rainey, *Institutions of Modernism: Literary Elites and Public Culture* (New Haven: Yale University Press, 1998), 108.

[23] See the section 'Milieux and Patronage' in my 'Ezra Pound and Italian Art', in *Pound's Artists: Ezra Pound and the Visual Arts in London, Paris and Italy*, ed. Richard Humphries (London: Tate Gallery, 1985), 121–37.

[24] It is employed as the epigraph to Kevin Jackson (ed.), *The Oxford Book of Money* (Oxford: Oxford University Press, 1995), iii, as if promising that his anthology may act as such a collaborative explanation.

aphorism as the epigraph of his poem entitled 'Money'. In an epigram first published under that same title in an April 1936 issue of *Poetry* magazine, Frost asserts that 'Nobody was ever meant / To remember or invent / What he did with every cent',[25] which is why Gioia can conclude:

> Money. You don't know where it's been,
> but you put it where your mouth is.
> And it talks.[26]

Bob Dylan, though, had already thought that because it gets dirty doing the rounds, and you don't exactly 'know where it's been', when it gets into your mouth 'money doesn't talk, it swears.'[27] Ben Lerner too attempted an explanation, after quoting Stevens's words, by adding that 'like money' poetry 'mediates between the individual and the collective, dissolves the former into the latter, or lets the former reform out of the latter only to dissolve again.'[28] What he appears to be saying is that in order for individuals to have social relations with collectives they need to have mediums of exchange in which they can engage in trading what is singular to them with what can be understood as valuable to others. Lerner is suggesting that both poetry and money perform such an interrelation of singular and plural, allowing us to trade across that barrier. But it would have to be said that if this is what he means, then poetry and money perform this feat in near incompatible ways and with vastly different consequences for both individuals and societies. Among the extortionate demands on poetry that Lerner explores, ones bound to fail in his Platonic model for why poetry may be so hated, is 'to propound a measure of value beyond money.'[29] Does Stevens's aphorism invoke such a project, or does it indicate rather why such a project would likely fail through contamination?

In 1995, the American poet William Matthews published a book of poems with a similar title to mine in which he linked two large nouns with an ampersand. His collection was called *Time & Money*, and along with other poems on different themes and topics, it contained two long meditations, one on each of these terms. In 'Money', Matthews also recalls Stevens's aphorism, reflecting upon it in this further poem on the money theme: 'if it's a kind / of poetry, it's another inexact way, / like time, to measure some sorrow we can't / name.' This idea of inexact measurements

---

25 Robert Frost, *Collected Poems, Prose and Plays*, ed. Richard Poirier and Mark Richardson (New York: Library of Congress, 1995), 282.

26 Dana Gioia, *The Gods of Winter* (Calstock: Peterloo Poets, 1991), 33.

27 Bob Dylan, 'It's Alright, Ma (I'm Only Bleeding)', track 10 on *Bringing It All Back Home* (CBS, 1965).

28 Ben Lerner, *The Hatred of Poetry* (London: Fitzcarraldo Editions, 2016), 110.

29 Ibid. 101.

for something else recurs in the chapters that follow, and the idea that it 'measures' something, a sorrow, which we can't name, only propels us further to find out how we might exchange a measuring device we can hold for a mysterious sorrow we can't.

In his 'Time' poem from this collection, Matthews naturally brings together the two themes of his book's title when he writes:

> Perhaps I should plan how to spend my
>
> time, but wouldn't that, like a home movie,
> prove but a way to waste the same time twice?
> Maybe time's just one more inexact way
> to gauge loss? But we keep more than we think.[30]

'I should plan to spend my / time', the poet asserts, collocating the terms of his title in the conventional verb and noun pairing, for *spending* is one of the verbs we most commonly use for the passing of time that matters or costs us. This is a further buried metaphor, and may help to explain the grip of the 'time is money', 'A is B' formula.

Matthews's idea of one thing being an inexact way of measuring another comes back with a vengeance in his 'Money' poem:

> Money's not an abstraction: it's math
> with consequences, and if it's a kind
> of poetry, it's another inexact way,
> like time, to measure some sorrow we can't
> name. The longer you think about
> either, the stupider you get,
>
> while dinner grows tepid and stale.[31]

When Matthews recalls and questions Stevens's 'Money is a kind of poetry', not only is it an inexact form of measurement for a loss, in this case a sorrow, but also, he says, the 'longer you think about / either' time or money, then 'the stupider you get', the reference to dinner being enough to suggest that an additional effect will be not only that you'll get older, but you'll also miss the ordinary pleasures of life, for your dinner will not be worth eating. The reason why this will happen, as with the names of his two poems 'Time' and 'Money', is that these are terms which draw attention to the fact that words have sense in their use as part of phrases and sentences, and if you take them out of such contexts, elevating them

---

[30] William Matthews, *Time & Money* (Boston: Houghton Mifflin, 1995), 13.
[31] Ibid. 55–6.

to the status of poem titles, for instance, and try to think about what they mean when standing alone in that fashion, then they will seem to be black holes, abysses of ungraspable profundity, and you will feel stupider in the face of them, for your thinking will have nothing on which to gain traction.

4. Poetry and insurance claims

The 'Money is a kind of poetry' formula may not be much less darkly profound, its two ocean-like words ambivalently ('kind of') conjoined with a copula. A first step might be to note that this aphorism is not simply reversible: 'Poetry is a kind of money' makes much less sense, and encounters even more instinctive resistance than what Stevens wrote.[32] That the 'tenor' and 'vehicle' of the metaphor, as they have been called, are not equivalents underlines that it is 'poetry' which is qualifying or seeking to explain something about 'money'. Such a thought has been reinforced in recent years by the equivocal term 'cultural capital', already adopted, derived from the writings of Pierre Bourdieu, and appropriated into critical discourse to mean that valued art objects with little obvious or immediate exchange value can nonetheless be 'traded' in a society because they can confer status on and fragrance to profitability derived from activities which deliver more economic capital and much less culture.[33] A publisher, for example, might decide to retain a poetry list not because it makes the firm large profits, but because it signals the sorts of cultural prestige that the company wishes to retain as part of its market position. 'Cultural capital' might seem to be a good idea for the revaluing of aesthetic knowledge and artifacts, but it has the dis-benefit of appearing to contribute further to the monetization of everything, even those things which appear to have fallen out of the clutches of consumer exchanges such as, to a large but not complete extent, poetry has in our day.[34]

But how, even imaginatively, can money be a kind of poetry? Among Stevens's uncollected prose are the short essays 'Insurance and Social Change' and 'Surety and Fidelity Claims'. These were written during the Great Depression and Roosevelt's New Deal, appearing respectively in the industry journals *The Hartford Agent*, October 1937, and *The Eastern Underwriter*, 25 March 1938. The first is an act of reassurance for private

---

[32] Compare Georg Simmel's reflections on the paired terms 'poetry' and 'truth' in *The Philosophy of Money* trans. Tom Bottomore and David Frisby from a first draft by Kathe Mengelberg (London: Routledge, 2004), 527.

[33] See Pierre Bourdieu, 'The Forms of Capital', in *Handbook of Theory and Research for the Sociology of Education*, ed. John Richardson (Westport, CT: Greenwood, 1986), 241–58.

[34] For a criticism of Bourdieu's project, see Jarvis, *Wordsworth's Philosophic Song*, 97.

insurance companies in a democracy, making comparisons between trading conditions in America alongside details of how insurance has been organized in Fascist Italy, Nazi Germany, Great Britain, and the Soviet Union. The second is an account of the human interest in the work of an insurance claim man who evaluates and settles for his company. Illuminating with regard to Stevens's thoughts on his professional life, they cast oblique lights on his work in poetry. Alan Filreis notes that Stevens 'held uniquely creative views'[35] on a bookkeeper who 'makes false entries in his books and keeps a memorandum of them and of the amounts embezzled', adding that it 'may seem morbid of an embezzler to keep a memorandum, yet many of them do'.[36] If the poet's creativity might so enter his insurance work, his claim evaluations can have entered his poetry too.

The first essay begins by noting that if 'each of us could put his hand on money whenever money was necessary: to repair damage, to meet any emergency, we should all be willing to stop so far as money goes.'[37] Stevens then underlines the difference between an intentionally fantastic (comparisons with H. G. Wells are made) universal insurance system and the fatal reality in which insurance must operate:

> The objective of all of us is to live in a world in which nothing unpleasant can happen. Our prime instinct is to go on indefinitely like the wax flowers on the mantelpiece. Insurance is the most easily understood geometry for calculating how to bring the thing about.[38]

Here the simile in 'to go on indefinitely like the wax flowers on the mantelpiece' might have already given the game away, and revealed the shabbiness in a desire for immortality. For even wax flowers fade and gather dust.[39] Pristine immortality would require others eternally to do the dusting, and not all of us would be certain that becoming an unnatural ornament in a bourgeois interior is the same as 'a world in which nothing unpleasant can happen'. But doubtless Stevens means to entertain as well as instruct, and this simile has a smile in it.

His imaginary scenario for total insurance is similarly equivocal in its formulation. He pictures an omnipotent being, unlike an actuary or

---

35   Alan Filreis, *Wallace Stevens and the Actual World* (Princeton: Princeton University Press, 1991), 43.

36   Stevens, 'Surety and Fidelity Claims', *Collected Poetry and Prose*, 797.

37   Stevens, 'Insurance and Social Change', *Collected Poetry and Prose*, 792.

38   Ibid. 793.

39   For Stevens's imaginative, material, and moral 'poverty', see Filreis, *Wallace Stevens and the Actual World*, 46–8.

underwriter who must measure risk before issuing a policy, a being who can pay the premium for total cover. Imagine

> that personality of the first plane who, at a stroke, insures all dwellings against fire; and who, without stopping to think about it, insures not only the lives of all those that live in the dwellings, but insures all people against all happenings of everyday life, even the worm in the apple or the piano out of tune. These are instances of insurance as it exists; and if they were not, there would be Lloyds or the future. There is no difference between the worm in the apple and the tack in the can of sardines, and not the slightest difference between the piano out of tune and a person disabled.[40]

I take it, though, that 'not the slightest difference' means that they are equally insurable, though also that in each case a liability limit would be calculated for the policy – perhaps less for the damage to your sensibility from your piano going out of tune, than the lifelong financial and human burden of caring for a disabled relative. The purpose of 'Insurance and Social Change' is to sketch out how the divine providence against all damage of that 'personality of the first plane' could come, in more earthly and limited terms, to be the business of national governments (it was Otto von Bismarck who first introduced national insurance in 1883), and to outline what the role of private insurance companies, like the one Stevens worked for, would be in such a scheme of things (one being to issue governments themselves with cover for damage to assets).

Yet, as the 'equality' of a piano out of tune and a person disabled suggests, in the actual state of things the insurers themselves would be taking greater risks of liability to pay out in the case of the latter, and the likelihood of a nationalized insurance scheme for permanently injured persons is much greater than for discordant pianos. Stevens quotes with relish a sentence from his company's 'Confidential Bulletin' to the effect that 'Cemeteries have been found by a number of offices to be a very definite market for the Hartford's All Risk Securities Policy', and he concludes:

> In short, then, the activities of the insurance business are likely, the greater and more significant they are, to make one reflect on the possibilities of nationalization, particularly in a period of unrest and the changes incident to unrest, a period so easily to be regarded as a period of transition. Yet the greater these activities are: that is to say, the more they are adapted to the changing needs of changing times (provided they are conducted at a profit) the more certain they are to endure on the existing basis.

[40] Stevens, 'Insurance and Social Change', *Collected Poetry and Prose*, 793.

Stevens assures his fellow claims men, thus, that even in the latter stages of the Depression, there is, provided profits can be made, little risk to their jobs, and, to rub the point in, his final flourish is to note that the survival of the company in such times depends upon the commitment to this cause of the workforce, for 'this exacts of each of us all that each of us, in his own job, has to give.'[41]

The challenges to making a profit that a claim man might face are given in hypothetical cases outlined in 'Surety and Fidelity Claims', and its relation to Stevens's poetry emerges in his interest not in the issuing of policies on the basis of calculated risks, but the evaluating of what is due to be paid out when damage has occurred:

> A family is killed by fumes from a gas stove in a cabin in a tourist camp. If the husband died first, this estate goes to A, B and C; if the wife died first, the husband's estate goes to X, Y and Z. The estate amounts to $50,000. You are on the bond of the administrator of the husband's estate. The $50,000 consists of cash on deposit in a bank which failed several years after you gave your bond. A, B and C will settle for $10,000, but X, Y and Z want $50,000. What had you better do?[42]

Not being in the business, I don't know the answer to such a question; but I imagine that the company might like to have it proved by autopsy that the husband died first, saving the insurance company $40,000 and helping with their profit margin. An even better solution might be that you prove there is no liability to cover damage caused by the failure of the bank. On the other hand, the company would have to be prepared in the event of the facts of autopsy proving either inconclusive or showing the sequence of deaths to be more expensive because of the intransigence of XYZ, that you might be obliged to try and persuade the latter to settle for the lower amount. However, none of these thoughts is quite Stevens's point. He is not asking exactly what you would or wouldn't do in any of the intricate circumstances he evokes. Rather, these complexities and the responses, ethical, commercial, and professional in nature, mean that, as he concludes, 'the most conspicuous element from the point of view of human interest in the handling of claims is the claim man himself.'[43] The evaluation of the complex situation made by this poet might align with that of the claim man by effecting a paying out of language to compensate for the discovery of damage incurred in, for instance, the poor wife and mother's death occasioning 'The Emperor of Ice Cream'.

---

[41]   Ibid. 796.
[42]   Stevens, 'Surety and Fidelity Claims', *Collected Poetry and Prose*, 798.
[43]   Ibid. 799.

The claim man appears on the scene in situations of loss, human, financial, and both together, as Stevens underlines:

> Then there is salvage: People would not so commonly be required to give bonds if they had money. This means that people are required to give bonds because they don't have money. From this point of view, the saying among claim men that often the only salvage recoverable lies in an advantageous settlement, is true. In any case, the recovering of salvage is closely involved with the treatment of claims. A man investigating a claim investigates at the same time the chance of getting the money back.[44]

Taken together, and understood as written by a poet, these observations on his professional life point to at least some reasons why Stevens could think that 'Money is a kind of poetry.' His working life was taken up with evaluation. He was involved in decisions about how much material objects in the world, including human beings, were worth insuring for, and in evaluating the risk of having to pay out on claims (the work of the actuary and underwriter). He would encounter the real consequences of those policies only if something went wrong in life, resulting in damage being done, losses being incurred, and their consequent insurance mitigation (the work of the claim man). Then he and his fellows would have to examine the cases and work out what if any of that insured matter could be regained in the salvage value of life (as when a failed bank's material assets might be offset against its monetary indebtedness), and how much could be regained by means of an 'advantageous settlement' – where the legatees agree to accept a fifth of what they might be due in better circumstances from a relative's estate.

Consider, in this light, another of his *Adagia*: 'After one has abandoned a belief in god, poetry is that essence which takes its place as life's redemption.'[45] That last word bridges between redeeming debts in financial exchanges and redeeming souls in an afterlife. But just as it isn't possible to believe in poetry as one might believe in a god, doubt has been cast upon the possibility of our being saved by this god-substitute too. Geoffrey Hill has called Stevens's remark an instance of that 'magnificent agnostic faith' which may be aligned with 'the tradition of Arnold and the Symbolists.'[46] T. S. Eliot challenged the effectiveness of that tradition in a 1927 review of I. A. Richards's *Science and Poetry*: 'Poetry "is capable of saving us," he says; it is like saying that the wall-paper will save us when the walls have crumbled.'[47]

---

[44] Ibid.
[45] Stevens, *Collected Poetry and Prose*, 901.
[46] Hill, 'Poetry as "Menace" and "Atonement"', *Collected Critical Writings*, 18.
[47] T. S. Eliot, 'Literature, Science and Dogma', *The Dial*, no. 82 (March 1927), 234.

Accepting Eliot's scepticism about money as a religion-substitute puts poetry into a position similar to that of money: it is an unreliable system of valuation that, if it is to access value, needs to be backed by greater resources of faith and trust, not merely in a human system but in one beyond us which gives more than just our economic system value. This is why economic calculations and recourses to 'the bottom line' imply underpinning values of the societies in which those calculations and recourses are made. Stevens's 'agnostic faith' reminds us that most of the poetry in our age has not had such sure collateral, and is, in this respect, like wallpaper holding up the wall, or paper without sufficient backing in gold, land, or other material wealth. Poetry and money have both been required to survive without such backing. Stevens's aphorism also effects a structure in which there is an idea of value in life with all its risk-related activities, then there are occasions of damage, of trauma, and of loss, including the loss or abandonment of faith, in which there may or may not be others to hold responsible. Then there is a secondary value, that of poetry, or the poet as claim man, appearing after the damage has been incurred. While poetry may not be able to offer salvation, perhaps it may provide some salvage.

Stevens's essay 'Imagination as Value' further suggests why the evaluation of insurance claims is not without its imaginative depths and relations to life's meaning when a belief in God has been abandoned. The most suggestive passage for help with his money-and-poetry adage is when he turns in passing to reflecting on 'the extent to which the imagination pervades life' and how 'it seems curious that it does not pervade, or even create, social form more widely'; but then, speculating, he notes:

> Perhaps, if one collected instances of imaginative life as social form over a period of time, one might amass a prodigious number from among the customs of our lives. Our social attitudes, social distinctions and the insignia of social distinctions are instances. A ceremonious baptism, a ceremonious wedding, a ceremonious funeral are instances.[48]

'The Emperor of Ice-Cream' represents, after all, a poor family's obsequies for their dead wife and mother made poetically ceremonious in the 'concupiscent curds' of its language.[49] To produce such ceremonious events

---

[48] Stevens, 'Imagination as Value', *Collected Poetry and Prose*, 732. The essay, from 1948, predates J. L. Austin's William James Lectures at Harvard in 1955, which became *How to Do Things with Words*, initiating Speech Act theory characterizing such 'ceremonious' occasions, later extending to John Searle's institutional facts, one of which is money.

[49] Stevens, *Collected Poetry and Prose*, 50.

as Stevens imagines in his prose above may require prodigious amounts of money, but the more telling point that he doesn't make is that among the most ubiquitous of social distinctions and their insignia is money itself – as William Empson illustrates in remembering Bertrand Russell giving a lecture where he 'brought out a coin, and the business about "me seeing my penny" was gone through' when 'somebody at the back of the room began to laugh, and it turned out that what he had got was half-a-crown.' The critic and poet then underlines how this complexly significant moment figures social distinctions and political values, for 'I thought it a very neat symbol of the Whig aristocrat and his democratic views; the actual value of the coin was a thing he would not have considered it polite to notice.'[50]

Geoffrey Hill, who versifies this incident in his poem 'Of Inheritance', intensifies the class condescension implied by noting that such 'prize apologists / for plebeian nobleness', who would have 'found it hard / telling one servitor from another', had 'spun / half-crowns to enlight- enment – *I take this penny*'.[51] Howard Nemerov's 'Money', subtitled 'An Introductory Lecture', similarly illustrates the exfoliating imaginative power of numismatic representation by spending 'a few minutes / upon the study of symbolism, which is basic / To the nature of money. I show you this nickel', he states, its representations of bison and native Americans serving to characterize the polity whose power supports the coin's circulation as a means for calculating the equivalence of different goods, though 'There is almost nothing you can buy with a nickel' and so it is 'becoming a rarity and something of / a collector's item',[52] and thus worth more than its face value. Imagination, however haplessly significant, has been employed in currency's production and design, whether as stamped metal or printed paper, and it further needs imaginative investments from all of those who take part in its economic exchanges to continue to facilitate their transactions of work and play.

5. Evaluating the experience of life

As we saw, the edge to Stevens's aphorism is in its elevating the value 'poetry' over the value 'money', for it says that money is one of poetry's kinds – that the qualities of interest and value and evaluation, of representation and transformation, that can be performed in poetry might also be found in

[50] William Empson, *The Structure of Complex Words* (1951; London: Penguin Books, 1995 edn.), 422.
[51] Geoffrey Hill, *Broken Hierarchies: Poems 1952–2012*, ed. Kenneth Haynes (Oxford: Oxford University Press, 2013), 233.
[52] Howard Nemerov, *The Collected Poems* (Chicago: University of Chicago Press, 1977), 369–70.

money. Stevens's poem from *Transport to Summer* (1947) called 'Attempt to Discover Life' appears to do just this:

> At San Miguel de los Baños,
> The waitress heaped up black Hermosas
> In the magnificence of a volcano.
> Round them she spilled the roses
> Of the place, blue and green, both streaked,
> And white roses shaded emerald on petals
> Out of the deadliest heat.
>
> There entered a cadaverous person,
> Who bowed and, bowing, brought, in her mantilla,
> A woman brilliant and pallid-skinned,
> Of fiery eyes and long thin arms.
> She stood with him at the table,
> Smiling and wetting her lips
> In the heavy air.
>
> The green roses drifted up from the table
> In smoke. The blue petals became
> The yellowing fomentations of effulgence,
> Among fomentations of black bloom and of white bloom.
> The cadaverous persons were dispelled.
> On the table near which they stood
> Two coins were lying – dos centavos.[53]

This ending recalls James Joyce's early story 'Two Gallants' from *Dubliners*, one it is hard to imagine Stevens had not read in 1947 – a tale in which a coin is similarly used to produce a mysteriously resonant close:

> Corley halted at the first lamp and stared grimly before him. Then with a grave gesture he extended a hand towards the light and, smiling, opened it slowly to the gaze of his disciple. A small gold coin shone in the palm.[54]

The word 'disciple' here evokes the betrayal of Jesus for those thirty pieces of silver, and if Stevens is recalling Joyce's story of an unscrupulously scrounging and corrupting person and his sidekick in his poem's close, then

---

[53] Stevens, *Collected Poetry and Prose*, 320–1. See James Joyce, *Dubliners*, ed. Terence Brown (London: Penguin Books, 1992), 54–5.

[54] James Joyce, *Dubliners*, ed. Terence Brown (London: Penguin Books, 1992), 54–5. For a note on the 'small gold coin' and how it gets into Corley's hand, see 266.

it may be helpfully tainting his poem with a more intimately penetrating analysis of monetary corruption and humiliation than would suit the message of 'Attempt to Discover Life'.

Placing coins at the ends of texts in this fashion cannot but have a monitory air, exacting its cost, as it were, as in Louis MacNeice's 'Charon', also likely to have been influenced by Joyce's story:

> And there was the ferryman just as Virgil
> And Dante had seen him. He looked at us coldly
> And his eyes were dead and his hands on the oar
> Were black with obols and varicose veins
> Marbled his calves and he said to us coldly:
> If you want to die you will have to pay for it.[55]

Threaded into this grimly apocalyptic scenario is the allegory, or 'parable' as MacNeice preferred to call them in his Clark Lectures, with its monetary theme signalled from the first: 'The conductor's hands were black with money: / Hold on to your ticket, he said, the inspector's / Mind is black with suspicion'. T. S. Eliot had not thought that 'death had undone so many' in this same city, less than half a century before, and MacNeice revisits the idea in a situation where the only thing for everyone to do is 'Take the ferry / Faute de mieux.' Charon, the ferryman named in the title who takes Virgil and Dante across the river Styx to Hell, turns out to resemble the bus conductor, as if the entire poem were a bad dream, for his hands are also 'black with money', but this time, ancient Greek 'obols'. So we put coins on the eyes of the dead to weigh down their eyelids, and if you want to cross this river too, you will have to pay the ferryman. Strangely like Stevens's poem, MacNeice's sets out on an ordinary bus journey through London, it would seem, but, rather than discovering life, he finds death, his own even, and in both cases these poets find themselves face to face with some small coins.

There is more than one place called San Miguel de los Baños in Latin America, but Stevens's poem alludes – if to anywhere – to the sulphur-bath resort in Cuba. It was prompted by his correspondence with José Rodríguez Feo, who, on 10 May 1946, wrote to 'My dear and most kind friend' that 'It was at dusk that I arrived from San Miguel de los Baños and tore the carefully packed package and in an atmosphere of roses and yellows and Uccello blues I perused the book.'[56] This volume was the Cummington Press edition of *Esthétique du Mal* (1945), but the combination of the place

---

[55] Louis MacNeice, *Collected Poems*, ed. Peter McDonald (London: Faber & Faber, 2007), 592–3 for this and the subsequent citations.

[56] Beverly Coyle and Alan Filreis (eds.), *Secretaries of the Moon: The Letters of Wallace Stevens and José Rodríguez Feo* (Durham: Duke University Press, 1986), 83.

name and the ambiguous flower-and-colour 'rose' looks to have prompted Stevens's evocation of a place he would never visit.

Having just read the poem in the *Quarterly Review of Literature,* Rodríguez Feo exclaimed on 30 November:

> There! I was surprised, and so pleased!, to see one commemorating my old bath resort: San Miguel de los Baños. How very fine of you, to pay homage to our little local villages. And that vision of the 'cadaverous person'; how magical the discovery! How come you see from so far-off those touching scenes? I have translated the poem and propose it to be included in this Winter issue. But tell me what are Hermosas?[57]

Stevens's brief reply on 10 December answers his question and reminds his correspondent of the role of 'fiction' in his poetry:

> I am glad to have your letter. Although I don't intend to reply to it today, perhaps I ought to explain Hermosas, which are a variety of roses. Of course, I don't know that Hermosas grow at San Miguel. But, then, probably nobody else knows. Besides, the San Miguel of the poem is a spiritual not a physical place. The question that is prompted by that poem is whether the experience of life is in the end worth more than tuppence: dos centavos.[58]

Best to trust the tale, not the bank teller. Those Hermosas might have been some kind of tasty delicacy, as the Spanish word would suggest, and hence Rodríguez Feo's question. In come the two deathlike figures, appearing to be locals, characterized sufficiently to suggest their strangeness; the entire poem is figured around a North American fascination with, and perhaps fear of, the Latin American south – as representing and threatening a richer life at the cost of a greater intimacy with death. They appear to make light of the roses, going up in smoke like a volcano, and then they go up in smoke too, being 'dispelled'. If the poem is set in 1946, the currency in the last line is Cuban money during the presidency of Ramón Grau. These coins are one hundredth of a peso each. But who or what are they for?

Filreis observes: 'The poem ends with an inconsequential tip and its obvious message: How easily are such social differences resolved in so natural a retreat.'[59] But perhaps its message is not so unproblematically 'obvious', and certainly the critic continues by reporting its Cuban reader's different interpretation, for, locating the poem with regard to the

[57]   Ibid. 89–90.
[58]   Ibid. 91.
[59]   Filreis, *Stevens and the Actual World*, 204.

correspondence between Stevens and Rodríguez Feo, Filreis notes that the young Cuban correspondent is 'interpreting this poem for himself after returning from his trip' and he 'did not concentrate on the way in which it suggests the wealthy young Cuban's resort as the site for such a dismissal'. Rather, he 'seemed to think the poem carried some message not generally on the differences between their two cultures but on the sentiment shared between them – on their friendship, as a sign of compensation for his failed "Attempt" to know Stevens more intimately.'[60]

Yet the 'site for such a dismissal', if it is obvious, is further caught up with and caught by ambivalences in the relationship of the USA with the Latin culture south of its border, and Stevens defended his work by suggesting that it had not been, in Filreis's words, 'intended to record his physical response to specific people, to a Cuban as opposed, say, to a Mexican or Argentine.'[61] In this light, the poem instances Stevens's idea that the imagination, like insurance cover, is a way of protecting us from life's unpleasantness, which includes the fact of inequalities of wealth, where, if the cadaverous are actually impoverished, our life is made poorer in that comparison and its aesthetic perfection is fatally tainted. But does 'Attempt to Discover Life' treat this economic contrast by using its imaginative power to dispel the poor pair?

The most important character in this poem is, perhaps, the one not described at all – the claim man as poet. This figure is entirely implied by the poem's voicing: he appears to be sitting in the same establishment and watching as the waitress performs the ritual of the hermosas. In the first stanza, since where these things are being assembled is not indicated, we can imagine the figure doing the describing is a customer and the things are piled before him. This assumption is then qualified in the second verse with the appearance of the cadaverous couple. Still, our narrator figure, further removed, is now watching them, and in the third verse he – there is no indication that this is not a male narrator – reports on what happens, only to leave the mysterious epiphany of the two coins on the table. Observing and reporting this scene with his detachment and enjoyment of a spectacle he appears not to understand, he renders it for readers in a mode that retains its mystery, in such details as the green roses going up in smoke. It would appear to be to this activity that the poem's title refers. It is the observer's attempt to discover life that is being exemplified.

But the poem's title suggests that this 'attempt' may not be successful, merely by stating that it is not a discovery of life. By the end of the third stanza much of the poem's content seems indeed to have gone up in smoke, in 'fomentations', which are 'applications of hot moist substances to the body to ease pain', such as might happen in a hot-spring bath; and gone up in smoke too are the two figures one of whom is compared to a dead body and the other who is wearing a black headdress. All that's left, it would seem, are the table and the two coins, which are described by Filreis as a tip, but that would have to be for the waitress. First the insurance man, who is of such interest in Stevens's two essays above, evokes life in the form of poetic colour and drama, as a series of events in narration. The implied observer sees this 'life' devoured and turned into nothing, which he also evokes, and then sees that it has resulted in a paltry payment or tip, and his efforts to value it in poetic terms have come down to a small sum of money.

Has life been converted into this form of payment or tip? Does the attempt to discover life only end in the discovery of life's passing, of its near worthlessness, its being consumed? Is imagination a form of insurance against the damages of life, and poetry the policy that can be signed off in the absence of any all-powerful insurer in the sky? The other side of this coin is that to add value by evaluating life and its risks as an insurance man does reveals the emptiness of a world not so evaluated. Dispelling poverty could mean dispelling life – the poor being, as the not-poor say, always with us, because without them we wouldn't be rich; and this might be why the poem's 'attempt' is just that, and has the air, in its final stanza, of so dishearteningly cheapskate a resolution.

CHAPTER THREE

Straitened circumstances

1. *Chaucer's complaint to his purse*

'There's no money in poetry, but then there's no poetry in money, either,' said Robert Graves, as if to cast aspersions on Wallace Stevens's adage.[1] The first part of Graves's assertion is widely attested. When in Scotland in 1619, Ben Jonson, conversing with William Drummond of Hawthornden, 'dissuaded me from poetry, for that she had beggared him, when he might have been a rich lawyer, physician or merchant.'[2] Three hundred years later, in 'Mr Nixon' from *Hugh Selwyn Mauberley*, first published in June 1919, Ezra Pound has his literary journalist advise: 'And give up verse, my boy, / There's nothing in it.'[3] There are, of course, exceptions to the rule. Alexander Pope secured his finances thanks to an immensely successful translation of Homer's *Iliad* (1715–20) that earned him two hundred guineas a volume from Bernard Lintot.[4] Byron's *Childe Harold* returned its publisher, John Murray, a huge profit, while *Don Juan* did help its poet go from the debt into which he had been born to the credit in which he died.[5] However, the contrast Jonson made in 1619, one repeated by Charles Simic in his article for the *NYRB* online in 2012, is the rule that such exceptions prove.

Whatever the circumstantial truth of the first part of his assertion, Graves's latter clause, that there is 'no poetry in money, either', is not the

---

[1] Frank L. Kersnowski (ed.), *Conversations with Robert Graves* (Jackson: University of Mississippi Press, 1989), 71.

[2] Ben Jonson, *The Complete Poems,* ed. George Parfitt (London: Penguin Books, 1996), 478.

[3] Ezra Pound, *Early Writings: Poems and Prose,* ed. Ira B. Nadel (New York: Penguin Books, 2005), 133.

[4] See Maynard Mack, *Alexander Pope: A Biography* (New Haven: Yale University Press, 1985), 267–8 and 416–17.

[5] See, for instance, Doris Langley Moore, *Lord Byron: Accounts Rendered* (London: John Murray, 1974), 180–1 and 224.

case. The poet himself couldn't resist the temptation, as a poem from his 1974 collection *At the Gate* evidences. Prompted by the decimalization of the British currency on 15 February 1971, '£. s. d.' laments the loss of the time-honoured names for the three types of coin: 'When *Libra, Solidus, Denarius* / Ruled our metallic currency, / They satisfied and steadied us: – / Pounds, shillings, pence, all honest British money.' What satisfied and steadied seems to have been the association of our power with that of the Roman Empire, as indicated by the adopted Latin names for those coins, with their basis in the values of precious metals: 'True, the gold *libra* weighed twelve ounces once. / The *solidus*, gold equally, / Worth twenty-five *denarii*', gave way, though, first to weighing less, then to unstable values, and then to 'paper promises':

> 'What happened to the *solidus*?' you ask me.
> Reduced at last to an unsilvered shilling
> Of twelve *denarii* – 'pence', or bronze money –
> It faded pitifully into the blue ...
> As for the *libra*, having done with gold,
> It languished among paper promises
> Based on hopes, lies and shrewd financial guesses.
> But mourn for the French *sou*, as is most proper:
> Three hundred ounces, once, all pure copper.[6]

The shilling may have 'faded pitifully into the blue' because the government of Edward Heath failed to conserve the old names for the tripartite currency that was then reduced to the binary and metric: one hundred pence in a pound. Sterling's name, which bears traces of its relation to precious metal, had been reduced to the green one-pound note of those days, though it is now once more a coin. Like John Wilkinson in 'An Episode for Sarah', Graves may be alluding in '£. s. d.' to 23 June 1972, when the Chancellor of the Exchequer, Anthony Barber, announced that the British currency would no longer be pegged to an exchange rate, but must find its level by being floated on the money markets, its value based on 'hopes, lies and shrewd financial guesses'.

Graves's observation with which I began may not quite mean that you can or cannot write poetry about money, but, rather, that money is the kind of subject that really, *pace* Stevens, doesn't have any 'poetry' about it. So there may not be much actual money in poetry, and there may be little or no metaphorically evaluative 'poetry' in money; but in this chapter I look at poems written between the fourteenth and the twentieth centuries in which

[6] Robert Graves, *The Complete Poems,* ed. Beryl Graves and Dunstan Ward (London: Penguin Books, 2003), 704–5.

money is the theme and its absence the concern. Like the rest of us, poets and poetry have been biographically and historically involved with the actualities of money, including ways in which these facts and circumstances have manifested themselves in poetry written in the hope of relieving shortfalls and monetary lack, by the request for support in patronage situations, or the production of work made to be sold into a literary marketplace. I consider various aspects of such situations in which poetry and money are intertwined. In so writing to request financial support, we find poets attempting to deploy what might be called their cultural capital in such a way as to improve their economic conditions.

Here, then, is a late poem by Geoffrey Chaucer in which he addresses his moneybag as if it were his mistress. The work is conventionally called 'The Complaint of Chaucer to his Purse', a title given it in manuscript copies, one its author will not have used:

> To yow my purse / and to noon other wight
> Complayn I / for ye be my lady dere
> I am so sory now / that ye been lyght
> For certes but yf ye make me / hevy chere
> Me were as leef be layde / vpon my bere
> For whiche vnto your mercy / thus I crye
> Beeth hevy ayayne / or elles mote I dye
>
> Now voucheth sauf this day / or hyt be nyght
> That I of yow / the blisful sovne may here
> Or see your colour lyke / the sonne bryght
> That of yelownesse / hadde neuer pere
> Ye be my lyfe / ye be myn hertys stere
> Quene of confort / and of good companye
> Beth hevuy ayayne / or elles moote I dye
>
> Ye purse that ben to me / my lyves lyght
> And saveour / as doun in this worlde here
> Oute of this towne / helpe me thrugh your myght
> Syn that ye wole nat bene / my tresorere
> For I am shave as nye / as is a Frere
> But yet I pray / vnto your curtesye
> Bethe hevy ayen / or elles moote I dye
>
> Lenvoy de Chaucer /
>
> O conquerour / of Brutes albyon
> Whiche that by lygne / and free eleccion
> Been verray kyng / this song to yow I sende

> And ye that mowen / alle *oure* harmes amende
> Haue mynde vpon my supplicacion.[7]

The ballade, with its three refrain-rounded stanzas followed by an envoi – indicated as sent to Henry IV in some copies – wittily begins by addressing the poet's purse as if it were a faithless lover, deploying language from unrequited love lyrics to beg for merciful treatment in its suit to 'my lady dere' who has become 'lyght', meaning short of coins and also wayward or loose. He asks her not to give him 'hevy chere', a sullen face, but to become more literally 'hevy', which will lighten his state, so that he can be supported by her. He wants to hear of his fortune improving before night comes, and that she will be filled with blissful sound and a yellow colour as of the sun, suggesting his need for some gold coins, to relieve him from the romantic death of being turned down by his love, and the actual death which, given his demise the following June, he fairly fears.

The line 'Oute of this tovne / helpe me thrugh your myght' has been the locus of some scholarly debate – which surfaces in the footnote to the word 'towne' from *The Norton Anthology of Poetry*, a text partly modernized and variant, which reads: 'Probably Westminster, where Chaucer had rented a house.'[8] This derives from an article by Andrew Finnel called 'The Poet as Sunday Man: "The Complaint of Chaucer to His Purse"', published in 1973, in which he dates the poem as written after the lease to this dwelling was taken out on 24 December 1399, thus placing its composition in the final year of the poet's life. That the cities of London and Westminster were, and still are, separate jurisdictions allows Finnel to argue that Chaucer is asking his purse to allow him to walk about freely, going from one contiguous town to the other.[9] However, in 'London and Money: Chaucer's *Complaint to his Purse*', John Scattergood offers an alternative dating and a simpler interpretation for the line, agreeing with Skeat that it means 'help me to retire from London to some cheaper place'.[10]

Scattergood dates the poem to the middle to late autumn of 1399, during the crisis around the deposing of Richard II and Henry IV's coronation on 13 October, the envoi to the new king securing that as the earliest it could have been composed:

---

[7] Geoffrey Chaucer, *The Minor Poems*, ed. George B. Pace and Alfred David (Norman: University of Oklahoma Press, 1982), 128–32.

[8] Margaret Ferguson et al. (eds.), *The Norton Anthology of Poetry*, 5th edn. (New York: Norton, 2005), 70.

[9] Andrew J. Finnel, 'The Poet as Sunday Man: "The Complaint of Chaucer to His Purse"', *The Chaucer Review* (Autumn 1973), 147–58.

[10] For a near contemporary poem about money and the city, see the anonymous 'London Lickpenny', in *London: A History in Verse*, ed. Mark Ford (Cambridge: Harvard University Press, 2012), 49–53.

Nevertheless, October, November, and early December 1399 must have been worrying months for Chaucer, so much so that once again, though old and possibly ill, he had to contemplate leaving his native city, this time not primarily for political reasons but for economic ones.[11]

In this light, the envoi's opening evocation to the 'conquerour / of Brutes albyon' and the explanation that he 'Been verray kyng' through his 'lygne / and free eleccion' serve the pragmatic function of declaring his allegiance to the new, true royal authority, justifying it by the tactful inclusion of conqueror and legitimate lineal heir and by the popular confirmation of parliament. He requests not so much charity from the monarch as that his 'grants and annuities', his pension, be granted him: it was in arrears from 29 September, and not paid until May 1400. In the meantime, he seems to have been tided over by the king's providing a partial advance on what was owed of £10 in February.[12]

The double addressees of the poem, first his purse and then the new king, turn the three stanzas and envoi into a justificatory public performance. Scattergood suggests the possibility of self-parody, and the editors for the Oklahoma edition note:

> The analogy between a purse and a courtly mistress is amusing in itself but also expresses an element of truth about Chaucer's situation. In his poetry he had often made fun of his lack of success in love; in this, perhaps his last poem, he carries on the old jest but with the wry acknowledgement that the purse *is* the true lady of a bourgeois official and poet who depends upon the smiles of his noble patrons. The plaintive flattery of the sovereign lady perfectly matches the tone of Chaucer's appeal to his sovereign lord in the Envoy: 'Haue mynde / vpon my supplicacion.'[13]

This self-parody or making fun of himself derives from the complicated business of simultaneously suing for help, which requires a degree of self-abasement, and, by means of the wit, retaining a sufficient degree of esteem to appear deserving of the help requested. To perform this balancing act is to deploy metaphorical figuration whose subject matter is humiliating, as in his being frequently unrequited in love, but whose

---

[11] John Scattergood, 'London and Money: Chaucer's *Complaint to his Purse*', in *Chaucer and the City*, ed. Ardis Butterfield (Woodbridge and Rochester, NY: D. S. Brewer, 2006), 173.

[12] From Scattergood, 173.

[13] Geoffrey Chaucer, *The Minor Poems*, 123.

poetic performance is winningly successful, as can be seen in a similarly circumscribed late-life begging poem by Ben Jonson where, as Marcel Mauss describes the general situation, 'charity wounds him who receives, and our whole moral effort is directed towards suppressing the unconscious harmful patronage of the rich almoner.'[14] The performance of worthiness in begging poems seeks to achieve such a 'suppressing' of the 'unconscious harmful patronage' while simultaneously entertaining, not driving away, the supportive Maecenas.

2. Rhyming for relief

Writing from the same city of Westminster more than two centuries later, Jonson addressed a late poem 'To the Right Honourable, the Lord High Treasurer of England', describing it in the composite title as 'An Epistle Mendicant' which is dated '1631', and in which he sues to his government for relief – a word that the poet puns on in order to evidence the worthiness in relieving him:

> My lord;
> Poor wretched states, pressed by extremities,
> Are fain to seek for succours, and supplies
> Of princes' aids, or good men's charities.
>
> Disease, the enemy, and his engineers,
> Wants, which the rest of his concealed compeers,
> Have cast a trench about me, now five years.
>
> And made those strong approaches, by false braies,
> Reduicts, half-moons, horn-works, and such close ways,
> The muse not peeps out, one of hundred days;
>
> But lies blocked up, and straitened, narrowed in,
> Fixed to the bed, and boards, unlike to win
> Health, or scarce breath, as she had never bin.
>
> Unless some saving honour of the crown,
> Dare think it, to relieve, no less renown,
> A bedrid wit, than a besiegèd town.[15]

---

[14] Marcel Mauss, *The Gift: Forms and Functions of Exchange in Archaic Societies,* ed. Ian Cunnison (London: Cohen & West, 1969), 63.

[15] Ben Jonson, *Complete Poems,* 215–16.

Though I won't be rehearsing arguments here for and against poems being able to make things happen or do things with words,[16] this poem evidently intends to do something: namely to provide its poet with resources for continuance in bedridden age. Ian Donaldson describes the context in which it will have been composed, though he does not, unfortunately, confirm whether these verses did result in an improvement in Jonson's finances.[17] What they do underline, by way of explanations for their own supplication, is that the writer has no other means of support than his writings, or his 'muse', and that in light of his bedridden condition, the inspiration to write and his other source of funding (aside from the generosity of patronage) cannot provide him with the means to go on.

As already suggested with regard to Chaucer's poem, there is skill, tact, and art in a begging poem, for it must illustrate the shameful state to which the poet has been reduced, but not succumb to self-pity, and simultaneously make a pitch as one of what are called the deserving poor – done by means of a performance which illustrates the quality of deservingness, at least to the extent of five triplet-rhymed tercets. Yet a begging poem has also to be a 'gift' to the patron and decidedly not a product for sale. The poem has to be, strictly speaking, worth both a lot less and decidedly more than the funds needed. It must not appear to be a product the poet is selling for the reward of the patronage, for this would be to remove the element of charity and generosity from the relationship proposed in the image of a powerful monarch relieving a besieged and starving town.

The poem proposes and sustains a metaphor drawn from his own enclosed and immoveable state, a metaphor that might have sprung from that pun on the word 'relief', which can be used to mean the giving of alms to relieve poverty, or the 'relief' of a besieged town by an allied army that marches up and drives away the surrounding enemy forces. Both of these acts would require the opening of a government's coffers, and relieving Jonson in his infirmity would have been cheaper than provisioning a military exploit in siege warfare. Perhaps his metaphor is intended to imply as much, but it is not the note that his final tercet strikes, for that would be to attribute motives of prudence to the royal purse, when what is needed is a generosity that will bring honour – not a reputation for good housekeeping – to the crown. The wit to sustain the metaphor and describe himself in the terms of siege warfare (those 'false braies, / Reducts, half-moons, horn-works, and such close ways') is part of his claim to deserve the support required, along with the dignity of utterance in the phrasing and rhyming of the

---

[16] For the arguments, see my *Poetry, Poets, Readers: Making Things Happen* (Oxford: Oxford University Press, 2002) and *The Sound Sense of Poetry* (Cambridge and New York: Cambridge University Press, 2018).

[17] See Ian Donaldson, *Ben Jonson: A Life* (Oxford: Oxford University Press, 2011), 402–8.

lines – the triplet rhymes themselves exemplifying a form of sustained and sustaining mutual support.

Though we don't know if Jonson's 1631 poem was effective in producing a donation to his funds, two years earlier King Charles I had provided him with the then princely sum of £100, as indicated in the title to 'An Epigram', addressed 'To K[ing] Charles for a Hundred Pounds He Sent Me in My Sickness', dated in the title '1629':

> Great Charles, among the holy gifts of grace
> Annexéd to thy person, and thy place,
> 'Tis not enough (thy piety is such)
> To cure the called King's evil with thy touch;
> But thou wilt yet a kinglier mastery try,
> To cure the poet's evil, poverty:
> And, in these cures, dost so thyself enlarge,
> As thou dost cure our evil, at thy charge.
> Nay, and in this, thou show'st to value more
> One poet, than of other folk ten score.
> O piety! So to weigh the poet's estates!
> O bounty! So to difference the rates!
> What can the poet wish his king may do,
> But, that he cure the people's evil too?[18]

Just as Chaucer had contrasted King Henry IV's being in a position to 'alle *oure* harmes amende' and, amongst all those responsibilities, to 'Haue mynde vpon my supplicacion', so Jonson brings together concern for the general public weal and the condition of an old and pensioned poet. Again the negotiation is complex in that it tacitly reminds addressed authority of its responsibilities and yet asks to be remembered and singled out amongst those manifold obligations to the state of the nation. Such interrelations between the private and the public purse may, in later centuries, occur in cases where straitened circumstances are still the subject, but not those specifically of the poet.

The indignities involved in begging poems, as indicated by Mauss, and the rise of the 'temporary poems' being published by Grub Street authors, according to Samuel Johnson's definition of the phrase in his *Dictionary*, help explain the disappearance of such works as Chaucer's and Jonson's requesting support from royal patrons.[19] The problems of writers and their finances are also heard in other writings of Johnson's, such as his 'Life

---

18 Ben Jonson, *Complete Poems*, 205–6.
19 Johnson's definition reads: 'GRU'BSTREET. *n.s.* Originally the name of a street near Moorfields in London, much inhabited by writers of small histories, dictionaries, and temporary poems; whence any mean production is called *grubstreet*.'

of Savage', and the couplets on patronage from 'The Vanity of Human Wishes':

> Yet hope not life from grief or danger free,
> Nor think the doom of man revers'd for thee:
> Deign on the passing world to turn thine eyes,
> And pause awhile from letters, to be wise;
> There mark what ills the scholar's life assail,
> Toil, envy, want, the patron, and the jail.[20]

About Pope's couplets in '*Of the* Use *of* Riches' where 'we eat the bread another sows' but 'how unequal it bestows, observe, / 'Tis thus we riot, while who sow it, starve', Colin Nicholson, noting an ambiguity of reference in 'riot', observes that 'far from passively suffering, the poor are rattling the bars of the couplet that denies them energy'.[21] Such complexities of poetic form are similarly present in Johnson's closing couplet, for a rhyme such as 'assail' and 'jail' encloses its scholar in the debtor's prison of its lines, but simultaneously rattles the bars by underlining them and their injustice in the ringing close. Johnson's commitment to frugality and self-sufficiency inflects his elegiac stanzas 'On the Death of Dr Robert Levet', in which the 'modest wants of every day' the 'toil of every day supplied'.[22] That poem's interest in the fate of the indigent poor foreshadows the explorations of rural poverty and individual integrity in poems by William Wordsworth such as 'Beggars' and 'The Sailor's Mother'.

3. Begging and lying in poems

Wordsworth's communing with nature is taken to be an unequivocal good, but, as one critic asks, what 'about need and suffering? We have heard much so far of a "reciprocity" which depends upon a continual overplus, but why should the account always be in credit?' This writer then defends the poet by turning to the constrained circumstances in which all values come to be expressed:

---

[20] Samuel Johnson, *Poems,* ed. E. L. McAdam, Jr. with George Milne (New Haven: Yale University Press, 1964), 99.

[21] Colin Nicholson, *Writing and the Rise of Finance: Capital Satires of the Early Eighteenth Century* (Cambridge: Cambridge University Press, 1994), 155, citing 'Epistle III To Allen Lord Bathurst *Of the* Use *of* Riches', Alexander Pope, *Epistles to Several Persons (Moral Essays),* ed. F. W. Bateson, Twickenham Edition, vol. 3 (London: Methuen, 1951), vol. 2, 83 and 85.

[22] Johnson, *Poems,* 314–15.

That the farmer in 'The Last of the Flock' loves his children more and more the richer he becomes; that Robert in 'The Ruined Cottage' stops loving his children so much when he loses his job: these are not judgments on the accidental badness of these characters but acknowledgements that there is no human virtue or pleasure which we can never be deprived of by material distress. Wordsworth made sure that readers of *The Prelude* knew what Raisley Calvert's money had done for the growth of the poet's mind; his sonnet acknowledging this debt affords one of the most impressive examples of Wordsworth's severe refusal of empty gesture in its failure to say almost anything about Calvert other than that he was sick and gave Wordsworth material help.[23]

These comments are keyed to an earlier account of how the Poor Laws required their recipients to be reduced to a level of absolute indigence in order to be considered deserving of charity. So the farmer has to lose all his sheep and become entirely unable to support his children to receive aid. Whether you have resources of intrinsic goodness as regards your children and dependents or not, you must be stripped of the means to express that goodness in order to be deserving of help to do it. The critic doesn't quite enforce this point as firmly as he might have done, because he wishes to discredit or dismiss the idea that the failure to love or care might come from 'badness of character', another way in which people in poverty can be regarded as 'undeserving' after all, and to underline that human values are always bound up with the conditions in which they may or may not be expressed.

By turning from his question in the paragraph above to the sonnet of Wordsworth's that is, in effect, a note of gratitude to a now dead sponsor, the continuity between the spiritual and material economics of the poet's subject are underlined, and the financial conditions within which he was able to write such poems:

> Calvert! it must not be unheard by them
> Who may respect my name that I to thee
> Ow'd many years of early liberty.
> This care was thine when sickness did condemn
> Thy youth to hopeless wasting, root and stem:
> That I, if frugal and severe, might stray
> Where'er I liked; and finally array
> My temples with the Muse's diadem.
> Hence, if in freedom I have lov'd the truth,

---

[23] Simon Jarvis, *Wordsworth's Philosophic Song*, 101.

> If there be aught of pure, or good, or great,
> In my past verse; or shall be, in the lays
> Of higher mood, which now I meditate,
> It gladdens me, O worthy, short-lived Youth!
> To think how much of this will be thy praise.[24]

Calvert's small legacy, given in 1794, contributed to Wordsworth and Dorothy's being able to live at Racedown, supporting thus the collaboration that would result, four years later, in the first *Lyrical Ballads*. The note struck above is that, being provided with this gift of material support, he could be free of the interest that would require him to bend what he said to the earning of a living. This is the logic that links 'if in freedom I have lov'd the truth, / If there be aught of pure, or good, or great, / In my past verse' to his being granted that relief from dependence, and thus links Calvert's crediting the poet's abilities to the truth that he may be found by readers to have expressed.

Through Calvert's will Wordsworth was promised £900, and even more than his generosity, which 'did not transform the financial situation – the money was released only fitfully and in small amounts', its meaning, Stephen Gill asserts, 'greatly affected Wordsworth's sense of possibilities':

> In putting such trust in him Calvert reinforced his image of himself when it most needed reinforcement and placed on him an obligation, which Wordsworth readily and optimistically received, to use his particular gifts of intellect and imagination for the betterment of mankind.[25]

Yet there is further interest in the relationship assumed but not articulated here between the 'trust' that the award of funds expresses and the 'obligation' that it placed upon the poet. For there are operative disjunctions implied in the articulation of the sonnet addressing Calvert too: his bequest is not 'investing in people' in the current corporate sense, where an audited return is implied, not least because it was awarded in a will (and he died a victim of tuberculosis in early January 1795) so any repayment – spiritual, for instance – could only be made to the memory of the dead friend; yet

---

[24] William Wordsworth, *Poems, in Two Volumes, and Other Poems, 1800–1807*, ed. Jared Curtis (Ithaca: Cornell University Press, 1983), 151–2. For an interpretation of what he calls 'the belated tribute to his benefactor' in the final book of *The Prelude* (1805, Book 13, ll. 349–67; 1850, Book 14, ll. 354–69), see Kurt Heinzelman, *The Economics of the Imagination* (Amherst: University of Massachusetts Press, 1980), 197–200.

[25] Stephen Gill, *William Wordsworth: A Life* (Oxford: Oxford University Press, 1989), 84.

Wordsworth, nevertheless, sees that it was not a strictly disinterested or indifferent gift. The idea was to provide the poet with the opportunity to dedicate himself to his art, and the values of the noun 'truth' and adjectives 'pure, or good, or great' may have been enabled by the bequest, but are not a calculated return on that investment – not least because literary artworks, and especially poems, can rarely be so securely evaluated at the point of production (as Wordsworth's if-clause acknowledges). It would require others to find the truth in what he had been able to write thanks to the trust in Calvert's bequest.

According to the Cornell editor, this sonnet was probably composed between 21 May 1802 and 6 March 1804, that's to say, after the *Lyrical Ballads* period, with the first longer *Prelude* in progress, and the shorter poems that would go into the two-volume 1807 publication in mid-flow. If its earlier proposed date were the case, this sonnet emerged at the same time as 'Resolution and Independence', that major statement about the fate of poets and the leech-gatherer's mode of subsistence. Wordsworth's being financially enabled to write poetry and his commitment to its truth (because not in anyone's pay)[26] also emerges in poems from the spring of 1802 where, as in 'The Sailor's Mother' and 'Beggars', the being deserving of funds and telling the truth about their straitened circumstances troublingly inflects these encounters with vagrancy and begging.

Yet what is the relationship between Wordsworth's indebtedness, his need of support, and his poems about indigent persons encountered on the road? The performances in begging poems by Chaucer and Jonson were inevitably nuanced with metaphorical strategies for maintaining self-esteem at the same time as requesting support so as to indicate that you deserve it. Some of these dynamics can be seen, with a reversal of the relationship between poem and need, and an identification with those lacking obvious means of support, in Wordsworth's poems that encounter beggars or begging, and in which the poet's own descriptive powers figure like a form of means testing – as here in the second and third stanzas of 'The Sailor's Mother':

> The ancient Spirit is not dead;
> Old times, thought I, are breathing there;
> Proud was I that my country bred
> Such strength, a dignity so fair:
> She begg'd an alms, like one in poor estate;
> I looked at her again, nor did my pride abate.

[26] Being in receipt of a government pension would, after all, be Byron's jibe in stanza 6 of the 'Dedication' to *Don Juan*: 'And Wordsworth has his place in the Excise', *The Complete Poetical Works*, ed. Jerome McGann, vol. 5, *Don Juan* (Oxford: Oxford University Press, 1986), 5.

When from these lofty thoughts I woke,
With the first word I had to spare
I said to her, 'Beneath your Cloak
What's that which on your arm you bear?'
She answered soon as she the question heard,
'A simple burthen, Sir, a little Singing-bird.'[27]

As the first stanza has it, 'One morning (raw it was and wet, / A foggy day in winter time)', the poet-speaker encounters 'A Woman on the road' and his imagination swells, as does his meter to pentameter and then alexandrine, at the sight of this fellow countrywoman: 'Majestic in her person, tall and straight; / And like a Roman matron's was her mien and gait.' He further promulgates his thoughts along this theme, for the association with the mothers of decimated Roman soldiers, as it might be, feeds and dramatizes for readers his representatively patriotic thoughts. Now, at the swelling of the final couplet, the poet encounters a diminished reality to check his 'lofty thoughts': 'She begg'd an alms, like one in poor estate' – and check he does, only to find nothing that will dent his 'pride': 'I look'd at her again, nor did my pride abate.'

It is on the basis of this unchecked pride that the poet-speaker asks his apparently means-testing question: 'Beneath your Cloak / What's that which on your arm you bear?' That he means to challenge her on why it is she's begging when she has something of value under her cloak, something which she might sell, perhaps, is underlined in the poem's variant texts down the years, for Wordsworth evidently havered over how overt he should be about her possibly covert means. Between 1820 and 1827 the line read '"What treasure," said I', and after reverting to a version without the 'treasure' word, it reappeared for one more reading in 1840: 'What treasure is it that you bear'. The revelation of the poem, that she is carrying the bird in a cage because her dead sailor son has left it to her, and its value as a treasure of his memory is too important for her to sell it as a bit of exchangeable treasure, is brought out of hiding by Wordsworth's pertinently impertinent question. This is, then, one of Wordsworth's attempts to discover life, and his descriptive language, not unlike Stevens's in the previous chapter, correlates description with evaluation, the evaluation of whether she is deserving of the alms that she has begged. In this poem, as in the earliest published version of 'Old Man Travelling', the encountered person gets the final and tacitly rebuking word, so we don't find out whether the woman's story renders her deserving of the poet-speaker's charity.

---

[27] Wordsworth, *Poems, in Two Volumes*, 77–8. See my 'Reparation and "The Sailor's Mother"', in *In the Circumstances: About Poetry and Poets* (Oxford: Oxford University Press, 1992), 9–23.

Immediately after drafting 'The Sailor's Mother' on 11 and 12 March, Wordsworth wrote another poem in which he encounters a strong-looking woman. Here is the first stanza of 'Beggars', which was written on the next two days of the same month:

> She had a tall Man's height, or more;
> No bonnet screen'd her from the heat;
> A long drab-colour'd Cloak she wore,
> A Mantle reaching to her feet:
> What other dress she had I could not know;
> Only she wore a Cap that was as white as snow.

Here it is as if the description of her clothing is not only intended to offer the reader a picture of the lady, who, the title would suggest, must be a beggar, but also that the quality and style of her garb is meant to tell us whether she is poor or not. The second and third stanzas, with their reference to her face 'of Egyptian brown', suggest that the poet-speaker thinks he has encountered a gypsy, not one of the neighbourhood figures that he had composed upon in 'The Old Cumberland Beggar',[28] for he is at pains to point out her foreigner-looking appearance:

> In all my walks, through field or town,
> Such Figure had I never seen:
> Her face was of Egyptian brown:
> Fit person was she for a Queen,
> To head those ancient Amazonian files:
> Or ruling Bandit's Wife, among the Grecian Isles.
>
> Before me begging did she stand,
> Pouring out sorrows like a sea;
> Grief after grief: – on English Land
> Such woes I knew could never be;
> And yet a boon I gave her; for the Creature
> Was beautiful to see; a Weed of glorious feature![29]

The situation outlined in the opening three stanzas of 'Beggars' is even more striking in its intersection of patriotic and charitable feeling. Once again the thought that a person wearing a cloak might be hiding something appears. The poet-speaker is sure she's lying for effect. This is the poem's theme,

---

[28] See authorial headnote in William Wordsworth, *Lyrical Ballads, and Other Poems, 1797–1800*, ed. James Butler and Karen Green (Ithaca: Cornell University Press, 1992), 228.

[29] Wordsworth, *Poems, in Two Volumes*, 113–14.

because when the two boys appear in the second part they are also accused of lying in that he knows, or claims to know, that they are her sons, though they claim that their mother is dead. Thus when they assail the poet-speaker with their 'plaintive whine' and he rebukes them by saying 'Not half an hour ago / Your Mother has had alms of mine', they assert that they are not the woman's children because their mother 'is dead', and when he replies 'Nay but I gave her pence, and she will buy you bread', they come back with 'She has been dead, Sir, many a day.' The poet-speaker then confronts them with what seems the poem's key issue: 'Sweet Boys, you're telling me a lie'. Yet it is the poet's assumption that they are lying; no confirmatory encounter with the woman *and* the boys happens, so the poem is deadlocked on their word against his. Yet Wordsworth concludes by noting that he is not offended by their lying, but rather charmed by an indomitable opportunism:

> 'It was your Mother, as I say – '
> And in the twinkling of an eye,
> 'Come, come!' cried one; and without more ado,
> Off to some other play they both together flew.[30]

But just as he gave the woman pence not because she needed it, but because she was beautiful, so he isn't offended by the boys' lying to him, because they do it so joyfully (and this is underlined in his return to the occasion many years later).[31] The theme is relevant to Wordsworth the poet, for lying to elicit funds might be thought a close analogy of what a poet who sells his wares into the book trade is doing, and the poet's anxieties over these poems, including the adjustments made especially to calibrate their relations to poverty and class and whether those encountered deserve charity, all indicate his awareness of this very analogy.

The relationship between truth-telling when begging and the independence to write truthful poetry is underlined in perhaps the most famous of these encounters, first drafted some two months later on 3–7 May 1802, perhaps a couple of weeks before the sonnet remembering Calvert's bequest. Having addressed the leech-gatherer he has encountered on the lonely moor but somehow failed to hear what he was saying, so much preoccupied with his own profession was he, again the poet-speaker finds

> My former thoughts return'd: the fear that kills;
> The hope that is unwilling to be fed;
> Cold pain, and labour, and all fleshly ills;

---

[30] Wordsworth, *Poems, in Two Volumes*, 115.

[31] See 'Sequel to the Foregoing [*Beggars*], Composed Many Years After', in William Wordsworth, *Shorter Poems, 1807–1820*, ed. Carl H. Ketcham (Ithaca: Cornell University Press, 1989), 231–3.

> And mighty Poets in their misery dead.
> And now, not knowing what the Old Man had said,
> My question eagerly did I renew,
> 'How is it that you live, and what is it you do?'[32]

Pressing upon Wordsworth's question is his thinking on Chatterton's suicide and the emotional troubles of his friend Coleridge, and on his representation of the question's being asked there presses his practice of encountering the indigent poor and turning those experiences into morally uplifting allegories, and his trusting in the cultural value of those poems for readers at the time and in an unpredictable future.[33]

Commenting on Ruskin's eloquently articulated beliefs about the 'intrinsic value of the wheat, the air, or the flowers', Geoffrey Hill writes of him bringing the 'intensity to his subject that Wordsworth in "Michael" or "Resolution and Independence" or "The Female Vagrant" or Book XII of *The Prelude* devotes to the unrecognized and publicly unfulfilled powers of men and women forced to live in various kinds of straitened circumstance.'[34] Though Ruskin may have been writing with the same intensity as Wordsworth, and though the intent of these poems may have been, as Hill asserts, to address 'the unrecognized and publicly unfulfilled powers of men and women forced to live in various kinds of straitened circumstance', what cannot be said about them is that they support Ruskin's assertion of an 'intrinsic value' either in naturally given phenomena such as air, or non-hybridized flowers, or in the added value of humanly cultivated strains of wheat. These encounter poems of Wordsworth's bid for their own value as art works by being particularly attentive to the evaluation of strangers' appearances, to the stories they tell about themselves, and, in the case of 'The Sailor's Mother' and 'Beggars', calculating the truth of their statements in the light cast upon them by the fact that each of them has, however unexpectedly, 'begg'd an alms'.[35]

---

[32] Ibid. 128.

[33] For more on the poetics and ethics of these encounter poems, see 'Burdens of Sound', in *The Sound Sense of Poetry* (Cambridge: Cambridge University Press, 2018), 120–39.

[34] Geoffrey Hill, 'Poetry and Value', in *Collected Critical Writings,* ed. Kenneth Haynes (Oxford: Oxford University Press, 2008), 486, citing *Munera Pulveris* in John Ruskin, *The Library Edition of the Works*, 39 vols, ed. E. T. Cook and Alexander Wedderburn (London: George Allen, 1903–12), vol. 17, 153.

[35] For the family, financial, and poetic disaster of John Wordsworth's drowning in the wreck of the *Earl of Abergaveny* in 1805, see Peter Swaab, 'Wordsworth's Elegies for John Wordsworth', *Wordsworth Circle*, vol. 45, no. 1 (Winter 2014), 31–8, and, drawing on his conclusions, my '"On the Power of Sound": the "*Moral*

4. Bounty and shame

Poets have not only been inspired to compose in and on the circumstances of their own or others' poverty. There are a great many poems entitled 'Money' which figure transitions from self-concern to others' relations with the medium of exchange, whether rich or poor or just-managing. Elizabeth Bishop wrote one of many such poems in the late 1930s or early 1940s, a particularly fertile period for works on this subject; but she wasn't sufficiently satisfied to publish it during her lifetime:

> Money comes and money goes,
>   Like a bird it flies,
> Its migratory habits stern
>   Both ignorant and wise.
>
> In the season, I have watched
>   Its wonderful gyrations,
> Swift and fierce, and boldly close
>   To human habitations.
>
> Under the arches of the vaults
>   Are built the hidden nests.
> What instinctive fears and faults
>   Govern those silver breasts?[36]

Though neatly turned in its three fully rhymed ballad stanzas, perhaps Bishop was right to withhold this twelve-line extended simile, which ends at the point where it would have had to answer its difficult concluding question. Nevertheless, 'Money' places the poem at odds with its eponymous subject, at a distance, as a bird-watcher might, so as not to scare it away, and yet that is what happens. The poem's accepted obligation to rhyme leads to a sexualized image in its final lines, where the access to money in the bank vaults is metaphorically compared to a hard, a silver-plated, a perhaps withholding fund of maternal nourishment, such as Adrian Stokes would elaborate in his poem 'Weathering'.[37]

Bishop did, however, allow asides about money into her authorized

---

Music" of Wordsworth at Work in Later Life', in *Poetry in the Making*, ed. Daniel Tyler (Oxford: Oxford University Press, 2020), 31–50.

[36] Elizabeth Bishop, *Poems, Prose, and Letters*, ed. Robert Giroux and Lloyd Schwartz (New York: Library of America, 2008), 215.

[37] See Adrian Stokes, *With All the Views: The Collected Poems*, ed. Peter Robinson (Manchester: Carcanet Press, 1981), 94. 'Weathering' is discussed in Chapter 9, 199–203.

oeuvre. Her 'Going to the Bakery', set in Rio de Janeiro, ends in an encounter with a particularly desperate beggar:

> In front of my apartment house
> a black man sits in a black shade,
> lifting his shirt to show a bandage
> on his black, invisible side.
>
> Fumes of *cachaça* knock me over,
> like gas fumes from an auto-crash.
> He speaks in perfect gibberish.
> The bandage flares up, white and fresh.
>
> I give him seven cents in *my*
> terrific money, say 'Good night'
> from force of habit. Oh, poor habit!
> Not one word more apt or bright?[38]

Cachaça is a distilled spirit made from sugarcane, so alcohol is knocking her over, while the bandage is offered as an explanation for the begging, prompting her to give seven cents in a very strong currency. Then the poem switches from one form of exchange to another, from coins to words. The description of that verbal performance as 'poor' implies an unexpected reversal, where the rich foreigner with her 'terrific money' is suddenly impoverished by the tacit humiliation in her patronage of the beggar, and the dependence of both on each is exclaimed about and questioned in its close.[39]

Gwendolen Brooks's 'The Lovers of the Poor'[40] brings home the tacit humiliations in place for those who enact the wounding of charity, as Mauss described it, for if 'charity wounds him who receives, and our whole moral effort is directed towards suppressing the unconscious harmful patronage of the rich almoner',[41] then the charitable inflictor of wounds is vulnerable to various forms of suppressive retaliation:

---

[38] Bishop, *Poems, Prose, and Letters*, 143–4. The next poem 'Under the Window: Ouro Preto' also references money in passing: 'NOT MUCH MONEY BUT IT IS AMUSING.'

[39] For the embarrassment of riches, see Randall Jarrell, 'Money', *The Complete Poems* (New York: Farrar, Straus & Giroux, 1969), 117; Charles Tomlinson, 'The Rich', *The Way In* (Oxford: Oxford University Press, 1974), 12; and the title poem from Frederick Seidel, *Widening Income Inequality* (New York: Farrar, Straus & Giroux, 2016), 116–18.

[40] Gwendolyn Brooks, *Selected Poems* (New York: Perennial Classics, 1999), 90–3.

[41] Marcel Mauss, *The Gift: Forms and Functions of Exchange in Archaic Societies*, ed. Ian Cunnison (London: Cohen & West, 1969), 63.

> Their guild is giving money to the poor.
> The worthy poor. The very very worthy
> And beautiful poor. Perhaps just not too swarthy?

Here those enhancing their self-esteem through good works are found to be tacitly preserving the differentiations of wealth, status, and racial identity that they would appear to be mitigating:

> Their league is allotting largesse to the Lost.
> But to put their clean, their pretty money, to put
> Their money collected from delicate rose-fingers
> Tipped with their hundred flawless rose-nails seems ...

Trailing off, Brooks voices the idea that the charity can be achieved without reducing the distance between the needy and the bountiful: 'Perhaps the money can be posted'. 'The poor' are always with us not least because of the prejudicial effect produced by nominalizing an adjective and putting a definite article in front of it. The lovers of the poor are bound to maintain the distance that is captured by the idea of posting the donations not least because of the linguistic usage by which they define their difference from those that they intend to help. The straitened circumstances and monetary difficulties that poets and others have experienced and how they have managed them in poetry has brought us face to face with the social and cultural dynamics of the mitigation of inequality by charity, and how poetry about poverty not one's own is also inevitably caught up in the problems besetting those lovers of the poor in Gwendolyn Brooks's poem. This, in turn, invites thought on ways in which the poet herself avoids those problems of the Lady Bountiful kind in her writings about poverty in Chicago.

The inequality Bishop encountered in Rio was just as pressing back home – in Chicago, for instance, as evoked in the depredated, quasi-sonnet 'kitchenette building' which forms the first section of Brooks's 'A Street in Bronzeville':

> We are things of dry hours and the involuntary plan,
> Grayed in, and gray. 'Dream' makes a giddy sound, not strong
> Like 'rent,' 'feeding a wife,' 'satisfying a man.'
>
> But could a dream send up through onion fumes
> Its white and violet, fight with fried potatoes
> And yesterday's garbage ripening in the hall,
> Flutter, or sing an aria down these rooms
>
> Even if we were willing to let it in,

> Had time to warm it, keep it very clean,
> Anticipate a message, let it begin?
>
> We wonder. But not well! not for a minute!
> Since Number Five is out of the bathroom now,
> We think of lukewarm water, hope to get in it.[42]

Through its rhythmical precision and refusal of metaphor, this reduced sonnet is removed from the trap that the ladies fall into in 'The Lovers of the Poor'. Brooks makes sure she is not going to succumb to the problems presented in that poem by her confident use of the first-person plural pronoun, in which either she is voicing (like a dramatic monologue) the experiences of those who live in this building, or she is identifying so closely with their condition that no distance, of the kind overt in Stevens's 'Attempt to Discover Life', emerges. Where almost all of the poetry about money in this chapter has revealed social and cultural differences figured in the degrees of access to money, in this poem the straitened circumstances are shared, and the poem benefits greatly from that unglamorous solidarity.

Mina Loy's 'On Third Avenue' also reduces to near invisibility the distance between her experience and perception of poverty. It begins with a quoted remark from one who does not wish her well ('You should have disappeared years ago …') and

> so disappear
> on Third Avenue
> to share the heedless incognito
>
> of shuffling shadow-bodies
> animate with frustration

Her poem has no first-person singular pronoun, as can be heard in the command-like second line of the poem 'so disappear', where a pronoun is expected. In amongst the 'shadow-bodies' the verbal consciousness moves, finding improvised forms with occasional rhymes for the vagrants, their 'hueless overcast / of down-cast countenances' and 'sweat-sculptured cloth' on 'irreparable dummies' like 'mummies / half unwound.' Yet though encountering urban poverty and being mixed with it, the poem accrues a figurative richness, which is intensified by contrasts in its second part, where she repeats the phrase 'Such are the compensations of poverty, / to see'. What is seen are a ticket-seller in the box office of 'a ten-cent Cinema' transformed into 'a Goddess / aglitter' and a lit trolley car going past with

---

[42] Brooks, *Selected Poems*, 3.

is passengers who become 'luminous busts', but 'lovely in anonymity / they vanish'.[43] Yet unlike in Brooks's 'kitchenette building', Loy's 'On Third Avenue', while locating its sensibility so as not to stage a difference of social perspective from its 'shuffling shadow-bodies', offers metaphorical figuration and transformative verbal imagining to provide her poem with its displayed resources.

5. Nothing but money

Philip Larkin's money poems give the impression that, while not having a worry about it, he has a problem with it. These two late works from *High Windows* (1974) might appear the consequence of the reluctantly cowed attitudes towards earning a living expressed in his two 'Toads' poems from *The Less Deceived* (1955) and *The Whitsun Weddings* (1964), and to sum up a life-weary grumpiness.[44] Yet he too, intentionally or not, is pointing towards issues of money and worth – problems about what money is for, and what its exchange value might be if we weigh it in any terms other than a money value. For behind the overt attitudes his poems voice, there is a questioning profundity and depth that he characteristically shrugs offs.[45]

'Homage to a Government' is among the only overtly political poems allowed into the oeuvre collected during the poet's lifetime:

> Next year we are to bring the soldiers home
> For lack of money, and it is all right.
> Places they guarded, or kept orderly,
> Must guard themselves, and keep themselves orderly.
> We want the money for ourselves at home
> Instead of working. And this is all right.[46]

Archie Burnett observes that this poem 'is concerned with the decisions of Harold Wilson's Labour government to bring home British troops

---

[43] Mina Loy, *The Lost Lunar Baedeker: Poems*, ed. Roger L. Conover (New York: Farrar, Straus & Giroux, 1996), 109–10.

[44] See 'Toads' and 'Toads Revisited', Philip Larkin, *The Complete Poems*, ed. Archie Burnett (New York: Farrar, Straus & Giroux, 2012), 34–5 and 55–6.

[45] Compare the lament of Larkin's Jewish 'biographer' Jake Balokawsky in 'Posterity', who 'makes the money sign' (*Complete Poems*, 86), with 'A Neglected Responsibility: Contemporary Literary Manuscripts', in Philip Larkin, *Required Writing: Miscellaneous Pieces 1955–1982* (London: Faber & Faber, 1983), 98–108.

[46] Larkin, *The Complete Poems*, 87.

from Aden, following a civil war there in 1965–67, and to disband the Far Eastern command and withdraw British forces from Singapore just before 1967.[47] He notes that the reason British troops were withdrawn is not because the government couldn't afford to pay for them, but because they had been ousted by the local independence movement's military actions. Disproving its historical accuracy is not his point, though: what the contested historical reasons do highlight and make even more prominent is the criticism of the country produced by dwelling on the money motive. This is then converted into a motif by means of the poem's dry, repeated phrases; and it is these that make it a starkly sour piece of polemic against the Labour government of the time.

The poem displays a consciously pointed use of enjambments to articulate lines of thought that the poet evidently doesn't like. We don't need him to tell us that the title is ironic, though he did just that in occasional writings cited by Burnett. In the first stanza there are two such phrases, and they turn on money (in both senses of that verb phrase). We are to 'bring the soldiers home', yes, but around the line end it is revealed that we are to do this 'For lack of money' and we want 'the money for ourselves at home', which might seem at least partially justified, though Larkin's dislike of a country which spends more on education than defence, also cited in the notes to his *Complete Poems*, again underlines the values-other-than-money theme – but then again around the line ending, we find that we want the money 'Instead of working'.

Whatever a reader might think of the poem's lamentingly late-colonial sentiments, its use of *rime-riche* is masterly, and the French name for this pairing of identical rhyme-words may have helped prompt this poem about the process of decolonisation (which, it might be noted, was by no means a process unique to that left-of-centre political party). The way its sound-sense amalgam works is pointed to in the third stanza, where 'the same' couplet-rhymes with 'nearly the same':

> Next year we shall be living in a country
> That brought its soldiers home for lack of money.
> The statues will be standing in the same
> Tree-muffled squares, and look nearly the same.
> Our children will not know it's a different country.
> All we can hope to leave them now is money.

The effect, though, is not particularly 'riche' in its employment here, because it rings hollow, as in the rhyming of 'money' with 'money'. Similarly, in the first stanza, to rhyme on 'all right' twice is to start the thought that it is not

---

[47] Ibid. 462.

all right at all. Nor does the poem begin to say that if they withdrew the troops for the right reason that would be all right, but evidently doing it for the wrong one is not. After all, why include 'Next year we shall be easier in our minds' at the end of the second stanza if not to draw attention to the impure motives even in wanting to have a clear conscience? Yet, putting aside the party-political slant of 'Homage to a Government', we can see that the more ubiquitous problem of what lies beyond money to grant *it* its value is informing the hollow-ring, the dead-echo of Larkin's rime-riche rhymes.

In the second poem, called 'Money', the character speaking doesn't appear to have any social connections such as would allow him to leave his money to his heirs:

> Quarterly, is it, money reproaches me:
>   'Why do you let me lie here wastefully?
> I am all you never had of goods and sex.
>   You could get them still by writing a few cheques.'
>
> So I look at others, what they do with theirs:
>   They certainly don't keep it upstairs.
> By now they've a second house and car and wife:
>   Clearly money has something to do with life[48]

Burnett reports that the poem was written between 11 and 19 February 1973, and that its earlier draft titles were 'Bank Statement', 'Financial Statement', and 'Prices & Incomes' – which characterize the movement of thought from his own mounting savings to the conclusion's melancholy detachment, as if the poet's position were as in an epigram from Cowper's 'Translations of Greek Verses' called 'On Late-Acquired Wealth':

> Poor in my youth, and in life's later scenes
>   Rich to no end, I curse my natal hour;
> Who nought enjoy'd, while young, denied the means;
>   And nought, when old, enjoy'd, denied the pow'r.[49]

The mismatching of this epigram, however melancholy, does assert the point of money, which, it implies, is to enable life and enjoyment while you can. A deeper problem in Larkin's 'Money' is in its epistemic detachment, its dividing the poet-speaker's life hopes and expectations from those of the others it characterizes in the two stanzas above. There the people he looks at with a wistful mock-envy, or disbelief, seem to know how to use it: 'By now

[48] Ibid. 94.
[49] William Cowper, *Poetical Works*, ed. H. S. Milford, 4th edn. with corrections and additions by Norma Russell (London: Oxford University Press, 1967), 570.

they've a second house and car and wife'. This line turns sourly ambiguous at the end when appearing to equivocate by the possible inclusive forward application of the adjective 'second' to the subsequent nouns ('car' and 'wife'), which are also forward-determined by the indefinite article 'a'. Are these people owners of a car or a 'second car', and are they married or remarried? And what, further, is the poem suggesting about the economic basis of matrimony? Is a second house or car the equivalent of a second wife?[50]

In the penultimate stanza, turning from the listing of desires, it offers another 1970s lament about inflation, devaluation, and the rising cost of living:

> — In fact, they've a lot in common, if you enquire:
> You can't put off being young until you retire,
> And however you bank your screw, the money you save
> Won't in the end buy you more than a shave.

The poem concludes by presenting the view from high windows other than those in the book's title poem, figured as a simile for what the sound of 'money singing' looks like:

> I listen to money singing. It's like looking down
> From long french windows at a provincial town,
> The slums, the canal, the churches ornate and mad
> In the evening sun. It is intensely sad.

But how is the song money sings related to the view of that provincial town, and how is a reader to relate to the poem's final sentence? What saves the poem from a bathos derived from not happening to share the values it gestures at is that the 'french windows' and the 'looking down' indicate that the view provided by money singing is from an economically elevated vantage point, so that 'looking down' may also be pitying, or being sentimental about the poor centre of town, and then 'intensely sad' may be bitterly ironic.

But if such a reading were in the right direction, wouldn't the second line have to read 'down on a provincial town', rather than 'at' it? Larkin's use of language here references his characteristic confidence in the linkage of word and thing, which is then brought into contact with two brief emotively subjective, and rhyming, remarks ('ornate and mad' and 'intensely sad'). These two comments are insecurely attached to the lists of objects that they

---

[50] For 'Wish I had some of the money back I spent on her', see Anthony Thwaite (ed.), *The Selected Letters of Philip Larkin 1950–1985* (London: Faber & Faber, 1992), 223.

characterize. The stanza neither manifests a dense and concrete language, one rich in vocabulary, nor a language that more confidently embraces abstraction and argument. Rather it offers, like a symptom of its money predicament, a language that had once been confidently referential, but has, as it were, lost its touch, and has unconfidently decided to hoard its cash, its cache of vocabulary, out of sight, in a bank or under a mattress, where inflation has been eating it away.

So the final sentence of the poem is 'intensely sad' on two levels: in the effect of 'money singing' on what is seen, and how it is registered. But why are the 'churches ornate and mad / In the evening sun'? The word 'mad' here is inescapably equivocating between 'crazy-looking' and 'angry-looking', and both of these are intensified by the 'evening sun' as if it were the last light from Arnold's 'sea of faith' withdrawing. It is as if the absurdity of an established church, and its compromised views of worldly wealth, appears even more painfully obvious in its decline, or that the complaint of religion against a seemingly valueless life (one in which there's nothing but money, and it is being eaten away by high inflation) is made even more hysterically 'mad' by religion's waning power over our consumerist and accumulatively motivated behaviour. Either way, since, as they say, you can't take it with you, the view from which money has alienated this poem's speaker may well appear 'intensely sad.'

CHAPTER FOUR

Indebtedness and redemption

1. *Paternal debt and repayment*

When in August or September of 1603 Ben Jonson's first son, also christened Benjamin, died suddenly of the plague at the age of seven, his father wrote an epigram that has an epitaph embedded in it:

> Farewell, thou child of my right hand, and joy;
>   My sin was too much hope of thee, loved boy,
> Seven years thou wert lent me, and I thee pay,
>   Exacted by thy fate, on the just day.
> O, could I lose all father, now. For why
>   Will man lament the state he should envy?
> To have so soon 'scaped world's, and flesh's rage,
>   And, if no other misery, yet age!
> Rest in soft peace, and, asked, say here doth lie
>   Ben Jonson his best piece of poetry.
> For whose sake, henceforth, all his vows be such,
>   As what he loves may never like too much.[1]

While with Drummond of Hawthornden in Scotland in 1618, Jonson recalled a dream about, and noted down the circumstances surrounding, this first son's death, giving the context in which he had come to write his farewell poem:

> When the king came in England, at that time the pest was in London, he being in the country at S[i]r Robert Cotton's house with old Camden, he saw in a vision his eldest son (then a child and at London) appear unto him with the mark of a bloody cross on his

---

[1]   Ben Jonson, *The Complete Poems,* ed. George Parfitt (London: Penguin Books, 1996), 48.

forehead, as if it had been cutted with a sword, at which amazed he prayed unto God, and in the morning he came to Mr Camden's chamber to tell him, who persuaded him it was but an apprehension of his fantasy at which he should not be disjected; in the meantime comes there letters from his wife of the death of that boy in the plague. He appeared to him (he said) of a manly shape, and of that growth that he thinks he shall be at the resurrection.[2]

Jonson sees the boy grown up in the dream, and dreams that the misfortune of his early death will, in eternity, be undone by the resurrection of the body and the life everlasting. His elegiac epigram's economic metaphor, sketched in the opening lines, guides its entire twelve lines. The special interest in the banking analogy, and whether it doesn't have a buried optimism, is touched on by J. H. Prynne in an essay on George Herbert's 'Love (III)' which comments on trading with God through 'special premiums or discounts or forward contracts'.[3] Does the fact that Jonson has paid back his 'debt' to the bank of Heaven mean that he's in better credit with God? Does it mean that he can hope to borrow again in the future? Is this how the 'lose all father' phrase works? Is he tempted not to borrow any more, because the repayment has been such a struggle? Is this how he learns not to 'lose all father', and thus achieve a better relationship with his God as regards 'getting and spending' children?

Ian Donaldson in his biography gives a possible source for where this 'redeeming' of debts and trust in a divine plan might have come from:

> The poem draws upon biblical as well as stoical wisdom, figuring the boy, like all loved possessions, as merely lent by heaven; as a debt that – like some strict Old Testament bargain – must now be punctually repaid. His thoughts may well have been prompted by the opening verses of Deuteronomy 15:
> 1. At the end of every seven years thou shalt make a release.
> 2. And this is the manner of the release: Every creditor that lendeth aught unto his neighbour shall release it; he shall not exact it of his neighbour, or of his brother; because it is called the Lord's release.[4]

A problem with this cancellation of indebtedness as applied to Jonson's poem is that it refers to a rule for the wiping out of debts that have lasted for

---

[2] Ibid. 468.
[3] J. H. Prynne, *George Herbert, 'Love (III)': A Discursive Commentary* (Cambridge: privately printed, 2011), 69.
[4] Ian Donaldson, *Ben Jonson: A Life* (Oxford: Oxford University Press, 2011), 179. He acknowledges Kathryn Walls, *Notes and Queries* NS 24 (1977), 136.

seven years and not been repaid. If this is indeed what the biblical passage means, then according to Jonson's poem, God ought not to have obliged the son to be 'repaid' to the lender; rather, the lender (God) should have been instructed to let off the debtor, and allow Jonson to keep his son. So the proposed biblical source doesn't appear to exemplify what Donaldson calls 'this austere philosophy'.[5] Perhaps these words from Deuteronomy did contribute to the poem's wording, with the implication that God might have broken his own scriptural rules as regards this debt forgiveness and cancellation scheme. Yet Jonson's poem is struggling with a compulsory payment on the precise date the debt becomes due.

'Seven years thou wert lent me, and I thee pay, / Exacted by thy fate, on the just day': this couplet rhyme, in lines 3 and 4, echoes faith in Christ's redemption. The metaphor has it that Jonson, on the day of his son's death, is obliged to repay the debt his birth and life incurred. The poet's sin, by hoping too much will come of his investment, is to have had other schemes for the boy than God's. Donaldson also notes the effect of the final spondees in the first couplet. The poem's 'austere philosophy is countered by subtle movements of mood and metre, as the poem shifts back and forth between calm acceptance and small resurgences of feeling: the last two syllables in each of its first two lines – "and joy", "loved boy" – gently resisting what appears at first to be a definitive statement of dismissal in the first four feet of the pentameter.'[6] True enough; but the poem's theme is the acceptance of God's design. Attending to the form of his own design, iambic pentameters with couplet rhymes, Jonson submits to the justness of the divine plan. The spondee 'just day', effective and affecting in its affirmation against metrical expectation, implies not only that Jonson must repay his debt, but that Christ also – who has paid the price before – will redeem the son. Such a thought cannot be in the Deuteronomy text, because it is dependent on the promissory dispensation of the New Testament. This acceptance and faith changes the boy's life from a mere beginning for one 'cut off' before 'his prime', into an emblem of a life's preordained pattern. The Christian attribution of a form to the life, redeeming the otherwise apparently wasted time, is effected by Jonson's lines, whose rhymes to this end form audibly completed shapes, aligning the poem's structure with the divine design, while the metrical stability of his pentameters audibly steadies as we read from the more pausing penultimate to the smoothly iambic final line: 'For whose sake, henceforth, all his vows be such, / As what he loves may never like too much.'

[5] Ibid. 180.
[6] Ibid.

2. Money in the temple

There was something reminiscent about the Occupy movement's encampment on the steps of St Paul's during November–December 2011 in London; and you wouldn't have had to remember *Mary Poppins* to sense the proximity of the cathedral and the financial district. What it was challengingly reminiscent of, and Church of England officials were not unaware of the association, was the biblical event pictured in many great works of art, such as El Greco's *Christ Driving the Money Changers from the Temple* (c. 1568). This occurrence appears late in the three synoptic Gospels, but in the second chapter of St John's, with the running head '*He foretelleth his death*' – suggesting that it was this interruption of business as usual which led the authorities to act against the self-proclaimed redeemer:

> And the Jews' Passover was at hand, and Jesus went up to Jerusalem, And found in the temple those that sold oxen and sheep and doves, and the changers of money sitting: And when he made a scourge of small cords, he drove them all out of the temple, and the sheep, and the oxen; and poured out the changers' money, and overthrew the tables; And said unto them that sold doves, Take these things hence; make not my Father's house an house of merchandise.[7]

Quite different from the 'Render unto Caesar' encounter with the Scribes and Pharisees, in which Jesus's mission sidesteps its potential political misunderstanding (because a trap),[8] here, rather, he has intervened in the religious, political, and cultural practices of his time, and committed what could be accounted a crime, certainly a 'breach of the peace', and if this happened twice, as some commentators suggest, then that corrupting of the spiritual place with secular trading had Jesus particularly incensed. If John's sequence is to be believed, then the Redeemer himself saw the relationship between what he had done and his coming martyrdom.

This episode, with its direct relationship to Jesus's death (sold for thirty pieces of silver, as alluded to in the second stanza of his poem 'Dialogue'), was of great importance to George Herbert. He named his collection of poems *The Temple*. Here is how St John interprets what has taken place:

> Then answered the Jews and said unto him, What sign shewest thou unto us, seeing that thou doest these things? Jesus answered and said unto them, Destroy this temple, and in three days I will raise it up. Then said the Jews, Forty and six years was this temple

---

[7] John 2: 13–16.
[8] Mark 12: 13, 16–17.

in building, and wilt thou rear it up in three days? But he spake of
the temple of his body. When therefore he was risen from the dead,
his disciples remembered that he had said this unto them; and they
believed the scripture, and the word which Jesus had said.[9]

This is the Gospel that opens 'In the beginning was the Word', and its
understanding of Jesus driving out the money changers is intimately
related to the verbal activity of making a promise and keeping it. When
he comes to what this radical act of disturbing the peace signifies,
John's allegorizing interpretation, placed in Jesus's mouth, concerns the
destruction of the central symbol of the Jewish faith and its replacement
in three days by this symbol of Christian redemption, his own resurrected
body. The interpretation then leaps forward to the disciples believing this
new anagogic interpretation of the scriptures, because Jesus's promise has,
they believe, been fulfilled, and, as a result, they can trust in the word of
God.

Christ driving the money changers from the Temple is, thus, a fatefully
definitive moment for the future history of Christendom, and it is not
an exaggeration to say that the terrible and tragic history of Europe's
relationship with the Jews can be derived from interpretations of this event.
Its connection to the motto of the stock market, the idea that 'our word is
our bond', is also troublingly involved in this occasion; and, in particular,
the difference between keeping your word in financial negotiations and
contracts, with its dependence on legally managed secular trust, and the
Word of God being kept through the sacrificial death and resurrection of
Christ.

David Hawkes has underlined how John's telling of the events could be
of particular importance for the Protestant interpretation of the Bible, and
he explores at length the role played by references to the Jews in Herbert's
poetry:

> *The Temple* announces the centrality of typology to its project in the
> very title, which alludes to the scriptural trope of the human heart
> as the temple of the Holy Spirit. This was an especially attractive
> figure for Protestants because of its facility for expressing the
> internalization of faith. The external, objective temple of the Old
> Testament is transcended by the internal, subjective 'temple' of the
> New, just as the external trappings of Catholicism are brushed aside
> by the interior faith of the Protestant believer.[10]

---

[9] John 2: 18–22.
[10] David Hawkes, 'Exchange Value and Empiricism in the Poetry of George Herbert',
in Linda Woodbridge (ed.), *Money and the Age of Shakespeare: Essays in the New
Economic Criticism* (New York and Basingstoke: Palgrave Macmillan, 2003), 88.

The role of metaphor is relevant here, because the Anglican sacraments are strictly metaphorical, where A is B only verbally, whereas Transubstantiation requires belief in a miraculous transformation of A into B. In *The Metaphors We Live By*, Lakoff and Johnson provide numerous instances of how the 'Time is Money' metaphor inflects speech, and they illustrate the 'Inflation is an Entity', 'Inflation is a Person', and 'Inflation is an Adversary' metaphors, as well as 'Ideas are Money', 'Wealth is a Hidden Object', 'Life is a Gambling Game' – only to skim the surface of their many examples.[11] A further argument for paying attention to such monetary metaphors is made by Hawkes when he challenges Douglas Bruster's distinguishing between 'two modes of New Economic Criticism', which he calls the 'reckoned' and the 'rash' in which '"Reckoned" criticism sees "the economic" as an object, "rash" criticism treats "the economic" as a metaphor'. Hawkes sees this as a false dichotomy and suggests that, like money, metaphor mongering is everywhere, either because in the past the economic was understood to be an integral part of the ethical life, or because, wherever you turn, there's no escaping it now:

> What Bruster calls 'the *Wall Street Journal*-sense of "economy"' is not remotely literal. He tries to define the 'literal' of 'economy' as a 'system involving money, credit, debt, profit, and loss,' but these terms do not refer to objective things; they are figurative terms for relations between people. The idea that certain modes of human behaviour can be isolated as 'economic' was invented by the political economists of the eighteenth century – economics, for Smith or Mandeville, is a separate 'sphere' from ethics. But it would never have occurred to the people of Renaissance England to separate the 'economy' from the rest of life, and such a separation is manifestly untenable in the postmodern environment, where the 'market' saturates every aspect of experience.[12]

Hawkes's intervention is, of course, polemically driven here, and since Bernard de Mandeville and Adam Smith imagined the separate sphere of economic theory, many have asserted that the ethical cannot be edited out – John Ruskin in *Unto This Last* or Charles Dickens in *Dombey and Son*, for instance. It is also odd to think that the postmodern dispensation in which market economics has saturated everything should reinforce the need to see literal and metaphorical understandings of money as not able to be dissociated, when neoliberal economics has seen a further attempt to

[11] See George Lakoff and Mark Johnson, *Metaphors We Live By* (Chicago and London: University of Chicago Press, 1980; rev. edn. 2003), 7–8, 26, 34, 48, 49, and 51.

[12] Hawkes, 'Exchange Value and Empiricism in the Poetry of George Herbert', 83.

claim the inescapability of a non-ethical 'invisible hand' monetary policy, whose freeing up of the international markets has, alongside other current phenomena, helped create the conditions in which it is possible to see sections of a population (the so-called 'left behind') as superfluous to the workings of 'the economy', and yet whose fate can then rebound in the form of fierce resentment, on the presumed agents of that economy, pressing, once again, urgent consequences concerning the ethics of non-ethical theories.[13]

3. *Love's usury*

In the first of his early 'New Year Sonnets', Herbert sets his art against secular love poetry. 'My God', he asks, does poetry 'Wear *Venus* Livery?' and 'Why are not *Sonnets* made of thee?' In the course of this reiterative questioning, he further demands of God: 'Cannot thy love / Heighten a spirit to sound out thy praise / As well as any she?'[14] As many have noted, this sonnet, written when the poet was seventeen, may have been prompted by the publication of *Shakespeare's Sonnets* in May of the previous year. The phrasing of the first five words in Herbert's eighth line looks inflected with the final couplet of Shakespeare's 130: 'And yet, by heaven, I think my love as rare / As any she belied by false compare.'[15] Not only does Herbert's sonnet borrow a little of its wording, it adapts the dramatist's swearing 'by heaven', thus tacitly evoking a spiritual and secular intersection, into its similarly swearing address to 'My God', and it further turns the 'false compare' criticism of other sonneteers in Shakespeare's poem into its own attack on the pack of them for neglecting to be inspired by religious as distinct from secular devotions (a theme that would recur in 'Jordan (II)', with is complaint about 'metaphors' that are 'decking the sense, as if it were to sell' – metaphorically inflecting them into the bargain).[16] Herbert's youthful exercise, sent in a letter to his mother from Trinity College, Cambridge, is faintly tainted too by the denigratory wording for others' mistresses misrepresented by their fictionalizing poets' similes in Shakespeare's 'My mistress' eyes are nothing like the sun'.

Yet as in this earliest attempt Herbert would adapt secular love poetry's tropes for religiously devotional ends, so in his mature poetry from *The*

---

[13] As Adam Smith put it, the individual who 'intends only his own gain' is 'led by an invisible hand to promote an end which was no part of his intention'; *The Wealth of Nations,* ed. Edwin Cannan (New York: Modern Library, 2000), 485.

[14] Helen Wilcox (ed.), *The English Poems of George Herbert* (Cambridge: Cambridge University Press, 2007), 4.

[15] Katherine Duncan-Jones (ed.), *Shakespeare's Sonnets* (London: Thomas Nelson and Sons, 1997), 375.

[16] *The English Poems of George Herbert*, 367.

Temple, the poet not only uses financial imagery in religious poems –
driving the money changers *into* his temple – but, to do so, as has been
widely noted, he adapts secular love poetry such as Shakespeare's, with its
frequently monetary notes ('Simply I credit her false-speaking tongue', for
instance, in Sonnet 138) so as to keep his own poetic feet treading firmly
'on the ground',[17] as here in Sonnet 30:

> When to the sessions of sweet silent thought
> I summon up remembrance of things past,
> I sigh the lack of many a thing I sought,
> And with old woes new wail my dear time's waste;
> Then can I drown an eye (unused to flow)
> For precious friends hid in death's dateless night,
> And weep afresh love's long since cancelled woe,
> And moan th'expense of many a vanished sight.
> Then can I grieve at grievances foregone,
> And heavily from woe to woe tell o'er
> The sad account of fore-bemoaned moan,
> Which I new pay, as if not paid before;
>   But if the while I think on thee, dear friend,
>   All losses are restored, and sorrows end.[18]

The volatility of the thought processes represented here is striking.
Though he is experiencing 'sweet silent thought', he nevertheless 'sighs
the lack of many things', and though his eye is 'unused to flow', still he is
overwhelmed by feeling and can 'drown an eye'. If these 'sessions' are also
court appearances, then they culminate in the ruling that in this seemingly
uncontrollable cycle of volatile emotions, cleared debts have to be cleared all
over again in a sequence of financial wordplay from 'tell' through 'account'
to 'pay': 'And heavily from woe to woe tell o'er / The sad account of fore-be-
moaned moan, / Which I new pay, as if not paid before'. Shakespeare's
emotional bookkeeping is at once both haplessly spendthrift and pointedly
penny-pinching.

After such volatile accountancy, the external intervention of the couplet
comes as an arbitrarily inadequate resolution: 'But if the while I think on
thee, dear friend, / All losses are restored, and sorrows end.' The emotional
indebtedness in the relationships has been configured financially, and it
may be that this economic metaphor, this dependence and indebtedness, is
simultaneously tainting the seeming compliment of the thinking-on-thee
– though given the emotional volatility portrayed, it isn't hard to imagine

---

[17] *Shakespeare's Sonnets*, 391 and 375.
[18] Ibid. 171.

such an escape route failing to work because implicated with the cycles of loss and repayment, as will indeed happen subsequently in Shakespeare's sequence. Sonnet 30 is one of many in which the richly figured negative states of the first twelve lines are not fully 'turned' by the intervention of the final couplet, and, as a result, the compliment of this turning to the friend leaves a faintly hollow resolution, as if, despite his eye being 'unused to flow', it is the sudden descent into grief from 'sweet silent thought' that remains with us, along with the legal battle over indebtedness and repayment that figures the predicament and establishes the stage for its not entirely certain-sounding resolution at the close.

Doing the accounts of his ambitions and lack of success, Shakespeare manages to escape from a cycle of self-pitying grief by thinking on his aristocratic patron, whose friendship provides him with all that he would otherwise have lost. Yet in this battle of conflicting thoughts, it is the saving grace of happening to think on his beneficent friend that sounds, in the shaping of the poem, convenient, and as if 'tacked on'. The technical weakness of the sonnet's closure prompts the thought that it is wishful, and its being so, within the sequence, will be borne out by subsequent complications. It might then be imagined as Herbert's task to convert such interventions from beings with greater wealth and loftier position, formally, into closes that can be relied upon, and Prynne again underlines how such a project is hedged about by calculations with financial overtones:

> There are some traditional interpretative schemes in which God's love is conditional, upon sincere contrition, full repentance, upon justification through faith, and eventual sanctification. But in Herbert's scheme the invitation is unencumbered by reckoning: there are no special premiums or discounts or forward contracts, it is an offer made out of pure love – and, as such, hard for the guest to believe or accept because hard for him to comprehend. Yet it is not an indifferent act, because it is motivated by God's will towards man, that man should return a pure love, if so he wills, as the matching response to God's willed offering.[19]

Prynne's subsequent and concluding speculations upon whether Herbert's project can be achieved in the terms of short lyric performances is also implicated in the strategies of adapting the secular love poetry of this poet's Elizabethan and Jacobean near-contemporaries with the staging of thoroughly and effectively resolved conclusions to lyrics. What might or might not make a qualitative difference between the endings of their poems

---

[19]   Prynne, *George Herbert, 'Love (III)'*, 69.

goes to the heart of relations between technique, feeling, and belief, and can be brought into focus by recalling a critical debate about the conclusions to some of John Donne's *Songs and Sonnets*.

Donne too repeatedly finds his mind moving to analogies with coins and coining, as in 'A Valediction: of Weeping':

> Let me pour forth
> My tears before thy face, whilst I stay here,
> For thy face coins them, and thy stamp they bear,
> And by this mintage they are something worth,
> For thus they be
> Pregnant of thee;
> Fruits of much grief they are, emblems of more,
> When a tear falls, that thou falls which it bore,
> So thou and I are nothing then, when on a divers shore.[20]

In 'The Canonization' he invites his interlocutor to 'Observe his Honour, or his Grace, / Or the King's real, or his stamped face / Contemplate'.[21] Herbert's use of financial imagery is further carried over from metaphysical wit, by which the 'most heterogeneous ideas are yoked by violence together', as Samuel Johnson put it.[22] Donne's only comment on his poetics is a metaphor that characterizes the art of ending a poem as the equivalent of minting a coin. After beating out the metal during the process of writing, the final line provides the hammer blow that makes it valuable and exchangeable: 'And therefore it is easie to observe, that in all Metrical compositions,' he asserts,

> the force of the whole piece, is for the most part left to the shutting up; the whole frame of the Poem is a beating out of a piece of gold, but the last clause is as the impression of the stamp, and that is it that makes it currant.[23]

In his essay called 'Farewell to Love', Christopher Ricks takes strong exception to the endings of Donne's poems for the ethics of their relations to women, to human sexuality, and to their own better passages in progressing towards those post-coital-like endings, which he sees as not

---

[20] John Donne, *The Complete English Poems*, ed. A. J. Smith (Harmondsworth: Penguin Books, 1973), 89.

[21] Ibid. 47.

[22] Samuel Johnson, 'Abraham Cowley', *The Lives of the Poets*, 3 vols., ed. John H. Middendorf (New Haven: Yale University Press, 2010), vol. 1, 26.

[23] *The Sermons of John Donne*, 10 vols., ed. George R. Potter and Evelyn Simpson (Berkeley and Los Angeles: University of California Press, 1953–62), vol. 6, 41.

merely saddened or disappointed, but misogynistic in their revulsions. Regarding the poet's comment on the coining of his conclusions, Ricks most frequently prefers thus the beating out of the metal to the stamping of it to make it legal tender in the final line. Donne is, the critic writes, 'corrosively unfaithful to his poems'.[24] The accusation is strongly argued for, both with close readings of the early secular love poems and coruscating comments on the indifference or apologetics of prominent Donne admirers. It is as if Ricks were saying that when it comes to the endings of some of his best-known love poems, Donne is, frankly, a counterfeiter.

'Love's Usury' is concerned, as are many of his most famous poems, with constancy and fidelity, and this poem metaphorically figures the terms of an activity officially proscribed by the Catholic Church. One reason why Ricks may not include this one in his indictment is that it works the necessary twist of a lyric in the reverse direction to the one he so dislikes. The corrosively cynical attitude to interpersonal ethics as figured by this poet's proposal for the practice of sexuality is present from the first:

> For every hour that thou wilt spare me now,
> I will allow,
> Usurious God of Love, twenty to thee,
> When with my brown, my grey hairs equal be[25]

The poem's title is itself a piece of metaphysical wit as defined by Johnson, and it trades on the scandalous association between the two possessively linked terms, an eventually equivocating bid for freedom in sexual relations which is tacitly contested by the historical ambivalence and conflict surrounding the place of usury in Christian doctrine. Dante had placed the usurers in the seventh circle of Hell in his *Inferno* Canto XVII, but Francis Bacon condoned it in 'Of Usurie' (1625) on the grounds that 'it is better, to Mitigate *Usury* by *Declaration*, then to suffer it to Rage by *Connivance*.'[26] He permits it because he sees that there will be borrowing and lending, and that there has to be recompense for risk, otherwise lending will stop and trade collapse.

Donne begins by striking a bargain in which for every hour of love he is allowed when young, he will pay back twenty when old – which would appear to give him the benefit of a lascivious youth and a very long and peaceful old age: 'Till then, Love, let my body reign, and let / Me travel,

[24] Christopher Ricks, *Essays in Appreciation* (Oxford: Oxford University Press, 1996), 49.

[25] Donne, *The Complete English Poems*, 69–70.

[26] Sir Francis Bacon, *The Essayes or Counsels, Civill and Morall*, ed. Michael Kiernan (Oxford: Oxford University Press, 1985), 128.

sojourn, snatch, plot, have, forget'. He'll love them and leave them, and get up to any trick to enjoy as many as he can while he can:

> Let me think any rival's letter mine,
> And at next nine
> Keep midnight's promise; mistake by the way
> The maid, and tell the Lady of that delay;
> Only let me love none, no, not the sport;
> From country grass, to comfitures of Court,
> Or city's quelque-choses, let report
> My mind transport.

But the hours of his youth can only be filled with love, it seems, if he is as unfaithful to all and sundry, taking the chances offered, or snatched, wherever they present themselves. Making the most of opportunities to love in youth, he appears to be arguing, requires the freedom to roam without constraint from love (the poem exploits the plain-sight ambiguity between the promiscuous act, the ideally constraining feeling of attachment to specific persons, and the address to the personified figure). Thus he says: I'll give the God of Love all the loyalty and twenty-fold repayment when I'm old, so long as he'll let me love anyone I like without consequence while I can:

> This bargain's good; if when I am old, I be
> Inflamed by thee,
> If thine own honour, or my shame, or pain,
> Thou covet, most at that age thou shalt gain.
> Do thy will then, then subject and degree,
> And fruit of love, Love, I submit to thee,
> Square me till then, I'll bear it, though she be
> One that loves me.[27]

Then he says, like a bold boast in the poem's close, that if the God of Love gives him all that freedom, he'll bear the burden of the deal, even when it comes to its enforcing, for thus he will have to lose in age the one who 'loves me'. The poem satisfies in so far as a reader might think he deserves the payback of an aged incapacity, but the argument may also be thought specious throughout. The metrical 'collapses' from pentameter to two-stress line at the end of the stanzas are prepared for in their second lines, which foreshadow the usurious swelling of the stanza, while the latter shortening counts the cost, the payback. But in the poem's close the coining hammer blow, the twist, is faithless because the argument is faithless – for he knows

[27] Donne, *The Complete English Poems*, 69–70.

it will cost him, and, I might reflect, not only him if *she* 'loves me'. Because the poem is arguing to be allowed its own faithlessness, a freedom from the constraints and reciprocal obligations in a contract figured by its stanzas' regularity, the coining at the end not only acknowledges that he will have to take on the burden of the usurious debt at high interest; it also turns the faithlessness argument against itself, suggesting, as high-interest debts will, that he might have been wiser to act differently earlier in life. In 'Love's Usury', because he is in danger at the close of losing his chance of a real and reciprocal love, the poem's 'corrosive' self-defeating turn corrodes its earlier shallowness and corruption.

Commenting on Donne's frequent punning on his own surname, Ricks allows that the shortcomings he finds in the secular love poems do not appear to apply to the holy hymns and sonnets: 'When Donne delivered himself over to Wotton, he and his name – 'have Donne' – could bow; when he delivers himself over to the supreme patron, he and his name kneel'; and he quotes 'When thou hast done, thou hast not done. / For I have more' from 'A Hymn to God the Father'.[28] Donne can't engage in the kinds of debating-society argument reversals of the secular love poems with so serious a matter as his salvation, and so his endings must turn upon themselves in proper self-denial, or self-abasement. His holy poems could only avoid being the work of a counterfeiter if they, as it were, were turning themselves in to the authorities at their closes.

4. Redeeming our debts

Donne was not the only divine who used coin images in his sermons: 'It fareth with *sentences* as with coins', wrote Bishop Lancelot Andrewes: 'In *coins*, they that in smallest compass contain greatest value, are best esteemed: and, in sentences, those that in fewest words comprise most matter, are most praised.'[29] Herbert's diction can be shown to have taken this advice, but are his endings designed to have coining-like interventions, derived from his knowledge of Donne's poetry, but absolutely without the faithless hollowness identified by Ricks? If his endings do convince, it will be on account of his handling relations between an evoked irresolution in the body of the poem and a discovered resolution in the sound-sense amalgams of its close.

Turning back to Hawkes's essay on Herbert and money, we find him considering the symbolism of the poet's poetry an attack on Baconian empiricism, and explicating the contentious significance of the Jews in his

---

[28] Ricks, *Essays in Appreciation*, 46–7.
[29] Lancelot Andrewes, *Selected Sermons and Lectures*, ed. Peter McCullough (Oxford: Oxford University Press, 2003), 108.

poetry as relating to the typological argument, where, once more, fetishism comes into play. In the sermon-like lines for 'The Church-porch', Herbert foresaw the difficulty Larkin sketches in 'Money'. He recommends that we 'Get to live; / Then live, and use it: els, it is not true / That thou hast gotten.' He concludes: 'Surely use alone / Makes money not a contemptible stone.' 'Never exceed thy income', he also recommends; and, later, 'By no means run in debt', asserting along the same lines that touching wealth and gold will not be sinful if you pass it on quickly, preferring a circulating economy to a stagnating, because miserly, one: 'Wealth is the conjurers devil; / Whom when he thinks he hath, the devil hath him'. Herbert illustrates this wisdom with the example of 'the scraping dame':

> What skills it, if a bag of stones or gold
> About thy neck do drown thee? raise thy head;
> Take starres for money; starres not to be told
> By any art, yet to be purchased.
>> None is so wastefull as the scraping dame.
>> She loseth three for one; her soul, rest, fame.[30]

'The Pulley' redeploys a number of these maxims and arguments, arguing that God's plan allows us this 'worlds riches', 'his treasure' and 'this jewell', and how 'both should losers be' if we 'adore my gifts in stead of me'. So, he decides, 'Let him be rich and wearie', so that if 'goodnesse leade him not, yet wearinesse / May tosse him to my breast.'[31] Herbert's economic and spiritual advice is thus an attempt to combine and accommodate the practicalities of life within an economy and the advancement of spiritual values towards an afterlife beyond that economic realm. Yet, as in the biblical parable of Dives and Lazarus, these realms of activity have ever been at stress, a stress emblematized in the twists and turns of Herbert's lineated arguments.

If the poet drives the money changers out of *The Temple* of his poems, he has had to put them there in the first place, in the form of those resorts to financial metaphors, outdoing Jonson's debt-repayment pun in his elegy for his son, as here in 'Avarice':

> Money, thou bane of blisse, & sourse of wo,
>> Whence com'st thou, that thou art so fresh and fine?
>> I know thy parentage is base and low:
> Man found thee poore and dirtie in a mine.

---

[30] *The English Poems of George Herbert*, 54–5.
[31] Ibid. 548–9.

> Surely thou didst so little contribute
>   To this great kingdome, which thou now hast got,
>   That he was fain, when thou wert destitute,
> To digge thee out of thy dark cave and grot:
>
> Then forcing thee, by fire he made thee bright:
>   Nay, thou hast got the face of man; for we
>   Have with our stamp and seal transferr'd our right;
> Thou art the man, and man but drosse to thee.
>
>   Man calleth thee his wealth, who made thee rich;
>   And while he digs out thee, falls in the ditch.[32]

Here the couplet rhyme that closes the sonnet, the way the miner is undermined, closes a metaphorical trap that is set in the poem's opening quatrain. Unlike Shakespeare's sonnet 30, whose couplet attempts a rescue with magical thinking, or the conclusion of 'Love's Usury', which achieves its resolution by flipping the coin and finding a faithful face upon it, Herbert's monetary metaphor resolves by drawing out an implication integral to the history of coining precious metals which figures his theme and its consequences. 'Avarice' thus exemplifies how the poet has to bring money into his temple poems so as to drive it out. There is a thoroughly appropriate implication in doing this, though, because by putting monetary imagery into the poems he confesses his own worldliness, or at least his knowledge of the world's ways, which entails his own need for the intervention of a scourging Jesus in his heart, a pattern illustrated here in the third verse of 'The Quip':

> Then Money came, and chinking still,
> What tune is this, poore man? said he:
> I heard in Musick you had skill.
> But thou shalt answer, Lord, for me.[33]

Yet, characteristically, Herbert's intervening Lord is not a jealous or wrathful God, not the Jesus who loses his temper in the temple and finds a scourge to whip the money changers out of his father's house. His God is, rather, as a rich man who can wipe out your debts through a generous self-sacrifice.

This is the Lord that appears in 'Redemption', a poem about which Louis MacNeice aptly comments that Herbert expresses 'his feelings about

---

[32] Ibid. 276.
[33] Ibid. 395.

86

redemption in an out-and-out allegorical sonnet in everyday diction and with images drawn from something so prosaic as real estate':[34]

> Having been tenant long to a rich Lord,
>   Not thriving, I resolved to be bold,
>   And make a suit unto him, to afford
> A new small-rented lease, and cancell th' old.
>
> In heaven at his manour I him sought:
>   They told me there, that he was lately gone
>   About some land, which he had dearly bought
> Long since on earth, to take possession.
>
> I straight return'd, and knowing his great birth,
>   Sought him accordingly in great resorts;
>   In cities, theatres, gardens, parks, and courts:
> At length I heard a ragged noise and mirth
>
> Of theeves and murderers: there I him espied,
> Who straight, *Your suit is granted,* said, & died.[35]

John Drury begins by noting how 'the momentous allegory, based on the two meanings of the title, emerges':

> The doubling of a nasty, all too common incident in urban life with the solution of the human predicament in the final, terse climax is astonishing and leaves the reader open-mouthed. The age-old contrast of simple country life with the vanities and squalor of the town was a well-established pastoral convention. As with all conventions, it is how it is used that counts. Herbert does it with a freshness born of sharp observation of both its aspects and the skill to turn them to urgent and deeply felt meaning.[36]

Herbert's method is, again, to integrate the turned argument, achieved in its final foot ('& died'), with the sustained metaphor of the entire poem.

---

[34] Louis MacNeice, *Varieties of Parable* (Cambridge: Cambridge University Press, 1965), 50.

[35] *The English Poems of George Herbert*, 132. Mildmay Fane composed a variation on this landlord and redemption theme. See 'My Country Audit' (1648), in *Seventeenth-Century British Poetry 1603–1660*, ed. John P. Rumrich and Gregory Chaplin (New York and London: Norton, 2006), 329.

[36] John Drury, *Music at Midnight: The Life and Poetry of George Herbert* (London: Penguin Books, 2014), 50.

His close doesn't turn upon, intervene in, or contradict the line of reasoning adopted; rather, it confirms it under a different interpretation, integrating the close into the whole design. Here, too, the place of the poem in a collection of Christian meditations is underlined, because the recognition of what *'Your suit is granted,* said, & died' means in the light of the different perspective is provided by the interpreting reader, for, aside from the ambiguous reference of 'Lord', the reading of its real estate metaphor is left implicit.

The most emblematic example of a mended relationship with a divine source of love and forgiveness is the full rhyme that concludes Herbert's 'Deniall', its final stanza mending the closing rhyme that had been lacking in the previous verses:

> O cheer and tune my heartlesse breast,
>   Deferre no time;
> That so thy favours granting my request,
>   They and my minde may chime,
>   And mend my ryme.[37]

This last stanza produces, thus, a formal answer to the prayer that it articulates. It follows that if poets have used monetary imagery to characterize their love relationships in poems, the same might be true of their poems about the love of God. However, the degrees of appropriateness or, as it might be, the tensions between the two registers are made more attenuated, or beaten more thinly, because of the differences of perspective in the idea of 'trust' involved in lending money to a poet, or lending him a son for seven years, or trusting that he will have achieved eternal life and will be reunited with his father with the resurrection of the body and the life everlasting. The qualm left by Herbert's beautifully finessed closes is whether they are instances of the most trusting good that human relations, relations of writer and reader, may collaboratively achieve, or whether, in so doing, they figure values beyond those that may be humanly experienced.

5. The parable of the talents

In 'The Church-porch' Herbert also advised that we should 'Spend not on hopes.'[38] But Samuel Johnson knew that we are fated to do just this:

---

[37]   *The English Poems of George Herbert*, 289.
[38]   Ibid. 55.

> Condemn'd to hope's delusive mine,
> As on we toil from day to day,
> By sudden blasts, or slow decline,
> Our social comforts drop away.[39]

'On the Death of Dr Robert Levet', of which this is the opening stanza, is a distinctly self-conscious poem, written in ABAB rhymed octosyllabic iambic tetrameter quatrains.[40] There is only one variation to this accentual syllabic pattern: line 5, 'Well tried through many a varying year', has ten syllables, while the words which produce the two-syllable variations are 'many a' and 'varying'. Further, the relationship between this self-consciousness and the poem's subject is figured in the first two lines of the penultimate stanza: 'The busy day, the peaceful night, / Unfelt, uncounted, glided by'. Levet lived, it suggests, in such an active and unreflective way that he didn't count the passage of time; but it also implies through its careful syllabic repetitions that Johnson *is* counting, in life and in the poem, for 'now his eightieth year was nigh'. The line 'Unfelt, uncounted, glided by' also emphasizes its distinctly counted and not gliding undercurrent with the commas between the second and third, and the fifth and sixth syllables, separating the adjectives from the verb-with-preposition.

So 'many a varying' performs its sense by varying the metrical pattern with the additional syllables of two anapestic feet in place of iambic ones. By contrast, 'Unfelt, uncounted, glided by' is an instance of the counter-mimetic, because the metrics and punctuation underline what is *felt* and *counted* by slowing the line with commas, counteracting the 'glided' enough to register an implicit contrast between literal temporal duration and the psychologically elastic time that insomniacs, for instance, and Johnson was one, experience. There is a more striking example of the counter-mimetic activated by the poem's recourse to negative constructions, in the antepenultimate stanza:

> His virtues walk'd their narrow round,
> Nor made a pause, nor left a void;
> And sure th' Eternal Master found
> The single talent well employ'd.

The self-conscious strategy in 'Nor made a pause, nor left a void' serves to express an unusual range of implied thoughts and feelings about an

---

[39] Samuel Johnson, *Poems,* ed. E. L. McAdam, Jr. with George Milne (New Haven: Yale University Press, 1964), 314–15 for this and subsequent citations.

[40] For an extended version of this account, see my 'The Edge of Satire: Post-Mortem and Other Effects', in *The Oxford Handbook of Eighteenth-Century Satire,* ed. Paddy Bullard (Oxford: Oxford University Press, 2019), 628–44.

apparently ordinary life and its value. Johnson's poem makes a pause at the caesura, and leaves a void of white paper at the line ending. The line thus tacitly expresses what it overtly denies. Levet was missed (by the writer, at least, and also by his many nameless friends in need), and the great gap made by his absence cannot be filled. This allows for an understanding of individual and personal uniqueness even in a form of modest social conformity – being both privately missed and yet publicly 'invisible', as it were. Such an 'irreplaceable invisibility', and the unique value of seemingly ordinary people, looks forward to Wordsworth's 'A slumber did my spirit seal' and the invisibility of the girl in the Lucy poems, written some fifteen years after Johnson's death.

Further self-awareness and self-criticism is implied in Johnson's allusion to the Parable of the Talents. This biblical allusiveness is an aspect of the poem that most who comment on it will pause over, as does one critic, who takes the wish for the deed in its dealings with the 'Eternal Master':

> Johnson strikingly reverses the Parable of the Talents in Matthew 25: 13–30. There the bad servant is eternally punished for burying rather than investing his absent master's gift as a single talent – a sum of money. Here Johnson knows that God will reward his friend who handsomely used God's humble but essential gift.[41]

Johnson does not presume to an assurance that his friend 'has handsomely used God's humble but essential gift'; though calling him 'a very useful, and very blam[e]less man',[42] he does not do God's judging for him. One way to construe this double-minded judging would be in the supposed 'intrinsic' and 'extrinsic' terms of aesthetic evaluation. Johnson's 'a very useful, and very blam[e]less man' is a human attribution of qualities, while praying for God's mercy upon Levet (or yourself) is a deferring of certainty about definitive evaluation to the all-seeing. Yet Johnson saw it as essential to Christian belief that human evaluation would never presume to encompass the divine – or as he puts it in 'The Vanity of Human Wishes': 'Still raise for good the supplicating voice, / But leave to heav'n the measure and the choice.'[43]

During his composition of 'On the Death of Dr Robert Levet', the poet keeps the idea of being buried in the ground as a running and, again, self-conscious theme throughout. Not only are we 'Condemned to hope's delusive mine' in the first line, working underground in the Roman lead

---

41 Howard D. Weinbrot, 'Johnson's Poetry', in *The Cambridge Companion to Samuel Johnson,* ed. Greg Clingham (Cambridge: Cambridge University Press, 1997), 38.

42 Samuel Johnson, *Letters,* ed. Bruce Redford, 5 vols. (Oxford: Oxford University Press, 1994), vol. 4, 6.

43 Johnson, *Poems,* 108.

mines,[44] but in line 6 we 'see Levet to the grave descend', as Johnson had done on 20 January 1782. Then in line 17 we hear how 'In misery's darkest caverns known, / His useful care was ever nigh', and Johnson then touches this burial in the ground theme again in the 'single talent' allusion to the Parable of the Talents. The biblical story is also an exercise in how to interpret a metaphor: 'For *the kingdom of heaven is* as a man travelling into a far country, *who* called his own servants, and delivered unto them his goods. And unto one he gave five talents, to another two, and to another one; to every man according to his several ability'. The first two servants 'went and traded with the same', doubling their money, but 'he that had received one went and digged in the earth, and hid his lord's money.' The climax of the parable seems on the face of it shockingly harsh:

> Then he which had received the one talent came and said, Lord, I knew thee that thou art an hard man, reaping where thou hast not sown, and gathering where thou hast not strawed: And I was afraid, and went and hid thy talent in the earth: lo, *there* thou hast *that is* thine. His lord answered and said unto him, *Thou* wicked and slothful servant, thou knewest that I reap where I sowed not, and gather where I have not strawed: Thou oughtest therefore to have put my money to the exchangers, and *then* at my coming I should have received mine own with usury. Take therefore the talent from him, and give *it* unto him which hath ten talents. For unto every one that hath shall be given, and he shall have abundance: but from him that hath not shall be taken away even that which he hath.[45]

This parable might seem hardly compatible with the teachings from which Ruskin took his title *Unto This Last*, in which the workers in the vineyard are all paid 'a penny a day' for different amounts of work, or, equally, that it 'is easier for a camel to go through the eye of a needle, than for a rich man to enter into the kingdom of God', or, again, the story of Dives and Lazarus.[46] Rather, the Parable of the Talents might go better with being advised not to hide your light under a bushel, or the parable immediately preceding that of the talents, which concerns the wise and foolish virgins and their lamps.[47]

It is a metaphor, though one in which the detail of the vehicle – the coin burial, the money markets, the lord being one who advocates the compounding of capital – painfully conflicts with the tenor, explained in

---

[44] Allusion to 'damnare in metallum' is noted in Samuel Johnson, *The Complete English Poems*, ed. J. D. Fleeman (Harmondsworth: Penguin Books, 1971), 228–9.
[45] Matthew 25: 24–9, and see also Luke 19: 12–28.
[46] See Matthew 20: 1–16, Matthew 19: 24, and Luke 16: 19–31.
[47] See Luke 11: 33–6 and Matthew 25: 1–13.

the rest of Matthew 25, that the servants investing and multiplying their talents are 'the righteous', about whom Jesus observes, 'I was thirsty, and ye gave me drink: I was a stranger, and ye took me in: Naked and ye clothed me: I was sick, and ye visited me: I was in prison, and ye came unto me.'[48] While the interpretation of the parable, including the illustrative instance that 'I was sick, and ye visited me', is appropriate to Johnson's elegy, nevertheless, even given this wholly metaphorical interpretation of a story cast in the terms of usury, the idea that the more you have the more you'll get and the less you have the even less you'll keep obliges a reinterpretation on the grounds that Jesus couldn't have meant *that*, could he?

Johnson does reinterpret and revalue the parable, deploying metaphors of his own, not least by having it that Levet exercised his single talent underground, in 'misery's darkest caverns' visiting the sick and dying. Thus, we might conclude, he invested it by burying it. He didn't put it out to the money markets to have it multiply by usury; he buried it in the ground, like the unworthy servant, but, unlike the reprimanded servant, he set to multiplying it in use in this subterranean form, as, Johnson might be implying, do all of us who work in 'hope's delusive mine'. This is how 'On the Death of Dr. Robert Levet' echoes a key question in 'The Vanity of Human Wishes' when that poem asks: 'Where then shall Hope and Fear their objects find?'[49] The tact required in understanding that 'sure' in 'And sure th' Eternal Master found / The single talent well employ'd', far from underlining that 'Johnson knows that God will reward his friend', rather does the opposite, introducing an uncertainty that needs shoring up with its 'sure'.[50] Johnson may have been hearing things in an earlier elegy, for Dryden had written: 'For sure our souls were near allied', though John Oldham being 'too little and too lately known',[51] the senior poet cannot be certain, and hence his used of 'sure'.

Yet this is not the only way that the parable is troubling for Johnson, as it has been for others.[52] Once again, the critic's desire to praise and protect his subject is blanking off an entire aspect of the poem's double portraiture. Here is the same critic on how Levet was rewarded for the value expressed by his life:

[48]   Matthew 25: 35–6.

[49]   Johnson, *Poems*, 107.

[50]   See Chester F. Chapin, *The Religious Thought of Samuel Johnson* (Ann Arbor: University of Michigan Press, 1968), with a discussion of 'faith' and 'trust' at 74–5.

[51]   *The Oxford Authors John Dryden*, ed. Keith Walker (Oxford: Oxford University Press, 1987), 245.

[52]   See John Ruskin, '*A Joy for Ever,*' being *The Substance (with additions) of the Two Lectures on The Political Economy of Art* (1857, 1880), in *The Library Edition of the Works*, 39 vols, ed. E. T. Cook and Alexander Wedderburn (London: George Allen, 1903–12), vol. 14, 98–9.

As the allusion to Matthew denotes, the Eternal Master also rewards Levet: 'Death broke at once the vital chain, / And free'd his soul the nearest way' – nearer to God, who welcomes Levet as a good and faithful servant who has entered the far country that is Heaven. Johnson's secular poem spiritually comforts the poet and the poet's readers. As Johnson says in his prologue to Oliver Goldsmith's *The Good Natured Man* (1768), 'social sorrow loses half its pain'.[53]

Yet part of Levet's virtue is in not thinking any such thing, nor thinking that he has been rewarded with good health, rather than that he happens to have it, and so doesn't notice time passing. However, to put it like this, being under the illusion that living a good life means receiving reward for it in knowing that you have done so ought to prompt the thought that the opposite must be equally true: if you are not conscious of having lived well, or harbour feelings of shame and guilt, and you are not enjoying a healthy old age, and you fear that you will die slowly and painfully, and you are feeling the bars of the temporal prison closing around you, then presumably that same Eternal Master is punishing you for having failed to invest your many talents properly. It is not all right, then, and not Christian, for Johnson as poet and man to identify himself with Levet's virtues. That too is presuming: he will have also known what the story of the two thieves who were crucified beside Jesus has been understood to teach, namely that we should neither presume nor despair. If Johnson were to think of himself and Levet as equivalents of the two thieves, then it is more than appropriate that he should pray God to 'have had mercy on' Levet and to add: 'May he have mercy on me.'[54]

Johnson's criticism of metaphysical wit, by which the 'most heterogeneous ideas are yoked by violence together',[55] draws attention to the conflicted values that those poets such as Donne and Herbert had been struggling to reconcile. The different perspectives in their work and Johnson's under which ideas of trust and promise, of indebtedness, payment, and redemption, have been employed point to a change of view about the possibility of conjoining and accommodating the human requirements for earthly continuance and the spiritual ones for everlasting life. 'Where then shall Hope and Fear their objects find?' Johnson asked in *The Vanity of Human Wishes*, and the cumulative force of his poem suggests that the 'where' is almost entirely out of this world.[56] Though Herbert had done his upmost to reduce the violence

---

53   Weinbrot, 'Johnson's Poetry', 39.
54   Samuel Johnson, *Diaries, Prayers, and Annals*, ed. E. L. McAdam, Jr. with Donald and Mary Hyde (New Haven: Yale University Press, 1958), 311.
55   Samuel Johnson, 'Abraham Cowley', in *The Lives of the Poets*, ed. John H. Middendorf (New Haven: Yale University Press, 2010), vol. 1, 26.
56   Johnson, *Poems*, 107.

required, in the lyrics, to yoke together those ideas of human and divine love even as he acknowledged the necessary cruelty in his Lord's suffering, Johnson's writings underlined the entire separation of those perspectives. The sense they could not strictly be connected found in Johnson's writings[57] had not been helped by the growth and change in the nature of money during what has been called the Financial Revolution, to which, with some of the poetry that it inspired, I now turn.

---

[57] For the infinitely definitive separation of the finite and the infinite, see 'A Review of Soames Jenyns' *A Free Inquiry into the Nature and Origin of Evil*', in Samuel Johnson, *A Commentary on Mr. Pope's Principles of Morality, Or Essay on Man*, ed. O. M. Brack, Jr. (New Haven: Yale University Press, 2004), 403–4.

CHAPTER FIVE

Poetic forms containing rampant money

1. *A South Sea Bubble ode*

'BRITANNIA's Lamentation, Occasion'd by the SOUTH-SEA; OR, The Second TOWER of *BABEL. A PINDARICK ODE*' is the first work in an anonymous pamphlet dated 1721 which contains three other poems. Though not all occasioned by the South Sea Bubble, they are each touched by its events in their manifest ulterior motive. It was later bound together as a nineteenth-century Pamphlet Book, with the words 'Miscellaneous Poems' printed on its spine, and containing nine items (not all of them poems), the first being 'Britannia's Lamentation'. There is no sign of authorship on the 1721 publication, perhaps because the pamphlet of four poems is a patriotic, or treasonous, piece of Jacobite polemic using the South Sea Bubble to invoke a fresh attempt to restore the British crown to the Stuarts. Among its three other poems is a hymn to the birth of Charles Edward Stuart, the Young Pretender, or Bonnie Prince Charlie, born on 31 December 1720 in Rome.[1]

'Britannia's Lamentation' begins with its title poem, an account of the consequences of the South Sea Bubble on the British nation. The first stanza prepares its panegyric by focusing on the inability of the Church of England to save the country, which further indicates that its author may have been a supporter of the Old Religion:

> If Pray'rs and Tears,
> The Shields, the Church of *England* only bears,
> In some great Exigence of State,

---

[1] Presented to the University Library Reading by Stratford Public Library in July 1952.

> Cou'd *those* have warded off the blows of Fate:
> We had not fall'n, we had not Sunk so Low,
> Under the griev'ous heavy Weight,
> The Pressures of the fatal overthrow.

This author competently manages the variable line-lengths and improvised rhyming of the English Pindaric as evolved from its Greek original in poems by Pindar celebrating athletes at ancient games, established in its flexible stanza conventions almost single-handed during the later decades of the previous century by Abraham Cowley.[2] The variable and improvised metrics and rhyme scheme is apt for the theme of speculation and risk – not least because the original odes and their occasions in sporting competition naturally involved the dangers of winning, falling, and failing. Cowley had supported the Stuart monarchy in the Civil War, and the emergence of his Pindaric mode can be related to problems of expression emerging from its defeat and exile: hence the appropriateness of an anonymous Jacobite Pindaric ode on the South Sea Bubble.

Mary Douglas has speculated about the involvement of those games and their celebratory odes with the economic structures of the time: 'Were the best young athletes and the best trainers in the pay of powerful patrons (as market theory would assume)? Did their patrons pay the poets for their congratulatory odes? There is certainly one instance of this in *Pythian* 10'. She adds:

> Evidence for betting is less direct. At Nemea, the presence in the late fourth-century stadium of contingents of spectators from Argos, Sikyon, Phlius, and Kleonai, is illustrated by the distribution of coins from these cities, and the fact that these are mostly small change may suggest that they were used for betting and gaming.[3]

Douglas thinks it praiseworthy that the book's authors have brought together poetry and sport. She finds that the two may be conjoined in the cultural management of risk and uncertainty, and in the establishing and promulgating of prestige. 'Britannia's Lamentation' highlights the venality of the risk-takers and the consequences of their actions as a means towards

[2] Ben Jonson's 'To the Immortal Memory and Friendship of that Noble Pair, Sir Lucius Carey and Sir H. Morison' is the only other such ode written in English during the seventeenth century. For an account of the English Pindaric's emergence and its characteristics, see David Trotter, *The Poetry of Abraham Cowley* (London and Basingstoke: Macmillan, 1979), 109–42.

[3] Mary Douglas, 'Conclusion: The Prestige of the Games', in *Pindar's Poetry, Patrons and Festivals: From Archaic Greece to the Roman Empire*, ed. Simon Hornblower and Catherine Morgan (Oxford: Oxford University Press, 2007), 398.

the celebration of the values implied in its hero, the King across the Water, recently back in his continental European exile after the failures of the 1715 and 1719 attempted restorations.

The combination of metrical and rhyme-scheme patterning within the conventions of an unpredictably improvised development serves this Jacobite poet well in dramatizing the lamentable inflating and bursting of the Bubble, while at the same time deploying the conventional line-lengths of English lyric and the strongly marked line ends closing on rhyme (it eschews unpunctuated enjambment) to assert the importance of measures and principles which may be thought to have prevented it, as here in its second strophe:

> Thro' all the Realms, the dark Contagion flew,
> Each gazing stood with eager Eyes,
> Imbibing Sympathetick Joys;
> From the Auraean Phantome to accrue:
> The Magazines were wont to hold,
> *Britannia*'s Stores of treasur'd Gold,
> Inexorable av'rice strait unfolds:
> All hurry'd, courting to supply,
> The boundless Prodigality,
> Did thro' three Kingdoms Passage force,
> Triumphant in its baneful Course,
> By vile seducers, loose and unconfin'd,
> No Guide was to Direct, or Precepts bind.

Once more the competence of the poet is manifest in the deployment of the form as a resistance to the articulated sense. These lines lament the conversion of 'treasur'd Gold' into stock rapidly rising in value and driven by 'Inexorable av'rice', while the rhymes on 'hold' and 'Gold', on 'force' and 'Course', and on 'unconfin'd' and 'bind' indicate a counteractive urge in the poet inviting controls that could have prevented the speculation and its consequences. Julian Hoppit has suggested, however, that the guides and precepts such as are here evoked were, in fact, in place before April 1720, when the scheme was authorized. The South Sea Company had been founded, he notes, in 1711 'to help the Tory government organise the National Debt and exploit public credit after nearly twenty years of expensive warfare.'[4] By late 1719 it had been taken over by the Whigs, who set up the South Seas scheme. These 'vile seducers, loose and unconfin'd'

---

[4] Julian Hoppit, 'The Myths of the South Sea Bubble', *Transactions of the Royal Historical Society*, vol. 12 (2002), 142. For criticism of this essay, see Pat Rogers, 'South Sea Bubble Myths', *The Times Literary Supplement*, 9 April 2014.

flaunt their freedom from this poet's appropriate leadership and values, ones simultaneously asserted and emblematically curbed in the couplet rhyme that closes the stanza: 'No Guide was to Direct, or Precepts bind' – the syntax directing as the rhyme contains.

The next strophe evokes, in the highest-flown pitch of the Pindaric, perhaps the greatest pyramid-selling speculative abyss in the country's economic history:

> Black was the storm our Isle o'erspread,
> Shot from the bosom of the *Southern-Sea*,
> A Prelude of the dark Catastrophe;
> Which struck at once the Empire dead:
> E'en Nature quak'd the Shock to bear,
> Substance soon transform'd to Air;
> From Fortune's Pinnacle her Fav'rites drop,
> And Sons Ennobled needed prop;
> Whilst Throngs of Wealthy crouding Prest,
> To be with Golden Shadows blest;
> Father, Son, and Brother,
> Rob'd, and Pillag'd one another,
> No Cautions cou'd Antisipate their Fall,
> The strong Delusion reign'd, Supreme o'er All.

Thus in the course of these two stanzas '*Britannia*'s Stores of treasur'd Gold' are a 'Substance soon transform'd to Air', indicating the ways in which the South Sea Scheme served to convert material wealth based in property and precious metals, into stocks and bonds, paper contracts not backed by any securities, which were then, after enormous growth during the earlier half of the year, to collapse in value in the autumn of 1720. Some of this value was transferred out of the country, as Swift noted in 'The Bubble':

> But these, you say, are factious Lyes
> From some malicious Tory's Brain,
> For, where Directors get a Prize,
> The *Swiss* and *Dutch* whole Millions drain.[5]

In 'The Bubble' rhymed tetrameter quatrains adapt the street ballad to figure the corrupting inevitability of the scheme's redistribution from the landed interest and the Tories to that of the traders in London and their ascendant political factions. King George I sold his gratis-provided holdings

---

5   Jonathan Swift, *Poetical Works,* ed. Herbert Davies (Oxford: Oxford University Press, 1967), 203.

in the scheme during the summer and at the top of the market, moving his profits to Hanover via Amsterdam, while the Canton of Berne benefitted substantially by selling before the fall began in September.

In addition to destroying the scheme for the establishment of a national bank for Ireland, which Swift also opposed, a further effect of the Bubble was to denude that country of coinage, helping to occasion a subsequent scandal in the form of Wood's Halfpennies. Irish speculation in the South Seas had resulted in many bankruptcies and drained the island of coin. As a consequence, trade was hampered by the lack of means. Wood's bronze half-pennies, minted in England and shipped to Ireland between 1722 and 1724, stimulated the production of much poetry and song, most famously from Swift's own pen. Herbert Davis's edition prints seventeen pages of 'Political Poems Relating to Wood's Halfpence', including these lines:

> There is a *Chain* let down from *Jove*,
> But fasten'd to his Throne above;
> So strong, that from the lower End,
> They say, all human Things depend:
> This *Chain*, as Antient Poets hold,
> When *Jove* was Young, was made of *Gold*.
> *Prometheus* once this *Chain* purloin'd,
> Dissolv'd, and into *Money* Coin'd;
> Then whips me on a *Chain* of *Brass*,
> (*Venus* was Brib'd to let it pass.)[6]

'Prometheus' was written in 1724, towards the end of the two-year period when Wood's money was legal tender in Ireland. In the footnote to a 1735 publication, *Venus* here is identified as a 'great Lady' 'reported to have been bribed by Wood.'[7] If it was 'Prometheus' in this allegory of Swift's, it was the South Sea Scheme that helped purloin the gold and silver from Ireland, in another form of redistribution, making way for an Englishman's brass. There was also the fear that increasing the amount of currency would depress the value of what there already was, a further means for impoverishment through inflation. The scandal over Wood's halfpennies may also be a case where poetry (and prose in the form of the 'Drapier's Letters') did help make something happen, because in light of the uproar caused, evolving into an outcry about Ireland's position in relation to the English crown, Wood's currency was withdrawn and he was compensated with a pension that he did not live to enjoy.[8]

---

[6] Jonathan Swift, *Poetical Works*, 278.
[7] Ibid.
[8] For an account of Swift's responses to Wood's scheme, see David Nokes, *Jonathan*

2. Politics and debt creation

Like the best of jeremiads, 'Britannia's Lamentation' can indulge for its own political ends the fraudulence, duplicity, and stupidity it abhors. It is further subject to historical ironies in that the strong illusions which reigned supreme in the stock-jobbing alleys of the Anglican and Whig city, and which members of the Patriot party also indulged, as Pope's satires on the scheme would note, could be matched by those that, evident as the poem unfolds, are energizing its lines (though the degree of illusion in Jacobite circles may be a result of both subsequent and Whig history).[9] The irreligion of the pyramid scheme is underlined by its analogy with that other great ungodly attempt to rise too high above the ground, the Tower of Babel:

> Deep was the Execrable Project Laid,
> For Hell it self the Combination made;
> The mighty Pile began to Rise,
> Like *Babel* Tow'ring tow'rds the Skies,
> 'S if Heaven, well as Earth they would Invade.
> When Lo! at Last,
> Th' undone affrighted Croud;
> Torn by its Blast,
> Proclaim'd the Cheat aloud:
> No sooner was the Myst'ry blown,
> But its Foundation gave a Groan,
> And down the amasing height,
> Under its Pond'rous Weight,
> Fell in, and Crush't the *British* State.

There are further ironies, for the British state would not in fact be crushed by the collapse of the South Sea Bubble, nor would it result in the return of the Stuart dynasty. It was, rather, part of what, with skilful management and protection of interests, would help Walpole rise to power and be the longest-serving prime minister in English history.[10] He had sold his South Sea shares at the top of the market, making 1,000 per cent profit.

'Britannia's Lamentation' then turns to reveal its ulterior motive, for while the country is bemoaning its fate and looking for a saviour, the author

Swift, a Hypocrite Reversed: A Critical Biography (Oxford: Oxford University Press, 1985), 280–96, and for his opposition to a national bank for Ireland, 268.

9   For the viability of a Stuart restoration at this time, see 'A Jacobite Opportunity: The South Sea Crisis and the Possibility of a Constitutional Restoration', in Eveline Cruickshanks and Howard Erskine-Hill, *The Atterbury Plot* (Basingstoke: Palgrave Macmillan, 2004), 56–90.

10   See John Carswell, *The South Sea Bubble* (London: Cresset Press, 1961), 259–64.

of the pamphlet calls upon the Stuart king to return from exile and save the country:

> Like *Egypts* Land our Isle was Left,
> Of Glory, Wealth, and Peace bereft;
> O'er whelm'd with Anguish and Despair;
> Great were the Thoughts of Heart,
> In ev'ry Eye a Tear,
> In every Loyal Soul a Dart:
> But Horrour and Destruction rowling on,
> As Billow after Billow press along;
> So *Albion* lyes, tost to and fro,
> Thus driven by disastrous Fate,
> The fatal Shock to undergo,
> Her crying Sins to Expiate.

This poet's allegiance is revealed by the strategic omission of the name in the last line of the poem's final section: 'Long Live and Reign Great------our Gracious King'. James III, as Jacobites would call him, had issued a declaration on 10 October 1720 from Rome in which a peaceful restoration (as in 1660) was proposed, George being in Hanover at the time; and plans were afoot in Europe to repeat a military attempt on the throne into 1721. This anonymous ode then appeals to the legitimate monarch, James, to return.

Yet the greatest unintended irony in 'Britannia's Lamentation', the thing it understandably cannot say, though probably understanding it, is that the South Sea Bubble had been evolved as a means to take over the national debt from the Bank of England, a private bank founded in 1694 to provide credit to the government of William and Mary to prosecute its war against France. That debt had been incurred as fixed bonds returning high interest, and the plan was to convert them into South Sea shares which could then float freely and lessen the government's debt burden. Walter Bagehot plainly stated in his *Lombard Street: A Description of the Money Market* (1873), when writing that without the aid of these emerging markets

> our National Debt could not have been borrowed; and if we had not been able to raise that money we would have been conquered by France and compelled to take back James II. And for many years afterwards the existence of that debt was the main reason why the industrial classes never would think of recalling the Pretender, or of upsetting the revolution settlement. The 'fund-holder' is always considered in the books of that time as opposed to his 'legitimate' sovereign, because it was to be feared that this sovereign would

repudiate the debt which was raised by those who dethroned him, and which was spent in resisting him and his allies.[11]

Not in all the books of that time, though, for we have seen from this pamphlet publication with its Pindaric ode in praise of the financial probity which would, it is assumed, be brought in by the restoration of the Stuarts – as Hoppit underlines:

> That revolution centred upon how the government established a permanent and funded national debt by employing parliamentary promises of future tax revenues to repay what had been borrowed. But initially there was much about this that was uncertain and experimental. Some of those problems were mainly administrative and organisational, but some were political, not least because of a potential threat to creditors of a Jacobite restoration.[12]

Here too the religious argument might not support the expectation that the new king would honour the debt, because his divine right would provide the moral authority and principle for the breaking of any such 'treasonous' contracts – once more driving a wedge between the terms of the analogy explored in the previous chapter around trust in secular contractual behaviour, and the interventions of the great account-keeper in the sky. It is a neat example of how indebtedness may be a means for the establishing of political acquiescence, and a source for a further unintended irony in this Pindaric ode.

The Jacobite theme revealed in the progress of 'Britannia's Lamentation' is underlined in the final verse of the second poem, 'AN ODE to the KING, ON THE *BIRTH of a PRINCE*', in which the disaster of the South Sea Bubble is cast into a providential light – at least as far as Jacobite sympathies were concerned:

> *South-Sea* might then be styled an useful Foe,
>   Rais'd up by Fortune to asswage;
> Those wider Ruins Daily seem to grow,
>   And Crush a more Destructive Rage:
> For wisest Patriots timely now foresee,
> From whence, and who must our Restorer be.

---

[11] Walter Bagehot, *Lombard Street: A Description of the Money Market* (Kitchener, Ontario: Batoche Books, 2001), 53–4. The Mississippi scheme of 1719, during which the term 'millionaire' was first coined, underlines that such speculations to relieve government debt were not confined to the English protestant succession.

[12] Hoppit, 'The Myths of the South Sea Bubble', 142.

Here the identification of the South Sea Bubble and its disaster with the Hanoverian settlement, the Church of England, and the mercantile and capitalist system in rapid development since the founding of the Bank of England only five years after the Glorious Revolution, all point to the politics and values of this anonymous, poetically competent author. Finally, in a third poem, '*BRITANNIA*'s Answer TO THE KING's DECLARATION', written in the heroic couplets and triplets most associated with the satire of the period, the anonymous poet once more makes the point:

> So once again, Your Strength in *Israel* Try,
> When their cow'd *Sanhedrim* shall prostrate lye;
> And to your Feet their slavish Necks shall yield,
> By *Bubbles* humbled, and by *South-Sea* peel'd,
> Then Reign Triumphant o'er *Britannia*'s Field.

'Britannia's Lamentation' must have been written after 20 October 1720, when James's declaration was issued, and the entire pamphlet will have appeared early in 1721, after the Young Pretender's birth. It suggests that the Old Pretender had declared he would not be making a further attempt on the throne, or that our poet thought this had happened, to which he then urged a change of mind, but one that did not ensue.

This anonymous poet would be on the losing side of this history. Yet opportunist outrage at the South Sea Company's corruption might also indicate the emergence of a decades-long risk-averse culture that, as John Carswell suggests in his ground-breaking history of the Bubble, served to separate by some forty or fifty years the Commercial and Industrial Revolutions that 'were undoubtedly part of the same process' as the Financial one; and he concludes by imagining an alternative history based on the idea that the speculative funding of projects had not been given so catastrophically bad a name by the events of 1720, for to 'delete the years of arrest conjures up all kinds of fancies', such as these poetical and literary allusions: 'Gray musing to the distant rattle of the threshing machine; Garrick acting by gaslight; and Dr. Johnson holding forth in his compartment as the Edinburgh train belches smoke and thunder across the countryside'.[13] Yet this experiment in national debt mitigation and speculative project-financing in the unregulated extremity of the South Sea Bubble would, in different guises, come to form a basis for first Britain's and then the world's growth-driven, manufacturing economies.

---

[13] Carswell, *The South Sea Bubble*, 272.

3. *Speculation and poetic form*

Anne Kingsmill, the future Countess of Winchilsea, had been a maid of honour at the court of James, Duke of York, and his wife Mary of Modena during Charles II's reign. There she met her future husband, Heneage Finch; and it was their loyalty to the Stuarts that led her and her husband to be exiled from court in 1688 and to retire in Kent. She too was moved to write a poem on the South Sea Bubble, one which concentrates upon the follies of her sex, who – she indicates here and elsewhere – are letting the side down with their frivolity and weaknesses, ones no different from their male investor counterparts when gambling in 'A Song on the South Sea'. It was written in 1720, the last year of her life:

> Ombre and basset laid aside,
>   New games employ the fair;
> And brokers all those hours divide
>   Which lovers used to share.
>
> The court, the park, the foreign song
>   And harlequin's grimace,
> Forlorn; amidst the city throng
>   Behold each blooming face.
>
> With Jews and Gentiles undismayed
>   Young tender virgins mix,
> Of whiskers nor of beards afraid,
>   Nor all the cozening tricks.
>
> Bright jewels, polished once to deck
>   The fair one's rising breast,
> Or sparkle round her ivory neck,
>   Lie pawned in iron chest.
>
> The gayer passions of the mind
>   How avarice controls!
> Even love does now no longer find
>   A place in female souls.[14]

---

[14] This text, first published in *The Hive* (1724), derived from the Lansdowne MS in the British Library, is printed in Roger Lonsdale (ed.), *Eighteenth-Century Women Poets: An Oxford Anthology* (Oxford: Oxford University Press, 1989), 26. It appears, with variant title and punctuation, in Anne Finch, Countess of Winchilsea, *Selected Poems,* ed. Denys Thompson (New York: Routledge, 2003), 80.

The lightness and lift of Finch's ballad stanza figures the speculative enthusiasm of the moment, while the predictable returning of the shortening form, the even-lined trimeters following tetrameters, underlines both the inevitability of folly and the comeuppances entailed. Finch, who can rhyme and pun on the implications of 'design'd' and 'kinde',[15] here concludes by linking the foolish 'controls' of being subject to speculative passion with the cost in 'souls'. Her poem is astonished and yet also entertained by the gullibility and public obsession with this stock market opportunity, while hardly letting on, aside from the 'cozening tricks', that things are going to go wrong. 'A Song on the South Sea' exemplifies Finch's even-handedness in satirizing the qualities in women that do not rise to her standards, as in 'On Myselfe'; and her composing here on speculative gain could then be seen as another of the petty things that she will not stoop to do. Her poem would hold itself aloof from what it mocks, yet does so by lightening its own modes.

Though Colin Nicholson doesn't refer to Finch's poem, he does touch on the theme in comments on a South Sea poem already encountered, Swift's 'The Bubble', and in his prose works as well, when noting that

> Women are busy too: figured as disappointed witches, 'the Female Troops' gather at the gaming tables, 'their Losses to retrieve', and contemporary newspaper accounts give us a flavour of the frantic pursuit of enrichment Swift is satirizing: 'Our South Sea ladies buy South Sea jewels, hire South Sea maids, and take new country South Sea Houses; the gentlemen set up South Sea Coaches and buy South Sea estates'.[16]

They were buying into material wealth on the credit of the stocks, which could thus be used as currency. This again points to the relationship between wavering or precarious trust in paper exchange, and the need to realize it in material things for them to count as wealth, promoting conspicuous consumption (though it hadn't been given that name at this stage) as a spur to economic development. This process is also noted in Finch's song in her stanza on the surrendering of material wealth in order to raise funds to gamble on the South Sea stock: 'Bright jewels, polished once to deck / The fair one's rising breast, / Or sparkle round her ivory neck, / Lie pawned in iron chest.'

15 See 'On Myselfe', in *The Poems of Anne Countess of Winchilsea*, ed. Myra Reynolds (Chicago: University of Chicago Press, 1903), 14–15.
16 Colin Nicholson, *Writing and the Rise of Finance: Capital Satires of the Early Eighteenth* Century (Cambridge: Cambridge University Press, 1994), 80.

Howard Erskine-Hill has drawn attention to the role of the South Sea Bubble in shaping Pope's satire on speculation.[17] The rhymed couplet form of Pope's epigrammatic epics sees him attempting to combine minutiae of local control with an expansiveness of large-scale structure, and the tension between the two helps account for Colin Nicholson's economic explanation for the 'failure' of Pope's form to curb and control the vastness of the proliferating corruption that he is able to imagine. The pun on 'containing' in this chapter's title promises to indicate how money has got under the skin of poetry too, and how, simultaneously, money might be prevented from overflowing, and overwhelming all by, in this instance, the reiterative local constraints of the form, as here in 'Epistle III To Allen Lord Bathurst *Of the* Use *of* Riches':

> Yet, to be just to these poor men of pelf,
> Each does but hate his Neighbour as himself:
> Damn'd to the Mines, an equal fate betides
> The Slave that digs it, and the Slave that hides.
> Who suffers thus, mere Charity should own,
> Must act on motives pow'rful, tho' unknown:
> Some War, some Plague, or Famine they foresee,
> Some Revelation hid from you and me.
> Why Shylock wants a meal, the cause is found,
> He thinks a Loaf will rise to fifty pound.
> What made Directors cheat in South-sea year?
> To live on Ven'son when it sold so dear.[18]

Nicholson comments further on the relationship of Pope's chosen form to his economic materials when he notes: 'Balanced verse portraits of parsimony and of prodigality bid for artistic equilibrium, while the power of the writing is triggered by characters treated as contemptible and threatening'; and he adds:

> Perhaps there was an element of self-recognition in that Pope's neo-classical proprieties and his sometimes venomous satire represent seemingly opposed characteristics, while his success in subordinating the passion of one to the reasonable form of the other is a mark of his couplet mastery. In several ways he forged a metre out

---

[17]   Howard Erskine-Hill, *The Social Milieu of Alexander Pope: Lives, Example and the Poetic Response* (New Haven and London: Yale University Press, 1975), 166–203.

[18]   Alexander Pope, *Epistles to Several Persons (Moral Essays)*, ed. F. W. Bateson, Twickenham Edition, vol. 3 (London: Methuen, 1951), vol. 2, 98–9. The passage is perhaps echoed in the 'hope's delusive mine' opening of Johnson's 'On the Death of Dr Robert Levet' discussed at the close of the previous chapter.

of – and often against – genuine and complicated antagonisms both private and public, and within these oppositions and conjunctions a fierce satire threatens to unbalance an embedded ethical programme designed to moderate the worst effects of corruption.[19]

The contradiction here, as in financial architecture designed to look like Greek temples, is that a classical theory of character and virtue, articulated through the principle of 'the golden mean', infiltrated by a fascination with its opposite, is preserved in imitative neo-classical guise – even as it laments discrepancies between substance and appearance. Pope's '*Of the* Use *of* Riches' is a poem simultaneously exercised by the myriad nature of money and the desire to put it to use, using it to good ends, and this means shaping it to them, then applying that value to the form of his poem and the way in which 'control' is one of the values most patently dramatized by the poet's couplets.

Entitled in full, but without the period variations of typeface and presentation, 'A Panegyrical Epistle to Mr. Thomas Snow, Goldsmith, near Temple-Barr: Occasion'd by his Buying and Selling the Third South-Sea Subscriptions, taken in by the Directors at a Thousand per Cent', John Gay's poem explores the analogy between the speculating of the poet and that of the projector:

> No wonder, if we found some *Poets* there,
> Who live on Fancy, and can feed on Air;
> No wonder, *they* were caught by *South-Sea* Schemes,
> Who ne'er enjoy'd a Guinea, but in Dreams;
> No wonder, *they* their Third Subscriptions sold,
> For Millions of imaginary Gold:
> No wonder, that their Fancies wild could frame
> Strange Reasons, that a Thing is still the same,
> Though chang'd throughout in Substance and in Name.
> But *you* (whose Judgment scorns Poetick Flights)
> With Contracts furnish Boys for Paper Kites.[20]

Grub Street poets had to try and live on fancy. Nicholson notes Gay's involvement with both speculative publishing and South Sea stock investments, the latter in which he was to lose money.[21] In his poem

---

[19] Nicholson, *Writing and the Rise of Finance*, 142–3.

[20] John Gay, *Poetry and Prose*, 2 vols., ed. Vinton A. Dearing and Charles E. Beckwith (Oxford: Oxford University Press, 1974), vol. 1, 281. On the basis of Gay's lines 11–12, 'When Credit sunk, and Commerce gasping lay, / Thou stood'st; no Bill was sent unpaid away', John Carswell speculates that 'Snow probably foreclosed, for his house survived to earn this tribute from Gay'; *The South Sea Bubble*, 196.

[21] For Gay's investing, see Nicholson, *Writing and the Rise of Finance*, 68–9.

addressed to the banker, Snow, the narrative shifts from Exchange Alley to Bedlam: 'A *Poet* enter'd of the neighb'ring Cell, / And with fix'd Eye observ'd the Structure well.' Gay only too evidently emphasizes the similarity and difference between the banker's structure of ungrounded inflation and these couplets, the latter self-secured with its metered rhyme, and in this madhouse the poet is tempted to invest: 'The Bard with Wonder the cheap purchase saw, / So sign'd the Contract (as ordains the Law.)' Gay's poem asks who is more deluded, the poet or the prospector, and in the end, the latter's speculation voiding, the banker asks to have his deal redeemed for a metal coin: 'Yet loth the Sum entire should be destroy'd; / 'Give me a Penny, and thy Contract's void.' But the poet gets the last laugh, reverting to an earlier and abstract mode of contract, the tally stick, by cutting more notches, and 'With just Resentment' he 'flings it to the Ground; / "There, take my Tally of Ten Thousand Pound."'[22]

Discussing 'A Panegyric Epistle', Nicholson notes that 'while the pentameter form of the poem's own contract of engagement with the reader remains constant, shifts occur in the literary name given to it at different moments in its utterance', and further,

> The poem's initial Horatian derivation involves an ironic invocation to Snow which then gestures at the close of the first stanza – with 'attend my Lay' – towards a kind of writing that had already evolved from an original signification of short lyric or narrative poem to become synonymous with *conte*. As the 'song' which then occupies lines 9 to 39 subsequently becomes 'the Moral Tale' about a banker and a poet in an insane asylum, Gay traces nominal shifts and changes in an unfolding continuity of narrative.

The critic associates this nominal instability in a poem written in the set form of pentameter couplets with 'the wealth of imaginative construction and the construction of imaginary wealth'.[23] While the metrical and formal 'agreement' with the reader is maintained, the promise of what genre of poem this might be is said to be radically flouted so as to imitate, mock, and so denounce the 'speculative' absurdities of both banker and poet, each of which, in their different ways, are engaged in slippages between 'imaginative' and 'imaginary'. But poets are not being mocked here, not least because their madness is proverbial and routine. What's more, the mad poet gets the last laugh on the mad banker, even while Gay may be attempting to earn by laughing at both. Nevertheless, is it true that because

[22] Gay, *Poetry and Prose*, vol. 1, 282.
[23] Nicholson, *Writing and the Rise of Finance*, 76.

an eighteenth-century poem maintains its rhymes, its relationship with a reader is reliable and trustworthy?

4. Paper credit and gold

The criticism of the South Sea Bubble's redistribution of wealth through a speculative project without material basis uses the values of gold or land as counters to wealth leveraged from airy nothings, and this points towards some two centuries of conceptual conflict about money's backing in gold or other precious metal. This conventional backing is still notionally present in the promise to pay the bearer on paper currency, and on the name 'pound' for English money. By contrast, paper currency based on forms of trust, on the 'promise' in their printed and not metallically stamped face value, has been subject to centuries of suspicion. The common assumption that material currencies gave way first to paper money backed by gold and then to fiat money founded on state credit has been challenged by Matthew Rowlinson, who provides anthropological evidence to argue that currency emerged as first imaginary money representing an abstract value to define tax debts for payment in produce.[24]

Nevertheless, as we shall see, a great deal of poetry in the eighteenth and nineteenth centuries is written in the belief that reliable wealth is material or metallic, and that paper money, as emblematically characterized by Peacock, is a fraud.[25] Here, for example, is Pope waxing satirically lyrical on the power of paper instruments, again from 'To Allen Lord Bathurst *Of the* Use *of* Riches':

> Blest paper-credit! last and best supply!
> That lends Corruption lighter wings to fly!
> Gold imp'd by thee, can compass hardest things,
> Can pocket States, can fetch or carry Kings;
> A single leaf shall waft an Army o'er,
> Or ship off Senates to a distant Shore;
> A leaf, like Sibyl's, scatter to and fro
> Our fates and fortunes, as the winds shall blow:
> Pregnant with thousands flits the Scrap unseen,
> And silent sells a King, or buys a Queen.[26]

---

[24] Matthew Rowlinson, *Real Money and Romanticism* (Cambridge: Cambridge University Press, 2010), 1–13.

[25] David Hume, for instance, discredits its benefit to commerce in 'Of Money', in *Essays: Moral, Political, and Literary,* ed. Eugene F. Miller (Indianapolis: Liberty Classics, 1985), 284–5.

[26] Pope, *Epistles to Several Persons (Moral Essays)*, 90–1.

Pope, too, is much addicted to end-stopping for the purposes of meaning control. There is only one instance above where he allows the sense to run over the line within a couplet: 'A leaf, like Sibyl's, scatter to and fro / Our fates and fortunes, as the winds shall blow'. The 'to and fro' of this international movement is figured by the formal variation. Of couplets that he calls 'the most celebrated lines in Pope's later writing, at least as far as the advent of the credit economy is concerned', Nicholson has this to say:

> Highly polished versification forges a self-containment for lines dense with satirical reference. In the phrase 'fetch or carry' and 'ship off' and the activity of buying and selling we watch the values and practices of commerce unsettle prevailing dispositions, while Pope annotates details of the trade in crowned heads and kingdoms as if they were commodities circulating in the markets of Europe.[27]

Yet there is a circularity here: the rise of the city merchants threatens the divine right of kings, and introduces the idea of a contractual monarchy, while this very innovation has to be defended against the urge to restore divine-right absolutists being supported by King Louis, who had his own Mississippi scheme to set his debts in order. The question is not whether the money is upsetting the traditional values, as that the interests of one part of the population are set against another, and both are attempting to deploy inventive monetary mechanisms to finance their interests. In a changing marketplace – as Pope, Swift, and Gay also knew – if you want to defeat your opponents you will have to compete with them and to finance that competition.

Nicholson observes that 'by the time of Pope's death in 1743, the political economy he sought to temper and redirect had demonstrated its irreversible triumph: his favoured couplet-form exposed as unequal to the task of disciplined restraint he had set for it.'[28] Pope's career as a poet, by this account, was defeated by the emergence of the market for stocks and shares, by paper money and the national debt, the Bank of England, and Walpole's ministry. However, as Nicholson also astutely notes, 'Pope has been described as the first English writer to achieve financial independence from the sale of his work', and he 'was adept at juggling his market to personal advantage' – and not only the market for translations of Homer:

> While publicly opposing the rapidly expanding financial systems and institutions of the time, like his friends and colleagues Pope participated in them and profited from the opportunities they

[27]   Nicholson, *Writing and the Rise of Finance*, 147.
[28]   Ibid. 11–12.

presented. So it becomes an interesting reflection upon subsequent literary canon-formation and the cultural valorisations it encodes that some of the most remembered voices from a time of the greatest explosion of financial and commercial activity England had hitherto seen, publicly set themselves determinedly at variance with what was happening, while privately seeking profit from it.[29]

Pope was able to benefit from what in his work he objected to, which would make him the same as any satirist, given that he was selling his works, and so profiting from what he was denigrating. But what follows from this is that, by the same token, he can't be said to have failed when 'his favoured couplet-form' was apparently 'exposed as unequal to the task of disciplined restraint he had set for it.' Pope's techniques were simultaneously being enlivened and vivified by the materials that he was subjecting to a 'disciplined restraint'. In such conditions, where a writer benefits from what he hates, it seems hardly fair to conclude that his failure to defeat his enemy has been an unmitigated failure, and this is because the planes on which the successes and failures are being played out, Exchange Alley and Parnassus, are not homologous spaces.

5. Serving Mammon

'Much have I travelled in the realms of gold'[30] is how John Keats, with both the classical golden age of poetry and perhaps *el dorado* in mind, begins 'On First Looking into Chapman's Homer' – although when he composed it early one October morning in 1816, paper money in Britain had not been convertible into that precious metal for nearly two decades, and debate literally surrounding the poem in Leigh Hunt's *The Examiner*,[31] where it appeared on 1 December, included discussion about returning to securing the currency on bullion holdings.[32] In 1797 the Bank of England had found its reserves of gold so reduced through the funding

---

[29] Ibid. 18.
[30] John Keats, *The Complete Poems*, ed. John Barnard, 3rd edn. (London: Penguin Books, 1988), 72.
[31] For magazine poems against paper money in these years, see Jeffrey N. Cox, *Poetry and Politics in the Cockney School: Keats, Shelley, Hunt and Their Circle* (Cambridge: Cambridge University Press, 1998), 201.
[32] Alexander Dick comments on the sonnet's relation to the establishment of a gold standard and the source of the 'realms of gold' phrase in Pope's 'Hereditary realms, and worlds of gold' from '*Of the* Use *of* Riches', in *Romanticism and the Gold Standard: Money, Literature, and Economic Debate in Britain 1790–1830* (Basingstoke and New York: Palgrave Macmillan, 2013), 26–35.

of the Revolutionary War against France that, rather than risk refusing to redeem paper notes with specie, it called upon Prime Minister Pitt to have the government back this necessity on patriotic grounds. By the Bank Restriction Act, British paper money would circulate un-convertible to gold until an act of 1817, the date at which the country officially went onto a gold standard (though the Bank would not be able to redeem its promissory notes in practice until 1823), and upon this standard monetary policy would remain until 1914.[33]

In his famous letter to Shelley of 16 August 1820, Keats draws upon the relation of poetic value to this precious metal, though in its unrefined state, when he suggests in light of his reading *The Cenci* (1819) that its poet might, in future writing, traffic a little more with the world by 'enriching' his work:

> – *an artist* must serve Mammon – he must have 'self-concentration' selfishness perhaps. You I am sure will forgive me for sincerely remarking that you might curb your magnanimity and be more of an artist, and 'load every rift' of your subject with ore.[34]

Shelley has cued the theme by writing to Keats on 27 July 1820 that 'I have lately read your Endymion again & ever with a new sense of the treasures of poetry it contains, though treasures poured forth with indistinct profusion', and this is 'the cause of comparatively few copies which have been sold'.[35] He apologizes for the style of *The Cenci* in which gold and money are entangled with the murder plot, as when Orsino speculates on whether he 'could take / The profit, yet omit the sin', thinking on how Cenci's 'daughter's dowry were a secret grave' while her father lives, and wishing he could 'despise danger and gold and all'. They are, as when in Act 4 ('each had a bag of coin' and 'The ladies Beatrice and Lucrezia / Tempted me with a thousand crowns'),[36] caught up in the play's ethical conflicts and illustrate it not in aureate imagery but in the matter of criminal motivation and guilt.

---

[33] For how these decisions in 1797 and 1817 inflected the meaning and symbolism of British money, see Rowlinson, *Real Money and Romanticism*, 50–4, and for William Blake's writing in relation to the bullion crisis of 1810, when gold became more valuable than gold coins, see Kurt Heinzelman, *The Economics of the Imagination* (Amherst: University of Massachusetts Press, 1980), 117–19.

[34] Hyder Edward Rollins (ed.), *The Letters of John Keats 1814–1821*, 2 vols. (Cambridge: Harvard University Press, 1958), ii, 322–39.

[35] Fredrick L. Jones (ed.), *The Letters of Percy Bysshe Shelley*, 2 vols. (Oxford: Oxford University Press, 1964), vol. 2, 579.

[36] Zachary Leader and Michael O'Neill (eds.), *Percy Bysshe Shelley: The Major Works* (Oxford: Oxford University Press, 2003), 342, 375, and 383.

In the spring of 1818 Keats had composed a couplet in one of the stanzas about the brothers' exploitative wealth from 'Isabella; or, The Pot of Basil', picturing those who 'all day in dazzling river stood, / To take the rich-ored driftings in the flood.'[37] Now the poet prefaces his exhortation by saying he can only judge of Shelley's poetry, not, then, his theatrical or social purpose. Commentators on this letter tend to understate its ambivalence, as when Rawlinson asserts that to 'be an artist, Keats thus claims, is to economize art'.[38] But, as we have seen, poetry and art are inevitably economized, and Keats's 'Mammon' allusions to the Sermon on the Mount and Edmund Spenser see him making a poetic claim against both Jesus and the polemic of the Cave of Mammon in Book 2, Canto 7 of *The Fairie Queene*.[39] But his indebtedness to Christianity and Spenser means that to 'serve Mammon' is a metaphor, and that while he hopes to 'gain' by publishing such work, he is not unaware of the contradictions implied in employing the Mammon of aureate imagery, loading every rift with ore, to lead a Sir Guyon, that Christian knight, beyond worldly temptation, as Spenser had done, with the hope of reducing his own financial embarrassment into the bargain.

Visualizing the Titans groaning in 'Hyperion: A Fragment' during the autumn of 1818, Keats loaded his own rifts by imagining the figures 'Dungeoned in opaque element, to keep / Their clenchèd teeth still clenched, and all their limbs / Locked up like veins of metal'.[40] But are his lines clogged with the raw materials of golden poetry, or trapped in hope's delusive mine? Rowlinson ramifies Keats's ambivalences in resisting poetry 'that has a palpable design upon us', which the poet called making 'a false coinage' in the same 3 February 1818 letter,[41] and in inviting Shelley, two years later, to unfurl his wings:

> Keats' representation of the poem as an end in itself thus differs from a pure or Kantian aestheticism. Rather it presents poetry as resembling money in having historically developed to become a means rather than an end – and then proposes a poetic that negates

---

[37] Keats, *The Complete Poems*, 242.

[38] Rawlinson, *Real Money and Romanticism*, 132. For the letter and its contexts, see Cox, 'Final Reckonings: Keats and Shelley on the Wealth of the Imagination', in *Poetry and Politics in the Cockney School*, 187–225.

[39] See Matthew 5: 24 and Edmund Spenser, *The Faerie Queene*, ed. Thomas P. Roche, Jr. and C. Patrick O'Donnell, Jr. (Harmondsworth: Penguin Books, 1978), 280–96. For a relevant interpretation, see Heinzelman, *The Economics of the Imagination*, 51–69.

[40] John Keats, *The Complete Poems*, 293.

[41] Rollins (ed.), *The Letters of John Keats*, vol. 1, 224 and 223.

this history. The poem becomes a gift that may not be given or money it is forbidden to spend.[42]

Yet money has not only been a means to an end, not only a representation of labour and other values, but also a commodity – especially, though not only, if it is coin using such precious metals that begin as 'ore'. Keats would be better understood as having recently experienced how his poetry appeared to have rapidly lost value when put into circulation; and, in reaction, he is encouraging himself and his fellow poet to compound their resources at a distance either from social purpose or devaluation in exchange; and he is figuring that projected greater security of value by association with the source of metallic currency. This does not mean that the poems thus figured cannot be given or exchanged, but that they will be 'worth more' when in either of these forms of circulation if created free from such transactional conditions.

Shelley's 'A Defence of Poetry' was a response to Thomas Love Peacock's 'The Four Ages of Poetry' (1820), which places poetry firmly in a marketplace of competing goods: 'like all other trades', poetry 'takes its rise in the demand for the commodity, and flourishes in proportion to the extent of the market'.[43] Peacock's language is itself inflected with the currency of muck and brass, for he sees poetry growing out of the 'natural desire of every man to engross himself' and praising 'how much gold' his patron has 'stowed away' in his house; or making a 'skilful display of the little knowledge that they have' which 'gains them credit for the possession of much more'; or mocking silver age versifiers of golden age rhymed clichés 'who took them on trust as meaning something very soft and tender, without much caring what'; and he sets 'the modern Parnassus far beneath' such exemplars of the 'all-in-all of intellectual progression' as unnamed 'politicians, and political economists', for instance, 'who have built into the upper air of intelligence a pyramid'.[44] Peacock's essay adopts the style of a comical knock-down argument; but there is little sign he means to suggest that those whose thought he opposes to the poets have been constructing a pyramid scheme on false credit and delusive trust, or issuing notes which he would satirize in *Paper Money Lyrics*, where in his 1837 'Preface' he writes of 'that arch class of quacks, who call themselves political economists'.[45]

---

[42]   Rawlinson, *Real Money and Romanticism*, 132.

[43]   H. F. B. Brett-Smith and C. E. Jones (eds.), *The Works of Thomas Love Peacock*, vol. 8 (London: Constable, 1934), 4. For this moment in relations between poetry and a mercantile, industrializing economy, see Rick Rylance, *Literature and the Public Good* (Oxford: Oxford University Press, 2016), 70–80.

[44]   Ibid. 4, 6, 17, and 24.

[45]   Ibid. vol. 7, 99.

The history of poetry's production hardly supports the assertion that it is only a 'commodity' that 'flourishes in proportion to the extent of the market', as the relation of his friend Shelley's creative efforts to the demand for them during his lifetime could manifestly have illustrated. Peacock's argument, though, basing the history of poetry in the terms of an evolving social competition, promises that poetry may well soon cease to exist, as it lacks sufficient market to be worth the effort of its production. His metaphors for the ages of poetry are derived from variously valuable minerals: first iron, then gold, then silver and, finally, bronze. Thus its best exemplars are traditionally and conventionally associated with aureate metaphors and the most valuable of precious metals – as in, for instance, the nineteenth-century anthology, *The Golden Treasury of English Songs and Lyrics* edited by F. T. Palgrave (1861), where Keats's 'realms of gold' sonnet would feature prominently, though the poet had given away more copies of the collection that first contained it than its publisher had been able to sell.

The golden age of poetry, according to Peacock, was that of Amphion and Orpheus, when poets were 'not only historians but theologians, moralists, and legislators'.[46] Perhaps echoing a suggestion from Imlac's description of the poet in Johnson's *Rasselas* (where the poet 'must write as the interpreter of nature, and the legislator of mankind'),[47] Peacock also provides Shelley with the term that he will use for the resounding close of his riposte, 'A Defence of Poetry'. He then goes through his entire cycle once more for the post-classical world, with the golden age as that of Shakespeare and English Romanticism as the current age of bronze, reserving his most knock-about criticism for contemporaries such as Wordsworth and Southey, as well as visitors to his *Nightmare Abbey* (1818), Coleridge and Byron. But he spares another visitor, the future author of *The Cenci,* from being named amongst these boobies. Shelley's poetic polemics against gold in *Queen Mab* (1813) and 'The Mask of Anarchy' (1819) would incline him to reject such routine modes of evaluation, which invite the terms that will denigrate the work of those contemporary poets with whom Peacock was personally friendly.[48]

Shelley's lines from *Queen Mab* articulate his views in fluidly lofty blank verse, where it is not the stopping but the flow that appears to be the mimetically evoked and threatening quality of commerce:

---

[46]   Ibid. vol. 8, 6.
[47]   Samuel Johnson, *Rasselas and Other Tales,* ed. Gwin J. Kolb (New Haven: Yale University Press, 1990), 45. This idea, derived from Orpheus's role, is attributed to Joseph Wharton in Kolb's note on the phrase.
[48]   For the publishing histories of *Queen Mab* and *Don Juan,* see William St Clair, *The Reading Nation in the Romantic Period* (Cambridge: Cambridge University Press, 2004), 317–38.

Hence commerce springs, the venal interchange
Of all that human art and nature yield;
Which wealth should purchase not, but want demand,
And natural kindness hasten to supply
From the full fountain of its boundless love,
For ever stifled, drained, and tainted now.

The poet goes on to denounce 'Commerce! beneath whose poison-breathing shade / No solitary virtue dares to spring', and decides that 'Commerce has set the mark of selfishness, / The signet of its all-enslaving power / Upon a shining ore, and called it gold'. He concludes that all levels of society have succumbed to this power, to which they are all enslaved, for 'in the temple of their hireling hearts / Gold is a living god, and rules in scorn / All earthly things but virtue.'[49] By 1819 and 'The Mask of Anarchy', Shelley could combine his hatred of precious metal fetishism with an abhorrence of paper money's role in the sustenance of the national debt and the funding of wars against the American colonists and then the French, seeing it as contributing to the economic deprivation of the labouring classes which had issued in the events of Peterloo. In a series of parallel answers to the question 'What is Freedom?' Shelley writes:

''Tis to let the Ghost of Gold
Take from Toil a thousandfold
More than e'er its substance could
In the tyrannies of old.

'Paper coin – that forgery
Of the title deeds, which ye
Hold to something of the worth
Of the inheritance of Earth.[50]

Yet here is Shelley as good as agreeing with Byron and their friend Peacock about the iniquities of a paper currency, and not only for the reasons of a fraudulent system of pseudo-trust, but because its purpose is to redistribute wealth away from 'the inheritance of Earth', which for this poet is shared between all those who inhabit it, and not only those who can manipulate currency so as to convert material things into speculative instruments and then, at an advantage, to convert them back

---

49 Geoffrey Matthews and Kelvin Everest (eds.), *The Poems of Shelley 1804–1817,* vol. 1 (London and New York: Longman, 1989), 312–13.
50 Jack Donovan et al. (eds.), *The Poems of Shelley 1819–20,* vol. 3 (London: Longman, 2011), 51.

into redistributed material things. Thus this poet attacks the tyranny of 'Wealth crying havoc!'[51]

Byron had perhaps read or discussed Keats's letter urging his friend Shelley to serve Mammon. He gives a twist to the idea in stanzas on money from *Don Juan* Canto 12 when asserting that the miser 'is your only poet' because passion 'pure / And sparkling on from heap to heap, displays / Possess'd, the ore'.[52] Like Shelley, he supports the rarity of specie against promissory paper notes. Yet as befits his satirically motivated narrating character, he is worldlier-than-thou in claiming bullion as the 'anchor' of currency:

> O Gold! Why call we misers miserable?
>   Theirs is the pleasure that can never pall;
> Theirs is the best bower-anchor, the chain cable
>   Which hold fast other pleasures great and small.
> Ye who but see the saving man at table,
>   And scorn his temperate board, as none at all,
> And wonder how the wealthy can be sparing,
> Know not what visions spring from each cheese-paring.
>
> Love or lust makes man sick, and wine much sicker;
>   Ambition rends, and gaming gains a loss;
> But making money, slowly first, then quicker,
>   And adding still a little through each cross
> (Which *will* come over things), beats love or liquor,
>   The gamester's counter, or the statesman's *dross*.
> O Gold! I still prefer thee unto paper,
> Which makes bank credit like a bark of vapour.

Yet in the couplet immediately preceding this miser's hymn to the reliability of gold, he asserts how 'money, that most pure imagination, / Gleams only through the dawn of its creation',[53] while later noting, apropos of a parliamentary closing session, that ''Tis not mere splendour makes the show august / To eye or heart – it is the people's trust.'[54] His improvised rhyming in the stanzas above might seem aligned with this miser's pleasure, so that 'miserable' and 'table' are held in place by the 'chain cable' that 'can

[51] See P. B. Shelley, 'Lines Written during the Castlereagh Administration', in ibid. 283.
[52] Lord Byron, *The Complete Poetical Works*, ed. Jerome McGann, vol. 5, *Don Juan* (Oxford: Oxford University Press, 1986), 497.
[53] Ibid. 495–6.
[54] Ibid. 520.

never pall'; but this being the only rhyme-word of the three which is drawn on by the flow of his syntax underlines the counter-pressure of instability and perpetual change giving vitality to his poem. *Don Juan* may be more tacitly aligned with the 'pure imagination' of money, and the politics of 'the people's trust' in institutions is what makes its 'show august'. Robert Charles Dallas wrote of *Don Juan* that, as Doris Langley Moore puts it, 'the poet had alloyed "his gold ore with the filthy dross of impure metal".'[55] Yet here it is not a Shelleyan social purpose that is debasing poetry, but the equivocations of a free-ranging mockery which in Canto 12 would close with a promise he did not live to keep to turn 'my best Canto … upon "Political Economy"' and, he advises his readers, 'Mean time read all the National-Debt sinkers, / And tell me what you think of your great thinkers.'[56]

Given that the author of *Queen Mab* had objections to the consequences of unbridled commerce, when in 'A Defence of Poetry', written in February and March of 1821, he comes to defend the poet's social and political value, Shelley does so by rejecting Keats's ambivalent recommendation in phrases that almost echo his words, phrases that the younger poet did not live to read (they were first published in 1840).[57] Writing about his own period, and the contemporary poetry that Peacock had described as produced in an age of bronze, Shelley retorted:

> The cultivation of poetry is never more to be desired than at periods when from an excess of the selfish and calculating principle, the accumulation of the materials of external life exceed the quantity of the power of assimilating them to the internal laws of human nature.[58]

Shelley takes up the very terms of Keats's letter when he writes that 'Poetry, and the principle of Self, of which money is the visible incarnation, are the God and Mammon of the world'.[59] Thus Keats's remark in the letter, after reading *The Cenci*, that he might '"load every rift" of your subject with ore' generates a further irony in the context of those lines from *Queen Mab*, for

---

55 Cited in Doris Langley Moore, *Lord Byron: Accounts Rendered* (London: John Murray, 1974), 184.
56 Byron, *The Complete Poetical Works*, vol. 5, 521 and 522. For Byron's loans to Shelley, see Langley Moore, *Accounts Rendered*, 251; and, for Keats's borrowing and lending, see Rawlinson, *Real Money and Romanticism*, 118–19, and Cox, *Poetry and Politics in the Cockney School*, 191–2.
57 See Roger Pearson, *Unacknowledged Legislators: The Poet as Lawgiver in Post-Revolutionary France* (Oxford: Oxford University Press, 2016), 7–30.
58 *Shelley: The Major Works*, 696.
59 Ibid.

the aureate praise of poetry encounters a panegyric against the fetish value and social effects of this metal worship. But Shelley was as sceptical as Peacock about paper money, which he described in 'The Mask of Anarchy' as 'Paper coin – that forgery'.[60]

According to Alexander Dick, the 'exhortation of *The Mask*, its invocation of hope and democratic reform, and its condemnation of the unjust legal system, especially with regard to economic self-sufficiency, point to a comprehensiveness that requires a mechanism of trust', and he adds:

> This is the part played by literature in Shelley's economic system. While Shelley did not necessarily advocate a gold standard or a moral standard, he did acknowledge the need for standards in the political administration of the people and their networks of communication and understanding, including money. In this respect, Shelley's poetry helped to entrench the idea of the standard that would, through the nineteenth century, dominate monetary policy and economics – in spite of the fact that Shelley himself might have found that suggestion abhorrent.[61]

Yet standards of trust and a gold standard are at odds not only in this critic's analysis of Shelley's politics, but in the controversies he explores around the value-stability and economic benefits of a paper currency. Writing on literature and money in defence of the former's social benefit, one leading advocate admits that despite 'continuing commercial success, and the personal fortunes made by some writers, the literary community has not usually had much of a good word to say about money.'[62] In this light, since the financial revolution in the decades after 1688, literature, and poetry within it, began to invent forms of compensatory counterargument. These extended from Pope and his circle through the Romantic period and its 'unacknowledged legislator' poets, into the Victorian age's societal and economic critics, whether with high Tory or Socialist affiliation. It survives through the modernists' alienation with their times, the Thirties poets' flirtations with communism, and even unto the counter-cultural poets who emerged in the latter decades of the twentieth century and beyond.[63] Yet getting their art off the gold standard would require more than a century

---

[60] *The Poems of Shelley 1819–20*, vol. 3, 51.
[61] Dick, *Romanticism and the Gold Standard*, 130.
[62] Rylance, *Literature and the Public Good*, 105.
[63] For the period's literary opposition to political economy, see Philip Connell, *Romanticism, Economics and the Question of 'Culture'* (Oxford: Oxford University Press, 2005).

of poets' writing in the light of money, and would only be achieved when the political economy had abandoned, by painful stages, money's stability as based on that precious fetish value.

CHAPTER SIX

For a vast speculation had failed

1. *Paper Money Lyrics*

On 20 July 1837, Thomas Love Peacock added a short preface to *Paper Money Lyrics*, a collection of poems originally composed in the winter of 1825–26, which concludes:

> Persons and things are changed, but the substance is the same; and these little ballads are as applicable now as they were twelve years ago. They will be applicable to every time and place, when public credulity shall have given temporary support to the safe and economical currency, which consists of a series of paper promises, made with the deliberate purpose, that the promise shall always be a payment, and the payment shall always be a promise.[1]

When Peacock writes that 'the promise shall always be a payment, and the payment shall always be a promise' he is expressing wry contempt for the deviousness of paper currency that is issued without sufficient backing in gold or other rapidly realizable assets. The verses in his collection are made of sounding brass with tinkling rhymes, as for example at the opening of 'Pan in Town', where he notes that because 'The country banks are breaking' and 'The London banks are shaking', 'Experience seems to settle, / That paper is not metal, / And promises of payment / Are neither food nor

---

[1] Thomas Love Peacock, *Paper Money Lyrics and Other Poems* (London: C. and W. Reynell, 1837), in *The Works of Thomas Love Peacock*, vol. 7, ed. H. F. B. Brett-Smith and C. E. Jones (London: Constable, 1931), 99–100. See Nicolas Shrimpton, 'Even These Metallic Problems Have Their Melodramatic Side': Money and Victorian Literature', in *Victorian Literature and Finance*, ed. Francis O'Gorman (Oxford: Oxford University Press, 2007), 17–38.

raiment'.[2] The same events inspired Thomas Moore in 1826 to compose a number of money poems, including 'Amatory Colloquy between Bank and Government', 'Dialogue between a Sovereign and a One Pound Note', and 'Memorabilia of the Last Week (March 1826)', poems versifying upon what does or does not back the currency, and which were published in *Odes on Cash, Corn, and Catholics* (1828).[3] Their concern with how money retains value, and trust is maintained, would haunt monetary policy as far as and beyond Churchill's return to the gold standard a century after these lyrics were composed.

The idea that money should be backed by gold or other precious metals encounters in poems written during the nineteenth century, such as those by Thomas Hood and Robert Browning given below, a criticism not unlike that motivating George Eliot's *Silas Marner* of miserliness and the unnatural love of precious metals. The poets in this chapter find themselves caught between a fear of unsupported currency and criticism of fetishistic hoarding. During Britain's greatest global wealth, poets got and spent their talents on isolating the complexities attendant upon riches and shortage. This chapter follows the boom-and-bust theme emblematically represented by South Sea Bubble into the nineteenth century, and starts further thoughts about unbacked speculations and the fetishizing of gold as means for securing paper currency and enabling international trade.

Around the turn of the nineteenth century there were nearly eight hundred privately owned banks issuing their own paper notes. Scores of them failed at the slightest hint of a panic and run. Between 1815 and 1830 more than two hundred private banks failed. There were epidemics of bank failures in 1825, 1837 – the years of *Paper Money Lyrics* – and in 1839 and 1842. The two interventions that helped begin the process of stabilizing the system of banking and currency were the founding in 1833 of the first joint-stock deposit banks, institutions which could redeem cheques but not issue currency, and Sir Robert Peel's Bank Charter Act of 1844, whereby no new bank could have the right to issue notes, and any bank which stopped making payments ('closed its doors') or amalgamated with a joint-stock deposit bank would lose its right to issue notes. By the same act, the Bank of England was restricted to issuing fourteen million pounds worth of fiduciary notes – that is, notes whose value depended upon (among other things) the user having faith in the value printed on

---

[2] Ibid. 101.

[3] A. D. Godley (ed.), *The Poetical Works of Thomas Moore* (London: Oxford University Press, 1910), 567–73; and for a critical exploration of the theme, see Alexander Dick, *Romanticism and the Gold Standard: Money, Literature, and Economic Debate in Britain 1790–1830* (Basingstoke and New York: Palgrave Macmillan, 2013), 145–9.

them.[4] Summing up these developments, Mary Poovey suggested that like 'economic and imaginative writing again, monetary genres could also be used to manage' what she calls the 'problematic of representation' which 'became visible – especially in periods in which the nation's money supply was imperiled or speculative manias gripped the nation'. This management is exemplified when the 1844 Bank Act 'fixed the relation between gold and the Bank of England's paper or when, in 1866, businesses' refusal to accept checks was interpreted as a sign that the Bank's paper was sound.'[5] Back in 1741 David Hume, no supporter of paper money, had asserted that 'Money' has 'chiefly a fictitious value', but the implications of such an insight are still working their way through the understanding of human institutions.[6]

Having faith in paper money: if public confidence is sustained, the currency retains its value whether backed or not because the promise is not tested; if the paper money is backed by gold or silver, the public can feel assured, but assured, be it noted, only upon an assumption that such rare metals are sufficiently hoarded and have themselves a stabilized value on commodity markets, a fetish or rarity value, derived, then, from the power to get hold of a particular, mutually admired, shiny, or at least shine-able, object. There is another source of metaphor and analogy here, one that appears if we ask, what might there be behind the currency of poetry, its language, to support it in retaining *its* value? For poetry such questions might, for instance, involve a poet's belief, or shaken belief, in the correspondence of words either with identifiable and understood material objects, or in authorized meanings, or precise definitions. What supports such beliefs is more nebulous: is it a shared practice, or common sense, a currency itself susceptible to shocks, or is it poets' confidence in their techniques, in poetic skill, a value that proves subject to, and in part dependent on, the confidence, competence, and beliefs of others? Or is it dependent upon faith in a God? This possibility will give value, for believers, to the material world and thus to the words which call it up, or, following the Gospel of St John, call it into being, as it gives a value to activities such as speculating on a machine for carving religious furniture, or writing poetry. Alfred Tennyson was familiar with both.

[4] See John Vernon, *Money and Fiction: Literary Realism in the Nineteenth and Early Twentieth Centuries* (Ithaca and London: Cornell University Press, 1984), 32.

[5] Mary Poovey, *Genres of the Credit Economy: Mediating Value in Eighteenth-Century and Nineteenth-Century Britain* (Chicago: Chicago University Press, 2008), 7.

[6] David Hume, 'Of Interest', in *Essays: Moral, Political, and Literary*, ed. Eugene F. Miller (Indianapolis: Liberty Classics, 1985), 297.

2. Speculations and hollows

The future poet laureate of Victoria's reign had received a bequest from his grandfather of two thousand five hundred pounds. He was given five hundred pounds by Arthur Hallam's aunt. In 1840 the poet met Dr Matthew Allen, who planned to develop a machine for carving wooden furniture. He was also the author of devotional literature. Tennyson invested his money in the scheme. In 1841 Dr Allen was duped by an agent and needed more capital to keep afloat. By 1843 the scheme had collapsed, and all Tennyson's money gone with it. Much of the investment was recovered in January 1845 because the poet's friend and brother-in-law Edward Lushington had insured Allen's life in Tennyson's favour. These events lie behind the poem 'Sea Dreams', written in December 1857, revised the following year, and published in January 1860.

Christopher Ricks is not impressed: 'An unconvincing poem, too timid for an exorcism.'[7] He thus exemplifies critical responses lending their support, or withdrawing it, from attributions of value. 'Sea Dreams' relates the language of faith and trust to the expression of feeling, where the unreliability of the former plays upon the instability of the latter. This is because the unreliability of the swindler's speech (his giving his word) has the same source as the volatility of expressed feeling: the words in both cases unbacked by a reliable and trustworthy word, a word secured in material wealth, or, for that matter, in stable human character or behaviour. The two are embroiled in lines where the 'city clerk, but gently born and bred'[8] reports a meeting in the street with the religious swindler who has tricked him out of his savings:

> 'My dearest friend,
> Have faith, have faith! We live by faith,' said he;
> 'And all things work together for the good
> Of those' – it makes me sick to quote him –[9]

The weakness of the poem doesn't lie here, though, but in the plot twists which allow the clerk's wife to extract forgiveness for the swindler from her husband: that is likely the timidity Ricks identifies, compounded by the 'baby song'[10] that the mother sings by the cradle of their child. The fascination of the poem is not there, but in the embroiling of two kinds of hollowness: the negative feeling of the clerk ('it makes me sick to quote

---

[7] Christopher Ricks, *Tennyson* (London: Macmillan, 1972), 182.
[8] Christopher Ricks (ed.), *The Poems of Tennyson*, 3 vols. (London: Longmans, 1987), vol. 2, 588.
[9] Ibid. 593.
[10] Ibid. 597–8.

him'), and the empty words of trust and faith, themselves characteristically conflating economic and religious claims.

T. S. Eliot, in his essay on *In Memoriam*, notes that the poet 'had nothing to which to hold fast except his unique and unerring feeling for the sounds of words', and that 'Tennyson's surface, his technical accomplishment, is intimate with his depths.'[11] The poet is reported to have said that 'scissors' was the only word of whose metrical form he was uncertain; but English monosyllables are dependent on contextual placing for their exact metrical and rhythmical roles. The poet's ability to compose depended thus on his skill in the face of such variable auditory values. Eliot's explanatory image points to the poet's one collateral. In 'Sea Dreams' there is a similar picture, evoking the state of the city clerk's investment:

> Their slender household fortunes (for the man
> Had risked his little) like the little thrift,
> Trembled in perilous places o'er a deep:
> And oft, when sitting all alone, his face
> Would darken, as he cursed his credulousness,
> And that one unctuous mouth which lured him, rogue,
> To buy strange shares in some Peruvian mine.[12]

Tennyson's lines tremble 'in perilous places o'er a deep'. The depths with which his technique's surface is in touch are accessed through those dangerous orifices, the unctuous mouth and the Peruvian mine, bottomless pits which, rather than giving out value, suck thriftiness in. 'By looking innocently at the surface', as Eliot notes, 'we are most likely to come to the depths, to the abyss of sorrow.'[13] 'Innocently' is equally relevant, for the clerk reports that his instinct was to distrust the swindler, but then he

> Fought with what seemed my own uncharity;
> Sat at his table; drank his costly wines;
> Made more and more allowance for his talk;
> Went further, fool! And trusted him with all[14]

The clerk wanted to believe the best of the man, not least because it fosters a feeling of his own 'innocence', his not being uncharitable to others. However, by 'looking innocently at the surface' we come 'to the depths',

[11] T. S. Eliot, 'In Memoriam', in *Selected Essays*, 3rd edn. (London: Faber & Faber, 1951), 337.
[12] *The Poems of Tennyson*, vol. 2, 588–9.
[13] T. S. Eliot, 'In Memoriam', 337.
[14] *The Poems of Tennyson*, vol. 2, 590.

as the clerk does, and find ourselves 'innocent' not in doing no harm, but in being not worldly wise, in being, as the clerk berates himself, a 'fool!'

The 'abyss of sorrow' appears from a mine that is not there: 'All my poor scrapings from a dozen years / Of dust and deskwork: there is no such mine, / None; but a gulf of ruin, swallowing gold'.[15] Tennyson's line ends on the key point, which is that failures of trust in investment schemes suck in more secure wealth, the gold, redistributing it elsewhere. There is no mine, no real abyss, only a fictional 'gulf of ruin', which is then proved real enough. The gulf is created by the swindler's empty words, his 'unctuous mouth'. Recalling Eliot's remark, though, and the 'abyss of sorrow', or that Tennyson 'had nothing to which to hold fast except his unique and unerring feeling for the sounds of words', what the poet hears is not a word's security, but its instability, and he is compelled to build the secured values of his lines out of the very insecurities that he most fears. For what is it that brings meaning to the swindler's 'My dearest friend, / Have faith, have faith!' but a renewal of our trust in the poem's whole context as we read these known-to-be-empty words. It is not that we have confidence in the voicing of these words within the dramatized narrative 'Sea Dreams' presents, but we do have sufficient confidence in the work of art that offers them, or, more precisely, in the timbre and structure of the lines that can contain them, this containing in poetic lines then returning us to the complexities in that word 'contain' encountered in the previous chapter. A poem may figure the renewal and restoration of trust even when demonstrating its absence, by having a structure from those same unreliable words, and the volatile and evanescent responses they deceitfully engendered.

For a poet writing about investments and losses, the poem's words, as Ricks's judgment suggests, take on the character of the stocks and bonds: they gain and lose value depending on our trust in them and upon their being able to stand for something upon which we may justifiably rely. Ricks points out the presence of the Allen affair in the autobiographical hinterland to Tennyson's 'history of a morbid, poetic soul, under the blighting influence of a recklessly speculative age',[16] his *Maud: A Monodrama* (1855): 'the fraudulent Dr. Allen had also had his investments in coal; Tennyson's feelings about this squalid débâcle could likewise be channeled into his story of how "a vast speculation had failed"'.[17] Again 'the abyss of sorrow' evokes an appropriate image, for in the opening of *Maud* we find a 'dreadful hollow', and a 'ghastly pit' where the protagonist's father's body was found. Meanwhile, Maud's 'old grandfather' who made his wealth in mining 'has lately died':

---

15   Ibid. 590–1.
16   Hallam Tennyson, quoting his father, cited in *The Poems of Tennyson*, vol. 2, 517.
17   Ricks, *Tennyson*, 247.

> Gone to a blacker pit, for whom
> Grimy nakedness dragging his trucks
> And laying his trams in a poisoned gloom
> Wrought, till he crept from a gutted mine
> Master of half a servile shire,
> And left his coal all turned into gold[18]

The speaker is disgusted by the way their money has been made in the exploitation of 'Grimy nakedness', but doubly so by his heirs who have not worked for their position. In this same section, Tennyson has his speaker associate the assumed vulgarity of displayed wealth with the sounds of words, for which he had a 'unique and unerring feeling'. The grandson is hearing voices lowered in simpering awe at his new house:

> Seeing his gewgaw castle shine,
> New as his title, built last year,
> There amid perky larches and pine,
> And over the sullen-purple moor
> (Look at it) pricking a cockney ear.[19]

His ear is differently pricked by 'gewgaw', or by 'perky' of the larches: he imitates his speaker's offence by accurately defacing the melody of his own lines. A self-consciously apologetic version of such technical precision appears in 'Sea Dreams' when the clerk, criticizing a nonconformist hell-fire preacher, refers to his 'loud-lung'd Antibabylonianisms'. The poet admits '(Although I grant but little music there)'.[20]

The puzzle of *Maud* lies in the relationship between the speaker's admitted mental state and the varying degrees of justice in what he says. Tennyson called the poem 'a little *Hamlet*',[21] and while there is method in the speaker's being mad, this madness infects the method. Chains of associated words and phrases link the separate sections; they dramatize the instability of the speaker's outlook, and associate the qualities he most admires in Maud with those he despises in her brother. So, of the brother, he reports:

> six feet two, as I think, he stands;
> But his essences turned the live air sick,
> And barbarous opulence jewel-thick
> Sunned itself on his breast and his hands.

[18] *The Poems of Tennyson*, vol. 2, 539–40.
[19] Ibid. 540.
[20] Ibid. 596.
[21] For this and citations in the paragraph, ibid. 517, 546, 549 (twice), 551, and 554 (twice).

Yet in the next section 'Maud's own little oak-room' is introduced, and she is described in it as 'like a precious stone / Set in the heart of the carven gloom'. The brother has left his estate, and the speaker imagines that in pursuit of 'fulsome Pleasure', he will 'drown / His heart in the gross mud-honey of town'; while, later, Maud's influence is dramatized by calling up a cedar, sighing perhaps for Lebanon, which has been 'fed / With honeyed rain and delicate air', and she has 'made my life a perfumed altar-flame'. Are these images of value 'barbarous opulence' or 'a precious stone'? Is it 'essences' that turn the 'live air sick' or 'a perfumed altar-flame'? Is it 'mud-honey' or 'honeyed rain'? The evaluative language of desire and disgust share points of focus and have vocabulary in common. They evoke a disturbed instability in the capacity to exemplify consistencies of value, and a mirroring inconsistency in the consciousness of the monodrama's speaker.

This speaker, we were told, has been rendered frantic by the death of his father, by the 'vast speculation that failed';[22] but the most prevalent symptom of his disturbance is this speculative tendency, as if nothing were good or bad but thinking made it so. The 'monodrama' allows its speaker's uncertainty about Maud and his relations with her, such as they are, to thrive because no word comes from her to reassure him or us:

> What, if she be fastened to this fool lord,
> Dare I bid her abide by her word?
> Should I love her so well if she
> Had given her word to a thing so low?
> Shall I love her as well if she
> Can break her word were it even for me?
> I trust that it is not so.[23]

But to speculate and trust is all the poem's speaker can do in these constraining circumstances. The paradox of Tennyson's language in *Maud* is that the multiplication of usages introducing instability into the character of responses to words such as 'jewel', 'honey', and 'gold' also enriches its diction. We saw Keats commenting on the thought-to-be-necessary enriching of every line with raw gold: '*an artist* must serve Mammon – he must have "self-concentration" selfishness perhaps. You I am sure will forgive me for sincerely remarking that you might curb your magnanimity and be more of an artist, and "load every rift" of your subject with ore.'[24] Yet Tennyson's golden diction is not the product of mining and refining; rather it comes from a later recognition that while words can be compared to nuggets, they

22   Ibid. 519.
23   Ibid. 551–2.
24   Hyder Edward Rollins (ed.), *The Letters of John Keats 1814–1821,* 2 vols. (Cambridge: Harvard University Press, 1958), vol. 2, 322–3.

may also be like Baudelaire's idea of common phrases in his *Fusées* (c. 1851): 'Profondeur immense de pensée dans les locutions vulgaires, trous creusés par des générations de fournis.'[25] Words can be rich in value because they may be significantly hollow, and this uncertainty at the core of the poet's medium, as in the behaviour of money in an economy, may be deployed as a sign of what the poet himself called the 'blighting influence of a recklessly speculative age.'[26] His achievement was to make vitally telling poems out of his sense of being blighted.

3. Jingling rhymes

Thomas Hood made a precarious living out of humour, the composition of comic rhymes, laughable puns, and grimly sad conclusions, as here in his 'Epigram: On the Depreciation of Money':

> They may talk of the plugging and sweating
>   Of our coinage that's minted of gold,
> But to me it produces no fretting
>   Of its shortness of weight to be told:
> All the sov'reigns I'm able to levy
>   As to lightness can never be wrong,
> But must surely be some of the heavy,
>   *For I never can carry them long.*[27]

Hood makes skilful play on two ways in which currencies can decline in value: by having precious metal values reduced, as noted in Graves's poem on the decimalization, or being caught in inflationary spirals. The relation of Hood's witty words to money was direct. He wrote and published annual miscellanies of what he called 'rich fun',[28] for his personal finances had collapsed at the end of 1834, partly due to the failure of an engraving firm; his situation was aggravated by a complete break with his wife's family over her near death from illness during pregnancy.

In February 1835 he wrote a pathetic letter to his friend C. W. Dilke outlining his situation: he owed between £200 and £300 without any

---

[25] Charles Baudelaire, *Oeuvres complètes*, 2 vols., ed. Claude Pichois (Paris: Gallimard, 1975), vol. 1, 650 ('Immense depth of thought in common phrases, holes hollowed out by generations of ants').

[26] Cited in Ricks, *Tennyson*, 148.

[27] Thomas Hood, *The Complete Poetical Works*, ed. Walter Jerrold (London: Oxford University Press, 1911), 395.

[28] Cited from the *London and Westminster Review* in John Clubbe, *Victorian Forerunner: The Later Career of Thomas Hood* (Durham: Duke University Press, 1968), 55.

immediate hopes of repayment. To avoid being imprisoned for debt, he left England with his family, hoping to live more cheaply while writing furiously to recover the lost financial security. He spent the next five years in Europe, first near Coblenz and then Ostend. In 1840, at the age of forty-one, he returned to England and began to write 'Miss Kilmansegg and her Precious Leg'. It first appeared in the *New Monthly Magazine* between September 1840 and February 1841. Hood's health, which was never good, had deteriorated in Germany; while writing the poem he was 'often ill, always poor'.[29] John Clubbe cites a 'doctor associate of the author', who concludes that Hood must have been 'in constant pain for at least the last seven or eight years of his life' and calls him 'a man of unusual determination and fortitude'.[30] Hood died, after a lingering illness, on 3 May 1845.

He was as good as addicted to rhyming. Two comments about his situation indicate this felicitous facility: 'no gentleman alive has written so much Comic and spitten so much blood within six consecutive years',[31] he said, 'obliged to set to work again, willy-nilly, well or illy'.[32] Both these rhymes, lamenting the need to work by illustrating it with forced rhymes, chime because the words have been deformed to fit: they express the effort required in the work of making joking wordplay, indicating the artifice of laughter (if Hood hadn't made it seem funny it wouldn't be and isn't really); they hint at damage done to the writer, for both the deformed words, 'spitten' and 'illy' refer to states of his own body; and they put a brave face on his predicament.

Such rhyming can produce ambivalent and downright negative responses in a reader. Of John Crowe Ransom's distych 'Sing a song for Percy Shelley / Drowned in pale lemon jelly', Geoffrey Hill observed:

> The particular acidity of his 'playfulness' on the subject of Romantic suffering is characterized in the poem 'Survey of Literature' by his rhyming the name Shelley with the phrase 'pale lemon jelly', but he does not come off from the confrontation with much credit. Shelley is Shelley and Ransom is silly.[33]

The relation of 'acidity' to 'playfulness' is apt to Hood's poetry and physical state, though 'acidity' might not be quite the word. Writing of

---

[29]   Ibid. 105.

[30]   Ibid. 231.

[31]   Cited from the *Athenaeum* (17 Oct 1840, 829), ibid. 34.

[32]   Peter F. Morgan (ed.), *The Letters of Thomas Hood* (Edinburgh: Oliver and Boyd, 1973), 284.

[33]   Geoffrey Hill, 'What Devil Has Got into John Ransom?', in *Collected Critical Writings*. ed. Kenneth Haynes (Oxford: Oxford University Press: 2008), 129.

that punningly named (kill-man's-egg) and rhymed title ('Miss Kilmansegg and her Precious Leg'), Arthur Symons praised the 'sting of its rhymes and the crackle of its puns' as 'perhaps the most accurate in the language.'[34] Ransom doesn't come off with credit because his joke-rhyme is a literary critical attitude making light of an actual death in a real Ligurian storm, an attitude shown to be trivially unserious by its mode of expression. Hood appears in a better light because he identifies himself with the technical effect he produces – his fate as a family man and a writer dependent upon his jokes coming off. Hood may be 'illy', but 'silly' he isn't.

William Empson, at the end of a short piece on rhyme in *Argufying*, lamely but accurately notes: 'All I can think of after this very rough attempt at surveying the conditions of a taste for rhyme is that people sometimes like it because it is easy and sometimes because it is difficult'.[35] It is likeable too when an impossibly difficult rhyming challenge is made to look easy, as in Byron's *sprezzatura* performance of wedding 'intellectual' to 'hen-peck'd you all'.[36] The apparent lack of strain creates the release of tension. It can please when the impossibly difficult is made no more than clumsily, or self-mockingly, manageable, as in Hardy's elegy for his first wife, 'The Voice', where he rhymes 'listlessness' with 'wistlessness' or, in a variant text, 'existlessness' – both serving as desperate remedies for a complex aftermath of loss.[37]

Byron's rhyming in *Don Juan* includes within its ambit of implication the humorous potential in being thought a notoriously philandering poet, mocking reader expectations, while Hardy's ghastly rhyme describes the wind taunting the poet's desire to believe he is being led on by a supernatural presence. His stanza is pinching itself. With rhyming, then, when we like it because it seems easy we are enjoying the writer's ability to appear to make light of constraints and conditions, while when it appears difficult we enjoy the sense of being subject to the world's conditions and making the best we can of them. These feelings are in alignment with the state of having or not having wealth: can you buy yourself liberty, are you seemingly free of the world's constraints by being able to have whatever you want (a golden leg, for example), or are you trapped by your

34 Arthur Symons, *The Romantic Movement in English Poetry* (New York: E. P. Dutton, 1909), 332.
35 William Empson, *Argufying: Essays on Literature and Culture,* ed. John Haffenden (London: Chatto & Windus, 1987), 136. See also Simon Jarvis, 'Why Rhyme Pleases', in *Lyric Theory Reader: A Critical Anthology,* ed. Virginia Jackson and Yopie Prins (Baltimore: Johns Hopkins University Press, 2014), 434–48.
36 Byron, *Don Juan* I, stanza 22, in Jerome McGann (ed.), *The Complete Poetical Works,* vol. 5 (Oxford: Oxford University Press, 1986), 15.
37 Samuel Hynes (ed.), *The Complete Poetical Works of Thomas Hardy,* 5 vols. (Oxford: Oxford University Press, 1982–95), vol. 2, 56.

circumstances into endless drudgery, like the woman in Hood's 'The Song of the Shirt'?

Empson makes another useful remark when he notes that 'a language which rhymes absurdly easily tends to make rhyme seem vulgar'.[38] He may be thinking of Japanese, a sound-poor language with innumerable homophones, or inflected languages where poets can rhyme on word-endings. In English the near complete lack of such inflected endings has meant that poets rhyme on the concept as well as the sound. There are constraints too: whether being compelled to match 'breath' with 'death' or being left without a dignified and un-clichéd rhyme for 'love'. Desperate straits can inspire desperate remedies, whether in financial affairs or rhyming. Empson's remark is particularly relevant to 'Miss Kilmansegg and her Precious Leg' because the facility of the rhyme can point up the vulgar display of nouveau riche prosperity, as at the young lady's christening:

> Gold! and gold! and besides the gold,
> The very robe of the infant told
> A tale of wealth in every fold;
>   It lapp'd her like a vapour!
> So fine! so thin! the mind at a loss
> Could compare it to nothing, except a cross
>   Of cobweb with bank-note paper.[39]

Hood's poem points up the analogy between aureate metals and literary language, as 'a regular piece of goldsmith's work, / Got the better of Goldsmith's diction'.[40] His is not only a punning satire on how the fetishistic desire for precious metals murders fecundity, for it evokes pathos at the heiress's absurd fate. She is as trapped in her circumstances as the seamstress in 'The Song of the Shirt' is in hers. This being trapped may be figured, for Hood and his work too, by rhyming.

Miss Kilmansegg makes a bad marriage to a rakish fortune hunter who kills her with the leg so as to steal it and use its money value to pay debts: 'If he found himself short in funds and stocks, / These rhymes will furnish the reason!'[41] Here is Miss Kilmansegg on the night of her death:

> Thus, even thus, the Countess slept,
> While Death still nearer and nearer crept,
>   Like the Thane who smote the sleeping –
> But her mind was busy with early joys,

---

[38] Empson, *Argufying*, 135.
[39] Thomas Hood, *Poetical Works*, 569.
[40] Ibid. 577.
[41] Ibid. 597.

> Her golden treasures and golden toys,
>> That flash'd a bright
>> And golden light
> Under lids still red with weeping.[42]

The salty 'sting' in her crying is a shock because it reminds readers that however much a fetish her leg is, she remains a person – though not for long. Her fate is inescapable: the rhymes tell us so. Hood identified himself, as noted, with the effects he produces. The account of Miss Kilmansegg's disastrous honeymoon describes with hyperbolic inappropriateness the advantages of being two in one, of doubling. Within two lines of writing 'double letters bring cash for the box', Hood adds: 'There's a double sweetness in double rhymes', while a dozen lines later, he sums up: 'And however our Dennises take offence, / A double meaning shows double sense'.[43] Hood defended his jingling rhymes and groaning puns; they were what attracted customers. Providing 'sweetness' and 'sense' in double measures, he provides twice as much poetic value for money. Upon fulfilling such promises of benefit depended his and his family's health and continuance. His rhymes simultaneously entrap his subjects in their fates and release both reader and imagined subject from them. They demonstrate the need both to recognize our own and others' predicaments and imaginatively to act with regard to them.

Such a mixture of the impossible and the possible attempts to wring the heart by ringing in the ear, as when 'The Song of the Shirt' reaches its close:

> Stitch! stitch! stitch!
> In poverty, hunger, and dirt,
> And still with a voice of dolorous pitch,
> Would that its tone could reach the Rich! –
> She sang this 'Song of the Shirt!'[44]

The penultimate line alerts readers to the poem's purpose as song, by doubting her song's power to 'reach the Rich', even as it articulates such a not entirely forlorn hope. A similar, more desperate entrapment and release is performed by the rhymes at the point where the woman in 'The Bridge of Sighs' commits suicide by drowning:

> Mad from life's history,
> Glad to death's mystery,

---

[42] Ibid. 599.
[43] Ibid. 592.
[44] Ibid. 626.

> Swift to be hurl'd –
> Any where, any where,
> Out of the world![45]

Baudelaire owed a debt to Hood and translated 'The Bridge of Sighs'. Prose poem XLVIII in *Le Spleen de Paris* is called 'Any Where Out of the World N'importe où hors du Monde'; it ends when the poet's soul echoes the cry of Hood's poem: 'N'importe où! n'importe où! pourvu que ce soit hors de ce monde!' The same cry reverberates more remotely at the close of Baudelaire's 'Le Voyage', a close addressed to death: 'Plonger au fond du gouffre, Enfer ou Ciel, qu'importe?'[46] Hood may have been in debt to the tune of between £200 and £300, but his grafting of popular song rhythms into English verse left other poets and many more readers indebted to his melodies. In 1837, he wrote 'Copyright and Copywrong' in support of a sixty-year protection bill, introduced into Parliament by Thomas Noon Talfourd, that failed. Clubbe points out that if 'copyright protection had given him a fair share of the income from the American sales of his books, his financial position would have been greatly relieved.'[47] But the debts of posterity are never and can never be repaid.

4. Fetishistic avarice

Robert Browning, like many poets before and after, associated success with gold. He wrote to Elizabeth Barrett on 11 February 1845 that a dozen pages of verse 'ought to bring me a fair proportion of the Reviewers' gold-currency'.[48] The comic gusto in Hood's writing, a vigour and speed of rhythm that forms an ill man's tribute to health and zest, may have had an influence on Browning's style. His 'Gold Hair: A Story of Pornic', written probably in 1862 and published two years later, shares a number of concerns with 'Miss Kilmansegg and her Precious Leg'. In both, the desire for gold is incompatible with, inimical to, taking part fully and humanly in life. The young lady of

[45] Ibid. 650.
[46] Baudelaire, *Oeuvres complètes*, vol. 1, 357 and 134 ('No matter where! No matter where! so long as its out of this world!' and 'Plunge into the abyss, Heaven or Hell, what matter?'). For 'Le Pont des Soupirs', see ibid. 269–71. For more on 'The Bridge of Sighs', Hood's economic predicaments, and relations between prostitution and writers' finances, see my 'On the Pavement', in *The Oxford Handbook of Victorian Poetry*, ed. Matthew Bevis (Oxford: Oxford University Press, 2013), 254–72.
[47] Clubbe, *Victorian Forerunner*, 58.
[48] *Letters of Robert Browning and Elizabeth Barrett Barrett 1845–1846*, 2 vols., ed. Elvan Kintner (Cambridge, MA: Harvard University Press, 1969), vol. 1, 18.

Hood's poem is murdered by her husband, and the poet's verdict of suicide, 'felo-de-se', suggests that it is her desire for conspicuous wealth, in the form of the golden leg with which she is struck, that causes her death. The central figure in Browning's poem differs from Miss Kilmansegg in two aspects. The girl from Pornic – it is a real story, gold having been found in the church of St Gilles in 1762 – is reported as too good for this world:

> Too white, for the flower of life is red;
>   Her flesh was the soft seraphic screen
> Of a soul that is meant (her parents said)
>   To just see earth, and hardly be seen,
> And blossom in heaven instead.[49]

The parenthesis in this stanza makes evident the difference between the poem's position and this idea of spiritual goodness. For Browning, moral qualities must be tested in experience, and he has numerous poems ('The Statue and the Bust' and 'Youth and Art', for example) which urge us to face life's spiritual challenges. The complicating factor here is that the girl does not seem to have a vice or a reason for vice, as Miss Kilmansegg – brought up in a family committed to the display of wealth – has. A second, related difference is that the girl does not want to show her gold. Rather, her desiring it coincides with a desire to hide it – as if it represented both vice and the wish to appear without sin. This combined fault then appears as the need to possess but not use properly, and coincides with another of Browning's regular concerns: the destructiveness of a compulsive desire to possess beyond reasonable limits.

There are two stanzas in which Browning describes the girl's hairdo as, though a first-time reader doesn't know this yet, a container for her gold:

> VIII
> The passion thus vented, dead lay she;
>   Her parents sobbed their worst on that;
> All friends joined in, nor observed degree:
>   For indeed the hair was to wonder at,
> As it spread – not flowing free,

> IX
> But curled around her brow, like a crown,
>   And coiled beside her cheeks, like a cap,
> And calmed about her neck – ay, down

[49] Robert Browning, *The Poems*, 2 vols., ed. John Pettigrew and Thomas J. Collins (Harmondsworth: Penguin Books, 1981), vol. 1, 759.

> To her breast, pressed flat, without a gap
> I' the gold, it reached her gown.[50]

The great drama of Browning's work revolves around the actions of reaching, stretching, grasping, holding, and letting go.[51] Here, this drama, also one of technique, is applied to grasping and releasing the gold – states of mind connected with miserliness and generosity. The girl's hair, a metaphor for the gold, is a wonder to behold; but it is made into a container for the stanza's rhymes. Every line of stanza 8 has end-stopped punctuation. It produces a stiffened motion, for 'indeed the hair was to wonder at, / As it spread – not flowing free'; and when he writes that the hair isn't so flowing, he doesn't enclose the stanza syntactically, but allows it to move stiffly, over into stanza 9: 'not flowing free', it pauses, then runs on 'But curled around her brow'. It is as if the movement of the verse is compensating for the action being staged, and it does this because evoking what's not admired. He would prefer it if the girl would let her hair down, for, as he writes earlier, 'Here, Life smiled, "Think what I meant to do!" / And Love sighed, "Fancy my loss!"'[52] But here, in stanzas 8 and 9, the rhymes act like pins, holding up the hair, and if you'd been allowed to touch it, it surely would have jingled. Though Browning doesn't rhyme comically on three or four syllables here, as he can and does, in, for example, 'Old Pictures in Florence', the triple rhyme enclosing the stanza and the use of only two rhyme-sounds does ring insistently, obsessively.

William Clyde De Vane, in *A Browning Handbook*, reports how George Eliot 'remarked to Browning one Sunday in 1864 when he called at the Priory that the motive of the girl's actions in hoarding the gold was not made sufficiently clear.'[53] Browning took away her copy of *Dramatis Personae*, which had appeared that year, and returned it later with the present stanzas 21 to 23 added. Thus the poet openly stated that the desire for gold is a substitute for religious feeling, sexual life, and relations with others. It removes her from experience: "'Talk not of God, my heart is stone! / Nor lover nor friend – be gold for both!'"[54] The inclusion of these three stanzas may not have improved the poem, or made 'sufficiently clear' the girl's motives. A better instinct might have been to leave the motivation mysterious but diseased, as it does still, yet now not so much clearly motivated as overtly moralized:

---

[50] Ibid. 760.
[51] See my 'Robert Browning's Grasp', from *In the Circumstances: About Poems and Poets* (Oxford: Oxford University Press, 1992), 198–238.
[52] Ibid. 759.
[53] William Clyde De Vane, *A Browning Handbook* (New York: Appleton-Century-Crofts, 1955), 286.
[54] Browning, *The Poems*, vol. 1, 763.

> Money, earth's trash and heaven's affront?
>   Had a spider found out the communion-cup,
> Was a toad in the christening-font?[55]

Barbara Melchiori interprets these lines as instances of the poet's aversion to Roman Catholicism, and quotes the description of the 'Scarlet Woman of Revelation',[56] interpreted by Protestants as the Church of Rome – 'having a golden cup in her hand full of abominations and filthiness of her fornication'.[57] The golden cup is the communion chalice and the abominations are the spider. Yet if so, what is Browning suggesting about the practical priest who uses the windfall of the girl's *louis d'or* for church restoration?

> But the priest bethought him: '"Milk that's spilt"
>   – You know the adage! Watch and pray!
> Saints tumble to earth with so slight a tilt!
>   It would build a new altar; that, we may!'
> And the altar therewith was built.[58]

Browning favours a balancing of impulses in life between the materialistic excesses of 'The Bishop Orders His Tomb at St Praxed's Church' and the false purity of the parents' view of their daughter in 'Gold Hair: A Story of Pornic', or between the false use of golden hair to substitute a fetish for experience, and a girl's mistreatment in 'Porphyria's Lover' where, not the rejection of being possessed, but an extreme of possessiveness occurs, again emblematized by what is done with her blonde hair:

> That moment she was mine, mine, fair,
>   Perfectly pure and good: I found
> A thing to do, and all her hair
>   In one long yellow string I wound
>   Three times her little throat around,
> And strangled her.[59]

Browning's theory of poetic truth is that we must come to the 'Perfectly pure and good' through experience of the humanly imperfect. In his symbol

---

[55] Browning, *The Poems*, vol. 1, 762.
[56] Barbara Melchiori, *Browning's Poetry of Reticence* (Edinburgh and London: Oliver & Boyd, 1968), 73.
[57] Revelation 17: 4.
[58] Browning, *The Poems*, vol. 1, 763. De Vane notes that the church at Pornic in which these events took place was destroyed in 1865, to make way for a new one, much to the poet's disgust.
[59] Ibid. 381.

of the gold ring at the opening of *The Ring and the Book*, he describes how the goldsmith mixes gold and alloy so as to make it workable, then uses acid to remove the alloy, leaving the pure yet humanly crafted gold. Palgrave published the first edition of *The Golden Treasury* in 1861, the year *Silas Marner*, George Eliot's novel of a miser transformed by love, also appeared.

Browning may have characterized money as 'earth's trash and heaven's affront' in 'Gold Hair: a Story of Pornic', but when in 1846 he was planning to elope with Elizabeth Barrett, he knew that, despite their shared superiority to monetary considerations, they could not live on air. They decided that Elizabeth must have her servant Wilson, who cost £16 per annum. Elizabeth had £8,000 in funds as well as ship and railway shares. Their yield of some £360 per annum would be handsome in Italy. Browning renounced any claim upon his future wife's money. The poet had a small allowance from his father and was concerned not to appear a fortune hunter. He wrote, hintingly, that though he will not touch her money, perhaps there would be a *'claimant* – who knows?' In the same 27 July 1846 letter, Browning admitted that 'I have only to be thankful that you are not dependent on my exertions.'[60] It would not be until at least 1855 and the publication of *Men and Women* that Robert Browning would begin to earn from those 'exertions' – his published verse.[61]

5. Ambivalence, resilience, and rhyme

Sitting in a café in a Venice piazza, the Spirit, or Mephistopheles as it had been in an earlier version, tempts the divided Dipsychus in Arthur Hugh Clough's poem of that name. It had been drafted in that same city in 1858, and celebrates being on easy street:

> As I sat at the café, I said to myself,
> They may talk as they please about what they call pelf,
> They may sneer as they like about eating and drinking,
> But help it I cannot, I cannot help thinking
> > How pleasant it is to have money, heigh ho!
> > How pleasant it is to have money.[62]

---

[60]   *Letters of Robert Browning and Elizabeth Barrett Barrett 1845–1846*, vol. 2, 906. For a fuller account, see Daniel Karlin, *The Courtship of Robert Browning and Elizabeth Barrett* (Oxford: Oxford University Press, 1985), 117–25.

[61]   For economic reflections on some of her publishing, see Alison Chapman, '"Vulgar needs": Elizabeth Barrett Browning, Profit, and Literary Value', in Francis O'Gorman, *Victorian Literature and Finance* (Oxford: Oxford University Press, 2007), 73–90.

[62]   F. L. Mulhauser (ed.), *The Poems of Arthur Hugh Clough*, 2nd edn. (Oxford: Oxford University Press, 1974), 241.

Clough was not comfortably off; he could not afford to be a poet by profession, as Browning was able to be, but spent his working life as a Fellow and Tutor of Oriel College, Oxford (1842–8), as Principal of University Hall, London (1849–51), and from 1853–61 as Examiner in the old Education Office. In October 1839, while still a Balliol graduate, Clough wrote that 'I am afraid … there is great likelihood of father's business breaking down before long.'[63] His father was a cotton importer whose trade with the Southern States of America through Charlestown to Liverpool fed the Lancashire cotton mills. The company failed in August 1841, and Clough immediately began to work as a freelance teacher to help the family finances. Clough's tutor, W. G. Ward, reported of the poet at Balliol: 'he told me that his pecuniary circumstances incapacitated him from giving wine parties' and that because he could not reciprocate, he did not like to accept invitations 'to wine with others.'[64]

'Spectator ab Extra', a longer variant version of 'How pleasant it is to have money', was published separately in 1862 and 1863. The second part, 'Le Diner', includes:

> Your chablis is acid, away with the hock,
> Give me the pure juice of a purple médoc:
> St Péray is exquisite; but, if you please,
> Some burgundy just before tasting the cheese.
>> So pleasant it is to have money, heigh-ho!
>> So pleasant it is to have money.
>
> As for that, pass the bottle, and d—n the expense,
> I've seen it observed by a writer of sense,
> That the labouring classes could scarce live a day,
> If people like us didn't eat, drink, and pay.
>> So useful it is to have money, heigh-ho!
>> So useful it is to have money.[65]

The Spirit is evidently a mammonist, while Dipsychus is one attempting to live temperately; but the spirit too, in its exploitation of exploded cant, satirizes worldly complacency, and the poet does not wholly identify his voice with either of the two speakers, using both rather to ventriloquize conflicting facets of a conscience in crisis. It is the method, writ large, of his best-known poem 'The Last Decalogue', where, in a parody of The Lord's

---

[63] F. L. Mulhauser (ed.), *The Correspondence of Arthur Hugh Clough*, 2 vols. (Oxford: Oxford University Press, 1957), vol. 1, 95.

[64] Blanche Smith Clough, 'Memoir', *The Poems and Prose Remains of Arthur Hugh Clough* (London: Macmillan, 1869), 18–19.

[65] *The Poems of Arthur Hugh Clough*, 699.

Prayer, he can both accommodate himself to, and distance himself from, the world's mutations of Christian teachings. Three of the couplets from this poem involve money: 'No graven images may be / Worshipped, except the currency' and 'Though shalt not steal; an empty feat, / When it's so lucrative to cheat' and 'Thou shalt not covet; but tradition / Approves all forms of competition.'[66]

The variations played on the Ten Commandments in this poem are clever enough to attract our interest, to tempt us by its smooth tongue. In 'How pleasant it is to have money', conspicuous consumption and the buoyant gusto of the poem's rhythms invite a complicit enjoyment. Yet, at the same time, the very length of the poem is designed, I would speculate, to give us a form of moral indigestion, as if to say 'this is just too much'. The repeated refrain and the jingling rhymes manifest an ambivalent character: they mimic a seductive confidence, but in their ringing hollow they show it to be ill-founded, and, finally, a little nauseous: 'Thus I sat at my table *en grand seigneur*, / And when I had done threw a crust to the poor'. If you even make an attempt to pronounce the French *'seigneur'* appropriately, here, the word will off-rhyme pointedly with 'poor'. It is as if while the lines, to our ears, rhyme neither felicitously nor with a facile click, their speaker thinks they do.

Remembering Empson's observation, probably derived from conversations about why Japanese poetry hardly ever rhymes, that 'a language which rhymes absurdly easily tends to make rhyme seem vulgar', Clough is able to insinuate vulgarity of attitude in the assumed social altitude of the poem's *parvenu* speaker. It is as if the poet, who knew what it was to want money, could rightly dismiss the slick financial triumphalism of this poem's voice, yet could not entirely escape from being attracted to careless ease. *Dipsychus* is a poem about being caught on the contrary barbs of the desire to live a good life and the desire to have a good standard of living.

In John Davidson's 'Thirty Bob a Week' every stanza 'wrings the heart', which is how the poet would describe Hood's 'The Song of the Shirt', a work he called 'the most important English poem of the nineteenth century', and Davidson explained:

> Only a high heart and strong brain broken on the wheel of life, but master of its own pain and anguish, able to jest in the jaws of death, could have sung this song, of which every single stanza wrings the heart. Poetry passed by on the other side. It could not endure the woman in unwomanly rags.[67]

---

[66] Ibid. 205.

[67] John Davidson, 'Pre-Shakespeareanism', in *The Man Forbid and Other Essays*, introduction by Edward J. O'Brien (Boston: Ball Publishing Company, 1910), 36. It was first published in *The Speaker*, no. 19 (28 January 1899), 107–8.

If Hood's rhyming combines being 'broken' and 'master of its own pain and anguish', his chimes entrap his subjects in their fates and release both reader and subject from them. 'Thirty Bob a Week' similarly dramatizes a combination of resilient yet deferential tones that attempt a balancing act not dissimilar to those performed by Chaucer and Jonson in their supplicant poems, though now an assumption of human equality has exacerbated the resentments to be managed in the structuring of power:

> But I don't allow it's luck and all a toss;
>   There's no such thing as being starred and crossed;
> It's just the power of some to be a boss,
>   And the bally power of others to be bossed:
> I face the music, sir; you bet I ain't a cur;
>   Strike me lucky if you don't believe I'm lost![68]

In his essay 'On Poetry', Davidson writes decidedly against rhyme. He believes that blank verse forms the height of poetic achievement, and that rhyme is a sign of decadence. Nevertheless, taking Shakespeare's Sonnet 73, he cites the four lines ending 'Bare ruin'd choirs, where late the sweet birds sang' and notes: 'The rhymes of this quatrain toll like a death bell' in which 'there is a feeling of effort, as of a thing achieved and it is the rhyme that achieves', admitting that it is 'beautiful, it is poignant'.[69]

The effort, and the tolling of a dead bell, can also be heard in the 'Thirty Bob a Week' stanza's music. It too sings a song of constriction, figuring the effort required to repeat it, assimilating and reliving the effort to continue that it shapes from the clerk's predicament. The second stanza, cited above, not only has the three entrapping rhymes culminating with 'lost!' but also rhymes on the same sound without its terminal consonant in 'boss' and 'toss'. There is, as it says, no question of luck in finding the rhymes here: the stanza is a model of the power that traps some and frees others. Its penultimate line, with the internal rhyme on 'sir' and 'cur', accelerates the financial constriction, yet also promises, in the new end rhyme, a development – but one crushed by the final line's discovery of a third, enclosing rhyme-word. Hood identified his fate with his poetic effects coming off; so too the clerk in Davidson's poem will 'face the music', and behind his speaker, also standing by his rhythm and rhyme, is the poet himself. This is the music of economic necessity, and someone else is calling the tune, compelling both speaker and poet to face it.

Yet both speaker and poet gain stature in the reader's eyes by recognizing this predicament and still pressing their case within the musical form of

---

[68] Andrew Turnbull (ed.), *The Poems of John Davidson*, 2 vols. (Edinburgh and London: Scottish Academic Press, 1973), vol. 1, 63.

[69] John Davidson, 'On Poetry' (1906), *The Poems of John Davidson*, vol. 2, 531–2.

this oppression. This manifests the need to maintain independence even when you are near the bread line. The predicament sounds within the poem's diction, a colloquial speech defended in the poem itself, though with an aside that might be thought out of character and situation: 'I ain't blaspheming, Mr. Silver-tongue; / I'm saying things a bit beyond your art'. Davidson takes a swipe at W. B. Yeats here, with whom he had quarrelled,[70] in the last lines of stanza 6 – which finesses its criticism by alluding to the literary man's occult enthusiasms and the first sonnet in Sir Philip Sidney's *Astrophil and Stella*: 'With your science and your books and your the'ries about spooks, / Did you ever hear of looking in your heart?' This momentary identification of the clerk's and the poet's situations is inseparably part of the poem's subject, embedded thematically in its technique.

Davidson's next verse opens with a reaffirmation of the speaker's pride in independence. He isn't begging for a handout here: 'I didn't mean your pocket, Mr., no'.[71] Davidson's dislike of rhyme, and his masterful use of it in 'Thirty Bob a Week' to dramatize enduring necessity, shows in the penultimate stanza, where the clerk knows he was not consigned by nature or God to live that life; rather, his society conveniently underlines that the place he knows is destined and defined. His only hope is to accept outwardly and inwardly resist. He must generate his own dignity and yet still show subservience: 'the difficultest job a man can do, / Is to come it brave and meek with thirty bob a week, / And feel that that's the proper thing for you.'[72]

Richard Le Gallienne recalled that Davidson 'found, as many another poet has done, that fame was more cry than wool, and that earning his livelihood continued as difficult as ever', noting a superficial paradox in his both registering and yet resisting 'reality':

> In this he was really no worse off than several of his famous contemporaries, but he had no bend in him, would not, or could not, stoop to journalism. A poet who insisted on reality in his work, he was incapable of adapting himself to those materialistic conditions with which the most inspired poet must compromise if he is to continue to exist.[73]

In 1894, seven days before he published his best known poem 'Thirty Bob a Week', Davidson complained to the publisher John Lane that his 'average

[70] See John Sloan, *John Davidson, First of the Moderns: A Literary Biography* (Oxford: Oxford University Press, 1995), 59–63.

[71] *The Poems of John Davidson*, vol. 1, 64.

[72] Ibid. 65.

[73] Richard Le Gallienne, *The Romantic '90s* (London and New York: G. P. Putnam's Sons, 1926), 147–8.

income from all sources for the last month or two had been at the rate of 35/– a week'.[74] He received a Civil List pension of £100 per annum in 1906, but in March 1909, seemingly because on top of his economic difficulties he found himself to be suffering from cancer, committed suicide by drowning in the sea off Penzance. T. S. Eliot, a one-time clerk in financial difficulties, wrote of Davidson's poem:

> I am sure that I found inspiration in the content of the poem, and in the complete fitness of content and idiom: for I also had a good many dingy urban images to reveal. Davidson had a great theme, and also found an idiom which elicited the greatness of the theme, which endowed this thirty-bob-a-week clerk with a dignity that would not have appeared if a more conventional poetic diction had been employed. The personage that Davidson created in this poem has haunted me all my life, and the poem is to me a great poem for ever.[75]

The debts of posterity are never – and never can be – repaid, as I noted of Hood's career, and certainly not in cash. Davidson's candour, his speaking out against 'Mr. Silver-Tongue', would ring the changes for developments in twentieth-century poetry.

The legacies of the British nineteenth century, for both better and worse, not only dominated and overshadowed the twentieth in this country, but have not yet been entirely outgrown. Clough's sitting in his Venice piazza might bring to mind not only Ezra Pound, but also the John Ruskin who, in the opening pages of *The Stones of Venice*, asks the tourist to 'behold in the brightness of their accumulated marble, pages on which the sentence of her luxury was to be written until the waves should efface it, as they fulfilled – "God has numbered they kingdom, and finished it"'. Ruskin draws the lesson for mercantile England, Tyre's and Venice's successor, as he argues, in the work's opening paragraph when he prophecies that the country 'which inherits their greatness, if it forget their example, may be led through prouder eminence to less pitied destruction.'[76]

Such risks of ruination were dramatized by the poems above either as great gulfs of emptiness where, as Colin Nicholson noted, the imaginative turns out to be imaginary, or where obsession with precious metals turns

[74] Cited from Sloan, *John Davidson, First of the Moderns*, 112.
[75] T. S. Eliot, Preface to *John Davidson: A Selection of his Poems*, ed. Maurice Linday (London: Hutchinson, 1961), also cited in R. K. R. Thornton (ed.), *Poetry of the 'Nineties* (Harmondsworth: Penguin Books, 1970), 78.
[76] John Ruskin, *The Stones of Venice*, vol. 1 in *The Library Edition of the Works*, 39 vols., ed. E. T. Cook and Alexander Wedderburn (London: George Allen, 1903–12), vol. 9, 59 and 17.

out to be a life-denying fetishism. The relation between these two failures lies in the nineteenth-century rules of international exchange, whereby currencies had stable equivalents depending on the amounts of bullion that national treasuries held. But in the century following the death of Victoria, currencies would cease to be so backed, as Nicky Marsh notes: 'the creation of a nationally standardized paper money, like the ending of the Gold Standard that it is inevitably associated with, was protracted and uneven and had different implications for writing in different moments and locations.'[77] Poetry too would slowly come off, and, with one vastly significant exception, stay off the gold standard. That exception, in the poetry and poetics of Ezra Pound, must now be confronted.

[77] Nicky Marsh, 'The Cosmopolitan Coin: What Modernists Make of Money', *Modernism / Modernity*, vol. 24, no. 3 (September 2017), 490.

CHAPTER SEVEN

Going off the gold standard

1. *A person of some interest*

Ezra Pound's 'Portrait d'une Femme', first published in *Ripostes* (1912), is from his London-based phase, written some eight years before encountering C. H. Douglas's *Economic Democracy* (1919), with its theory of Social Credit.[1] The poem is inflected with values and judgments that call upon a monetized vocabulary to colour its pointedly judging portrayal of what may be an art-loving society hostess:

> Your mind and you are our Sargasso Sea,
> London has swept about you this score years
> And bright ships left you this or that in fee:
> Ideas, old gossip, oddments of all things,
> Strange spars of knowledge and dimmed wares of price.

As Johnson's elegy for Robert Levet implies, descriptions of others are – by back-projection along the line of sight – simultaneously portraits of the describer. While Pound may have thought he was creating a Henry James-like social satire on a wealthy hostess, its satirical thrust implies that the speaker is *not* an instance of what is portrayed. Pound's Hell being 'a Hell for the *other people*, the people we read about in newspapers, not for oneself and one's friends', as T. S. Eliot noted,[2] his rendering that otherness in the poem's voicing leaves it vulnerable to the thought that this is a haplessly un-self-aware self-portrait. An unsympathetic commentator might take the following as an account of *The Cantos*' method: 'Ideas,

---

[1] For the role of economics and commodity in the 1912–14 moment, see Lawrence Rainey, 'The Creation of the Avant-Garde', in *Institutions of Modernism: Literary Elites and Public Culture* (New Haven: Yale University Press, 1998), 10–41.

[2] T. S. Eliot, *After Strange Gods* (London: Faber & Faber, 1934), 43.

old gossip, oddments of all things, / Strange spars of knowledge'. Many accounts of the late Cantos have come, in effect, to this conclusion.[3]

Pound's unfolding of financial vocabulary hints at more than artistic patronage, and indicates a reason other than the repetition of r-sounds in its opening line for why this poem may have been rejected by *The North American Review* after its submission in January 1912:[4]

> Oh, you are patient, I have seen you sit
> Hours, where something might have floated up.
> And now you pay one. Yes, you richly pay.
> You are a person of some interest, one comes to you
> And takes strange gain away

Is she purchasing the interest of a lover? It remains obscure what is being paid for. The lady may be a faded and second-rate benefactress, a financial supporter of the arts whose reward is contact with the creative, such as the poet-speaker. A sexual undercurrent is hard to miss, and the 'pay ... interest ... gain' sequence implies that social and sociable exchanges have been monetized, compromising both parties, while the speaker's 'placing' of the *femme* portrayed tacitly exculpates him from being touched by these 'rare ... riches' – and yet tainted by association with such bric-a-brac he is:

> Idols and ambergris and rare inlays,
> These are your riches, your great store; and yet
> For all this sea-hoard of deciduous things,
> Strange woods half sodden, and new brighter stuff:
> In the slow float of differing light and deep,
> No! there is nothing! In the whole and all,
> Nothing that's quite your own.
>   Yet this is you.[5]

The final four syllables may access a touch of sympathy with the character portrayed, but only because the patronized is now patronizing – and why does Pound employ the French title?[6] Perhaps it is to distance the portrait

---

[3] See, e.g., Richard Sieburth, 'In Pound We Trust: The Economy of Poetry/The Poetry of Economics', *Critical Inquiry*, vol., 14 no. 1 (Autumn 1987), 142–72. For a sympathetic but not uncritical account, see Peter Makin, *Pound's Cantos* (London: George Allen & Unwin, 1985), 101–21.

[4] Noted by the editor in Ezra Pound, *Early Writings: Poems and Prose*, ed. Ira B. Nadel (New York: Penguin Books, 2005), 351.

[5] Ibid. 45–6.

[6] For a discussion of non-translated titles in modernist poetry, see my '"I like the Spanish title": William Carlos Williams's *Al Que Quiere!*', in *Modernism and*

and place its failure overseas, in the world of *fin de siècle* decadence, which the poet-speaker also repudiates, even if still capable of that perhaps symptomatic 'dimmed wares of price' formula, a form of locution castigated by Pound as technically inept and *passé* soon afterwards.[7]

'Portrait d'une Femme' posits a relationship between the 'worth' of her second-hand knowledge (indicated by 'dimmed wares of price', 'pay', 'richly pay', 'some interest', 'strange gain', 'riches', 'great store') and the devalued diction, the poem's tarnished language. In a mimicking of *passé* literary talk, Pound implies an analogy between the language of poetry and money in which the former is contaminated by its metaphorical relation with the latter, tainted by the observation that the exchanges of the currency in an economy are subject to fluctuating value, depreciation, or inflation. Even if its satirical slant functions as a casting off of a persona, or implication that the only solution, first for the benefit of poetic language, and then with regard to the economy and society as a whole, is to disconnect poetic language from such 'drift' and 'floating down' in a stagnant sea of inertial mediocrity – so as to stabilize it on other, deeper, firmer grounds. Yet it was precisely the problem of guaranteeing value, and keeping it free from the risks of exchange, such as this one with a person taken to be of lesser value, that would effect a profoundly self-damaging contradiction in the poet's poetic politics, his political poetics.

2. Churchill's return to Midas

Part IV of *Hugh Selwyn Mauberley* (1920) does not contain the first use of the word 'usury' in Pound's poetry. As Richard Sieburth noted, in the early poem 'Octave' the poet employs the word metaphorically (as Donne had done in 'Love's Usury'), but with an aureate pre-Raphaelite halo: 'these golden usuries / Her beauty earns as but just increment'.[8] *Mauberley* includes a portrait of a society hostess, too, in the Lady Valentine from part XII, whose inadequate aesthetics and cultural contribution brings to a conclusion the first section of the sequence, one in which Mr. Nixon has, in part IX, advised his interlocutor to 'give up verse, my boy, / There's nothing

Non-Translation, ed. Jason Harding and John Nash (Oxford: Oxford University Press, 2019), 86–103.

7 See my '"Written at least as well as prose": Ford, Pound and Poetry', in *Ford Madox Ford: Modernist Magazines and Editing,* ed. Jason Harding (Amsterdam and New York: Rodopi, 2010), and Pound's advice not to 'use such an expression as 'dim lands *of peace*', a phrase in Ford's 'On a March Road (Winter Nightfall)' from *Face the Night* (1904), in 'A Retrospect', *Literary Essays,* ed. T. S. Eliot (London: Faber & Faber, 1954), 5.

8 Ezra Pound, *Collected Early Poems* (London: Faber & Faber, 1977), 146. See Richard Sieburth, 'In Pound We Trust', 144–5.

in it.'[9] Soon after Pound had encountered Major Douglas's book serialized in the pages of *The New Age* between June and August of 1919, the poet has the soldiers of the Great War come 'home to old lies and new infamy; / usury age-old and age-thick / and liars in public places.'[10] He would believe it demonstrated that, under usurious capitalism, there was a catastrophic relation between its economic life and the arts: 'with usura the line grows thick / with usura is no clear demarcation'.[11] So he put it in Canto 45, denigrating the baroque and lamenting the decline of the quattrocento spirit in painting, but he must surely have had the poetic line in mind as well. Yet the assumption that the two lines quoted above are not themselves 'thick' or lacking 'clear demarcation' has not been shown, and nor is it clear how to evaluate the thickness or clarity of Pound's own lines.

The poet's ever more shrilly arcane, dogmatic, and compounded assertions regarding language, money, politics, and value, and how they impacted upon his techniques as a poet, are manifest in the following passage from Canto 78. Here in the *Pisan Cantos* he reiterates, in encoded scraps, elements of his monetary beliefs, his still present (though entirely forlorn) hopes for the introduction of Social Credit, and his imaginary assumptions about Mussolini's interest in such ideas with regard to the monetary reform of the fascist state:

> Geneva the usurers' dunghill
>   Frogs, brits, with a few dutch pimps
> as top dressing to preface extortions
>   and the usual filthiness
> for detail see Odon's neat little volume
>   , that is, for a few of the more obvious details,
> the root stench being usura and METATHEMENON
> and Churchill's return to Midas broadcast by his liary.
>   " No longer necessary," taxes are no longer necessary
> in the old way if it (money) be based on work done
>   inside a system and measured and gauged to human
>   requirements
> inside the nation or system   道
> and cancelled in proportion
>   to what is used and worn out

---

[9] Ezra Pound, *Early Writings*, 133.

[10] Ibid. 130.

[11] *The Cantos of Ezra Pound*, 4th collected edn. (London: Faber & Faber, 1987), 229. For a representative selection of Pound's writings on economics, see Ezra Pound, *Selected Prose 1909–1965*, ed. William Cookson (London: Faber & Faber, 1973), 159–324, and for his monetary-rhymes, see *The Poems of Alfred Venison* (1935), in Ezra Pound, *Collected Shorter Poems* (London: Faber & Faber, 1984), 258–73.

à la Wörgl.   Sd/ one wd/ have to think about that
but was hang'd dead by the heels before his thought in proposito
came into action efficiently[12]

The passage begins with a scatological diatribe against the Swiss banking system, located in Geneva (rather than Zurich, for instance) so as, perhaps, to associate it not with German-speaking institutions, but French protestant ones and the rise of capitalism. A line of nationalistic slurs singles out some western seaboard Europeans ('Frogs, brits, with a few dutch pimps') as being the culprits for the rise of this 'usual filthiness' – presumably the emergence of a credit-based projecting economy during the later seventeenth and eighteenth centuries, the so-called Financial Revolution, encountered above with relation to the South Sea Bubble. Odon Por was an Italian writer on economics and Fascism whose 'neat little volume' – his *Politica economico-sociale in Italia* (1940) – offered examples of what Pound found repellent (in a bodily sense) with regard to the behaviour of those operating the usurious system as thus identified.

'METATHEMENON TE TON KRUMENON, as I think Aristotle remarked'[13] is a phrase spoken by Pound in his wartime broadcasts from Rome, one drawn from Aristotle's *Politics*, and taken by the poet to refer to the intentional variation of a currency by changing the amount of precious metal in it. 'Churchill's return to Midas' is his shorthand for the policy instituted by Winston Churchill, then Chancellor of the Exchequer, to return sterling to the gold standard at a deflationary equivalence in 1925. The British currency had gone off this standard at the outbreak of the First World War and Churchill was attempting to return the pound to the system by which national monies had been related and international trade facilitated before the war destroyed its basis. This policy of attempting to guarantee the exchangeable value of paper money by backing it with a fixed amount of bullion was much criticized at the time,[14] among the errors being the fixing of the conversion rate so high. The passage's collage of sources is

---

[12]   Pound, *Cantos*, 481–2. Explications are indebted to John Hamilton Edwards and William W. Vasse, *Annotated Index to The Cantos of Ezra Pound* (Berkeley and Los Angeles: University of California Press, 1975), and the annotated edition of *The Pisan Cantos,* ed. Richard Sieburth (New York: New Directions, 2003).

[13]   Ezra Pound, 'Financial Defeat: U. S.', broadcast 26 March 1943, in *'Ezra Pound Speaking': Radio Speeches of World War II,* ed. Leonard W. Doob (Westport, CT: Greenwood Press, 1978), 263. For the translation, 'if those who use a currency give it up for another', and commentary on the phrase's source in Aristotle's *Politics*, see Edwards and Vasse, *Annotated Index to The Cantos of Ezra Pound*, 265–6.

[14]   Keynes was also critical of the return to the Gold Standard. See 'The Economic Consequences of Mr Churchill', *Activities 1922–1929,* in *The Collected Writings of John Maynard Keynes,* vol. 19, 357–453.

thus caught between two anathema-like principles: that the currency should be based on a fixed relation to the hoarding of fetishized metal (primarily gold, but also silver) and, equally, that private banks could create money out of nothing by printing paper.

Pound refers to Churchill's policy error a number of times in the *Pisan Cantos*, as here in Canto 77:

> " And with the return to the gold standard " wrote Sir Montagu
> " every peasant had to pay twice as much grain
>   to cover his taxes and interest "
>
> It is true that the interest is now legally lower
> but the banks lend to the bunya
> who can thus lend to his victims
> and the snot press and periodical tosh does not notice this[15]

Sir Montagu Norman was governor of the Bank of England between 1920 and 1944. 'Bunya' means 'money-lender' in Hindi. The association of 'usury' and 'liars in public places' in *Mauberley* is thus ever less temperately reiterated, as is the association between a disliked form of economic behaviour and the failure of newspapers and public prints to reveal the facts as Pound saw them. Yet the corruption of language cannot be reduced to the idea that others are not saying what you believe, and that the supposed failure to do so is not merely an index of *their* legitimately held beliefs, but a form of cover-up or complicity in the evil. Pound's language, though, is itself corrupted by the corruption it seeks to expose. He may think that 'snot press and periodical tosh' is telling it straight, but the rage ('snot' and 'tosh') has blurred the image.

Pound's reference to Churchill's 'liary' in Canto 78 intends to imply that the Prime Minister of Great Britain had, as Chancellor of the Exchequer in 1925, ulterior motives for making this decision, which places him with the usurers and the corruptors of language. Pound is insinuating that money should be a fixed amount of exchange-power, correlating useful work with human needs, and controlled by the state for the benefit of the population. The ideogram, derived from the Confucian *Analects*, a text Pound had with him in his Pisan detention, means 'the truth, the path, the doctrine', and is itself a fetish-like countersign, 'guaranteeing' the value of what he asserts. The passage then turns to the reiteration of his views on Social Credit and the projected utopian economics whereby money will be based on 'work done' with 'human requirements' as its measure, and then will stop being money, or credit, when 'used and worn out'.

---

[15] Pound, *Cantos*, 474.

Wörgl is a small town in the Austrian Tyrol whose mayor, between 31 July 1932 and 1 September 1933, issued its own 'stamp scrip' or *Freigeld*, the face value of which had to be sustained by the payment of an additional tax at regular intervals, encouraging circulation and stimulating economic activity – and thereby exemplifying for Pound the practicality of his monetary ideals.[16] The person hanged by the heels is again Mussolini, who, in his 1933 meeting with Pound, on hearing the poet expound his ideas for monetary and economic reform, flattered his visitor by saying that he would think about them: 'Sd/ one wd/ have to think about that'. Nothing in Mussolini's economic policy, or his alliances with Italian corporations such as Fiat, suggests that he did other than fob off the American poet.[17] Despite Mussolini's continuing popularity in some quarters, his credentials as an enlightened despot remain unproven.[18] The cited passage concludes by suggesting that had it not been for Mussolini's defeat and death at the hands of the partisans as he attempted to across the Swiss border, he would have gone on to introduce Pound's preferred policy. A reader is to understand that the poet's aspirations for monetary reform beginning with fascist Italy were destroyed by the usurers – with the victorious Churchill (as exemplified by his mistaken policy in 1925) at their head.

The commentators in the *Annotated Index* note of the poet's monetary ideas: 'Pound's economics are often thought to be medieval (in both the chronological and derogatory sense)'.[19] But it's not the medievalism that is the problem: it's the assurance of a special insight into a global conspiracy. Rather than dismissing his 'Ideas, old gossip, oddments of all things' and 'Strange spars of knowledge', we might look to his poetic technique ('I believe in technique as the test of a man's sincerity'),[20] to the aesthetic and ethical basis for these lines. Pound's claims for the value of his economic theories are invested in their being the equivalent of the Chinese ideogram

[16] It was the Austrian Central Bank that brought the experiment to an end. Richard Arkwright had issued his own 'Cromford dollars', silver coins minted in Mexico City in 1802 which had been captured by British ships during the Napoleonic Wars and, because of a shortage of silver coinage in Britain, over-stamped with the value of 4 shillings and 9 pence exchangeable for goods in the village. A rare example discovered by a metal detectorist in 2016 can be seen in the Derby Museums.

[17] See Canto 41 for a snippet of their meeting, and for a fuller account, see A. David Moody, *Ezra Pound: Poet, A Portrait of the Man and His Work*, vol. 2, *The Epic Years 1921–1939* (Oxford: Oxford University Press, 2014), 136–7.

[18] See Christopher Duggan, *Fascist Voices: An Intimate History of Mussolini's Italy* (Oxford: Oxford University Press, 2013), 418–35.

[19] Edwards and Vasse, *Annotated Index to The Cantos of Ezra Pound*, 265.

[20] Ezra Pound, 'A Retrospect', in *Literary Essays*, ed. T. S. Eliot (London: Faber & Faber, 1954), 9. Sincerity, though, can be no guarantee of freedom from delusion.

in the passage above (their being 'the way', 'the truth', 'the doctrine': a value derived from some purported facts) as in 'for detail see Odon's neat little volume'. This first name-dropped reference indicates another feature of the lines' backing, the 'work done' – Pound's researches. Their highly idealistic, moralized purpose and the desire to base economics on 'human requirements' are by no means despicable; yet, despite any good sense that may inhere in these Aristotle-cum-Confucius-supported fragmentary economic assertions, it is hard not to feel that the virtue they may contain is fatally mixed with scatological revulsion and fantasy. As with the language of 'Portrait d'une Femme', these lines can't help seeming to be 'strange spars of knowledge' that 'might prove useful' and yet 'never prove'.

Alongside the ironies of Pound's social engagement, wrecked for at least two gross errors, namely his delusions about Mussolini and his anti-Semitism[21] – ones, though, that cannot be separated from his core poetic and cultural beliefs and values – there is a deep irony in the poet's views on the health of poetic language as related to his economic fixations. His poetics are themselves involved in an idea of 'fixation', whereby value in the arts, the value of some art works, both the labour and the outcome, is a permanent worth, analogous with his theory of money as one in which the value of currency is backed, secured, and fixed by credit on the assumed value of things in themselves, especially when literally 'natural' (the town's pasture lands, in the case of the Monte dei Paschi di Siena, for instance).[22] His mistake, aside from thinking that you could go wrong for a single mistake ('Muss., wrecked for an error'[23]), rather than an entire outlook and its consequences in conduct, was in thinking that these two values, in art and in money, were coherently correct and virtuous, because equally well backed by something other than the fluctuations of opinion, scarcity, need, and desire. His theory of the ideogram is an instance of such 'natural' backing for poetic language.

Pound believed that in the 'pictogram', the 'etymology' of a Chinese character meant that a river is seen in the character for 'river', and a mountain in the character for 'mountain', making each character able to preserve the poetic truth-value of uses because bound to a form of pictorial correspondence. The 'foot' radical, for instance, is included as the base of the character for 'the way' above. But there is no more than a metaphorical relation between a human foot and the correct way of a philosophical system (not least because going down 'the primrose path of dalliance' or

---

21 For an account of this relationship, see Leon Surette, *Pound in Purgatory: From Economic Radicalism to Anti-Semitism* (Urbana and Chicago: University of Illinois Press, 2001).

22 For a sympathetic account of Pound's interest in the Monte dei Paschi bank in Siena, see Moody, *Ezra Pound: Poet,* vol. 2, 212–20.

23 Pound, *Cantos,* 795.

the term 'error' themselves employ implicit foot metaphors too). His idea, as expressed in the *ABC of Reading*, was that whereas Chinese 'HAD TO STAY POETIC; simply couldn't help being and staying poetic', the poetry in his own language presented as 'a column of English type', *that* 'might very well not stay poetic.'[24] Pound the worker, was, in effect, blaming his Anglophone tools.

But the error of Churchill's going back onto the gold standard in 1925, while now almost a truism of economic history and a view of Pound's which is by no means that of a 'crank', sets his theory of supported value in both money and language against an attempt to provide secured value – albeit a fetishistic one – and, in the interests of a more humanly productive idea of money and economic activity, against the idea of Indian farmers being strangled by debt. Such a criticism in the field of monetary policy attacks the grounds of his own poetics: what he dislikes in Churchill's policy is an analogy of, or close to the workings of, what he believes makes his lines have a better access to the truth of nature and life than, say, those of Swinburne or Wordsworth. This notion is, and has been, reinforced by the view of Imagism as itself a fetishistic poetic theory, because of its prioritizing of the 'concrete' over the 'abstract', emblematically present, for instance, in William Carlos Williams's 'No ideas but in things'.[25]

3. Currencies backed by nature

Whatever the *japonisme* or *chinoiserie* in Ezra Pound's haiku-like epigram 'In a Station of the Metro', he certainly doesn't have 'th' Eastern idea' about determiners.[26] The Chinese and Japanese languages have no articles, definite or indefinite, at all. Yet Pound was capable of thinking that telegraphese-style poetic lines with much reduced articles and no verbs

[24] Ezra Pound, *ABC of Reading* (London: Faber & Faber, 1951), 20–2.
[25] Richard Sieburth tracks the aureate metaphors in Pound's earliest poetry and their survival into the first 30 Cantos. For his account of Imagism's economics and the converting of a gold fetish into a thing or nature fetish, see 'In Pound We Trust', 146–9, and for Williams's practice in light of Pound's monetary ideas, see Kurt Heinzelman, *The Economics of the Imagination* (Amherst: University of Massachusetts Press, 1980), 243–51.
[26] At the start of Canto 84, Pound recalls Senator Bankhead describing Roosevelt as 'stubborn az a mule' who 'got th' eastern idea about money' (*Cantos*, 537) – a reference, perhaps, to the conflicted need for easy credit from the West's many precarious banks and for well-backed currency and secured institutions in the East during the opening up of the frontier after the Civil War. As a 'credit-crank' Pound was more inclined to support the Western need for currencies of any kind (e.g., tobacco) than the Eastern need for copper-bottomed banks and money.

would have more 'vigour' if freed of such 'clutter'. In 'D'Artagnan Twenty Years After' he writes: 'If *le style c'est l'homme*, the writer's blood test is his swift contraposition of objects'; and, to exemplify his point, he offers 'The footsteps of the cat upon / The snow: / Plum blossoms.'[27] Yet the stylish shift from two lines of nouns determined by definite articles to an indefinite plural, signified by an absence of article in conjunction with the added 's', exemplifies the difference between Pound's ideogram-inflected poetic theories and his Anglophone technical skills. As noted, Japanese, while it has grammatical and therefore meaning-bearing determiners, doesn't have articles, plurals, or, in the way English does, possessive pronouns. As a result, an English-language poet translating Japanese poems interprets them by interpolating articles, possessive pronouns, and other 'little words', while the skill and sensitivity of the translator shows simultaneously in the degrees of interrelated 'naturalization' and 'making strange' that is achieved, the former shaping a reception-context in which the latter can be understood and appreciated. Thus Pound's poetic practice in his Chinese translations and his imitation of Japanese poetic forms shows acute sensitivity to those far from useless little words, a sensitivity that runs counter to much that he suggests in his pronouncements on ideograms and the ideogrammatic method in, for example, *The Chinese Written Character as a Medium for Poetry* and the *ABC of Reading*.

Among the most famous and much discussed of Pound's shorter poems is 'In a Station of the Metro', a poem about which he also wrote much self-promotional and literary polemical prose. In doing so, though, he says nothing about his deployment of English articles and a deictic determiner. Here's how the poem, including title, appeared when collected in *Lustra* (1916):

IN A STATION OF THE METRO

The apparition of these faces in the crowd;
Petals on a wet, black bough.[28]

The title's use of articles establishes a standard by which the rest of the poem might be appreciated. Readers encounter an indefinite location (*a* station) in a definite urban transport network (*the* Métro). This is the conventional way of employing articles in a narrative, first references being to an indefinite place, which is then made more specific, is defined, by an additional reference. This narrative procedure is itself a kind of fiction,

27 Ezra Pound, *Selected Prose 1909–1965*, 422, and see, for the original version of this haiku and its moment of composition as reported by Victor Plarr, 'Vorticism', in *Gaudier-Brzeska: A Memoir* (1916), in *Early Writings*, 286.

28 Pound, *Early Writings*, 82.

because the person who is in 'a station' usually knows which one it is (the disorientation produced if he weren't might be enough to prevent him from perceiving the crowd as he does). In any case, Pound elsewhere mentions what station it was: 'Three years ago in Paris I got out of a "metro" train at La Concorde'.[29] The indefinite article in the title has, then, two roles: it establishes a conventional narrative relation with a reader, and it indicates that the specific station is not of significance to the poem, though the fact that it is an underground station will be. The title indicates a certain *outre Manche* poetic chic (there are underground stations in London, where the poem in this form was first published), though that is not a flavour conveyed by his use of articles.

The poem reverses this ordering of article-use, not from indefinite to definite, but the other way around, from '*The* apparition' and '*the* crowd' to 'Petals' (an indefinite plural) and then the indefinite singular '*a* wet, black bough.' The definite articles – to specify a singular experience – are reinforced by the one deictic in the poem: '*these* faces'. This specifying, as an initial move in conveying an experience, contrasts with Pound's prose account of the poem's occasioning perception:

> Three years ago in Paris I got out of a 'metro' train at La Concorde, and saw suddenly a beautiful face, and then another and another, and then a beautiful child's face, and then another beautiful woman, and I tried all day to find words for what this had meant to me, and I could not find any words that seemed to me worthy, or as lovely as that sudden emotion.[30]

The conventional way to recount such an event is to refer, as Pound does, to seeing '*a* beautiful face'. Richard Aldington paid Pound's poem the homage of parody in the year following its 1913 American publication, but he hadn't spotted that the poem depends so on the switching of articles around the line end, for his first line 'The apparition   of these poems   in a crowd' doesn't sustain the article contrast in the original.[31]

David Moody reminds us that the poem appears to be, almost, in the form of a Japanese *haiku* – though, again, its similarity to such poems must be framed by its differences. Reading 'In a Station of the Metro' does raise a question about Moody's interpretation of the faces being seen: 'not as the dead but as if reborn in the next year's almond or olive blossom'. The pretty interpolation of what blossoms they might be (if it's a *haiku*, cherry

---

[29] 'Vorticism', published in *Gaudier-Brzeska: A Memoir* (1916), in *Early Writings*, 284.

[30] Pound, *Early Writings*, 284.

[31] 'The apparition   of these poems   in a crowd: / White faces   in a black   dead faint' was published in *The Egoist* on 15 January 1914, cited here from ibid. 359.

would also be likely) reminds us of more information Pound regarded as superfluous – just as he didn't state that line 2 takes place 'as if' a year later. Another interpretation is to associate the figures with the line from Dante's *Inferno* that T. S. Eliot was to make his own in *The Waste Land* about a decade later: 'I had not thought death had undone so many'.[32] The very prolixity of the commentary on this little poem and its possible significances, as for instance in Moody's speculation, draws attention to the 'indefinite' condition of the concluding lines, opening the poem up to a response, requiring a certain indeterminacy, or indefiniteness, which is effectively created by the poet's highly skilled use of articles.

The crucial contradiction, then, is that Pound's support for a state-controlled currency not backed by gold, including Wörgl-like stamp script, and similar experiments in what is called *fiat money* – quantitative easing, as practiced by the Bank of England in the wake of the 2008 Credit Crunch, is a current form of it – ought to have led him to 'contract-style' thinking about money in its symbolic relations and its circulatory functions; and 'contract-style' interpreting, including the understanding of article-use, is what readers are practicing in reading Pound's short poem. His being against the fetishism of 'gold' and the Marxian idea of money as a commodity with a value (as well as a symbolic representation for price) ought to have made him a contractualist. But such an institutional, speech act, idea of money as something 'uttered' by a national bank, without the incurring of private profit, did not provide him with a sufficiently metaphysical assurance of value fixity, and this raises the issue of Pound's self-evaluation.

The deep contradiction about the gold standard for the poet is that his misunderstanding of his own poetics led him to fetishize the material base of his techniques (though his fetish was 'nature' and the exact definition of individual words) and to believe that he could dispense theoretically, though not in residual gesture and practice, with the conventions of grammar and syntax, working in rhythmically 'charged' fragments, and so make the truth of his poetry especially, and his writings more generally, invulnerable to the collaborative and strictly equal role of readers, readers producing the sense of the work in and for themselves. This is not Pound's idea of the relationship between writer and reader, however; for, as he puts it, in discourse 'what matters is / to get it across e poi basta' [and then enough].[33] This is made analogous with the 'intaglio method' where the sense is impressed into the wax, or, similarly, readers have become the material that

---

[32] T. S. Eliot, *The Poems*, 2 vols., ed. Christopher Ricks and Jim McCue (London: Faber & Faber, 2015), vol. 1, 57.

[33] Pound, *Cantos*, 486. For Sieburth's use of this passage to contrast his interest in money's function with neglect of economic production, see 'In Pound We Trust', 166.

is coined by the stroke of the moneyer. Pound's arguments took him away from gold, and fetish value, and towards theories of money in which the collaborative belief of users in the system is essential to its workings (loss of confidence in a country's economic management, or its politics, will alter its currency's exchange value nearly instantly on the markets, as attention to the news on any particularly turbulent day will show). Extreme cases, as in the Venezuelan crisis of 2018–19, lead to the sorts of hyper-inflation that render a nation's money as good as useless.[34]

Pound's economic and monetary ideas, with their wish to increase well-being and challenge injustice, were vitiated by his failure to understand that such monetary ideas depended upon a symbolic and contractual idea of money as fiduciary, as based on, however uncertainly, trust. Yet here there is a further bifurcation of sense, for in the case of Pound we re-encounter the two different kinds of 'trust' that had emerged in the secular and religious ideas of 'redemption'. When Sieburth concludes that 'In Pound we trust', as a part of his symptomatology, he cites the poet's 1933 judgment of Mussolini as 'artifex' and 'belief' in what he intends to do. But this turns out, as in Canto 78, to be a one-way trust, by which we surrender our will (and judgment) to the leader's, or the poet's. The trust that he doesn't invoke is that which functions mutually, where neither abandons will or judgment, and where the sustenance of trust, as in keeping promises, is indexed to performance.

However much technique may evidence sincerity, the only thing it can be tested to evaluate is a person's performance. But Pound propagandized for first a poetics and then an economics which would not be dependent upon equal cultural exchanges with individuals, whether readers or economic actors, but which would fix value on the natural, the substantial, and the timeless. It would fix it through technique not understood as transactional, but as autonomous and authoritative. Yet his use of articles in 'In a Station of the Metro' is necessarily collaborative, because playing both with and against conventional usage. He committed himself to nature and natural process as his metaphorical fetish, supported by his account of the Chinese written character and, later, a partial and fetishizing interpretation of the Sienese Monte dei Paschi bank.[35]

---

[34] In 2018, Venezuelans crossing the border into Colombia would give away bundles of currency as souvenirs in exchange for anything useful that locals would offer them.

[35] Recent research suggests that the bank's security on the pasturelands around the town was never practically evoked and that control of the bank by the Sienese aristocracy vitiated the civic virtuousness towards which founding it might have aspired. See Maura Mordini, 'Pound e l'Archivio di Stato di Siena: Note sulle storia del Monte dei Paschi', in Ezra Pound, *The Fifth Decad of Cantos: Siena, The Leopoldine Reforms* (Rimini: Raffaelli Editore, 2006), 119–23.

Yet this natural support for the poetry in his language, with its privileging of a 'picture theory' of meaning that could dispense with words whose function is strictly syntactical, words which don't 'picture' anything – words such as 'is' and 'the' – meant that his poetics was an equivalent of the gold standard, while his ideas for economic justice were off it. This is why his public career, which might be said to have reached its height in his broadcasting from Rome and Salò during World War II, is a disastrous instance of poets as unacknowledged legislators, and, further, illustrates how the contradiction between his poetics and his monetary theories focuses down, finally, upon the fact that his technique could at times enable and at others severely limit his poetry's collaborative relations with its readers. This is how usury, or his obsession with it, did, in effect, thicken the line in Pound's own work, whether the method of *The Cantos* or his epistolary and polemical prose.

4. A Peace passing understanding

In '*The Waste Land*: A Keynsian Epic?' Tom Paulin reports the evidence that Eliot knew John Maynard Keynes's *The Economic Consequences of the Peace* (1919),[36] the only book by the economist the poet claimed to have read. Paulin asserts that detail from Keynes's account of post-conflict Europe contributed to the waste and desert imagery in Eliot's poem. Yet, with the exception of a passing reference to working with German banks, Paulin does not address in detail ways Eliot's poem might have been influenced either by its poet's own work for Lloyd's Bank on the revaluation and renegotiating of pre-war debts with European countries whose economies had been devastated, or the precariousness and complexity of his own domestic finances during the years in which the poem was conceived and completed.[37]

Nor does Paulin discuss the economics of *The Waste Land*'s publication, including the unusual financial negotiations involved in its appearance in America, which including a meeting in the lawyer John Quinn's office where *The Dial* agreed in advance to award Eliot its annual prize, and to buy copies of the first book publication, as a means of paying him for the right to publish the poem almost immediately prior to its appearance in book form.[38] Nor, most disappointingly, given Paulin's questioning title,

---

[36]   In Eliot, *The Poems*, vol. 1, 675–7.

[37]   See 'Introduction' to T. S. Eliot, *The Waste Land: A Facsimile and Transcript of the Original Drafts Including the Annotations of Ezra Pound*, ed. Valerie Eliot (London: Faber & Faber, 1971), ix–xxix.

[38]   See Lawrence Rainey, 'The Price of Modernism', in *Revisiting* The Waste Land (New Haven: Yale University Press, 2004), 71–101.

does the critic provide any evidence for the influence on the poem of Keynes's economic ideas and principles. Does *The Waste Land*, for instance, offer any economics-inflected solutions to the predicaments of European cities and civilizations which it so vividly provides objective correlatives for?

There are manifest convergences of interests and viewpoint between the two works. Keynes declares himself to have become a European when attending the Paris peace talks in 1919. 'Gerontion', it has been suggested, draws upon Keynes's account of the character of Clemenceau at the peace talks; yet perhaps the most striking possible allusion concerns more the description of Wilson's failure to appreciate the problem of bringing his high ideals into dialogue and negotiation with European nationalist interests in the form of the French president's attempts to 'win' the peace treaty for France in its long-term rivalry with Germany. 'We had indeed quite a wrong idea of the President', Keynes writes, and adds: 'We did not figure him as a man of detail, but the clearness with which he had taken hold of certain main ideas would, we thought, in combination with his tenacity, enable him to sweep through cobwebs.'[39] But, as Eliot has it in 'Gerontion', inflecting his passage with the word 'profit':

> These with a thousand small deliberations
> Protract the profit of their chilled delirium,
> Excite the membrane, when the sense has cooled,
> With pungent sauces, multiply variety
> In a wilderness of mirrors. What will the spider do,
> Suspend his operations, will the weevil
> Delay?[40]

The Hall of Mirrors in the Palace of Versailles is where the German Empire was declared in 1871 and the treaty ending the Great War signed on 28 June 1919. Paulin's aim is to identify Keynes's characterization of the French president with Eliot's own character and sexuality: 'To return to [*The Waste Land*] after reading Keynes is to realize that in it Eliot is anatomizing that "dry sterile", punitive intellect he shared with Clemenceau' and he does this, we are assured, in order to reach out 'to an ethic of mercy and forgiveness'.[41]

Eliot had himself raised the issue in 'Gerontion', asking: 'After such knowledge, what forgiveness?' Paulin cites at length Eliot's letter to his

---

[39] John Maynard Keynes, *The Economic Consequences of the Peace,* in *The Collected Writings of John Maynard Keynes,* vol. 2 (London and Basingstoke: Macmillan, 1971), 25.

[40] T. S. Eliot, *The Poems,* vol. 1, 33.

[41] Tom Paulin, *Crusoe's Secret: The Aesthetics of Dissent* (London: Faber & Faber, 2005), 323.

mother in which he pairs and contrasts the French and American presidents in exactly the terms Keynes does in his book on the peace, noting that 'the one strong figure was Clemenceau, who knew just what he wanted, and that Wilson went down utterly before European diplomacy.'[42] Wilson couldn't 'sweep through cobwebs', in Keynes's words, because the spider would not 'Suspend his operations' in Eliot's. The poet was not identifying himself with Clemenceau, as Paulin would polemically have it, but dramatizing the predicament of an American in Europe as, you might say, a warning to himself, for 'I believe that Wilson made a great mistake in coming to Europe', as Eliot concluded to his mother; and he cannot have been unaware when writing such words that this was his father's view of his own recent behaviour in staying in London and marrying an English woman.[43]

Eliot's theory of 'the mind of Europe' in 'Tradition and the Individual Talent' has its economic correlative too. Keynes's account of the continent makes a number of literary allusions, also suggestive of the objective correlative method, such as to Hardy's *The Dynasts*, but also Greek and Shakespearean tragedy, while the clothing of self-interest in internationalist terms is characterized by means of the witches' speech in *Macbeth*. The economist also outlines the benefits of the gold-backed fixed exchange-rate system of pre-war European currencies, and notes the difficulties connected with this system's collapse. Eliot's job in the bank was directly connected with this problem, in that he was tasked with working out how pre-war loans could be re-calculated and the debts they represented be repaid. In this light, the passage in *The Waste Land* that includes allusions to Wagner's *Das Rheingold* is thought to relate to the problem of how money is to be backed after the First World War.[44]

What became *The Waste Land* had originally set out to be a good deal more directly satirical about contemporary society than it ended up being, and Pound's contribution to that transformation was significant. Yet, nevertheless, the issue of animus in the poem's representations cannot help coming up, and being linked to the question of Eliot's prejudices, addressed with such care by Christopher Ricks.[45] One of those problems,

---

[42]   T. S. Eliot, *The Letters,* vol. 1, *1898–1922,* ed. Valerie Eliot (London: Faber & Faber, 1988), 368.

[43]   For Empson on how anti-Semitic lyrics edited out of *The Waste Land* relate to his familial conflicts, see 'My God, man, there's bears on it', *Using Biography* (London: Chatto & Windus, 1984), 195–7.

[44]   T. S. Eliot, *The Poems*, vol. 1, 674–5. Ricks and McCue's note on the gold standard may be slightly misleading, because it appears to suggest that the country was on this standard during the war. By suspending the gold standard in 1919, they must mean that the country did not go back onto it after the end of hostilities, for it had been suspended in 1914.

[45]   See Christopher Ricks, *T. S. Eliot and Prejudice* (London: Faber & Faber, 1988); Anthony Julius, *T. S. Eliot, Anti-Semitism and Literary Form* (Cambridge:

already encountered in Pound's poetry and ideas, is the relation of his worldview with words about Jews, as manifested in one of the most contentious passages in 'Burbank with a Baedeker: Bleistein with a Cigar': 'The rats are underneath the piles. / The Jew is underneath the lot. / Money in furs.'[46] The satiric animus, which Eliot would come to criticize in Pound but perhaps insufficiently recognize in himself, was to represent identified moral opprobrium with 'correlative' others. It is Jews in the lines above, and homosexuals in the proposition made by 'Mr. Eugenides, the Smyrna merchant, / Unshaven' who 'Asked me in demotic French / To luncheon at the Cannon Street Hotel / Followed by a weekend at the Metropole.'[47] The purchasing of heterosexual favours from prostitutes is similarly associated with money when 'The nymphs are departed. / And their friends, the loitering heirs of City directors; / Departed, have left no addresses.'[48] He similarly places at a provincial distance textile business war profiteers when describing in a simile and an aside the 'small house agent's clerk' as 'One of the low on whom assurance sits / As a silk hat on a Bradford millionaire.'[49]

Eliot would point out in *After Strange Gods*, which contains its own notorious passage about 'free-thinking Jews', that hell was a 'Hell for other people' in Ezra Pound's *Cantos*.[50] Empson's way of addressing these satirical portraits in *The Waste Land* was to take them back home to the poet himself, to include him in the portraiture, as it were, and include him thus in his own Hell: 'Eliot wanted to grouse about his father, and lambasted some imaginary Jews instead (as a backroom boy at Lloyds, doing rather technical work, and living very quietly, he was not of course regularly meeting the millionaires).'[51] Eliot was thus also concerned with the question of what supports value in both money and poetry, but his implied answer is distinctly at odds with Pound's.

5. The dominant vice of our time

Eliot certainly had more direct practical experience of money than did Ezra Pound. Out of his experiences at Lloyds Bank, with their concomitant

Cambridge University Press, 1995); and Bryan Cheyette, 'Eliot and "Race": Jews, Irish and Blacks', in *A Companion to T. S. Eliot*, ed. David E. Chinitz (Oxford: Wiley-Blackwell, 2009), 335–49.
[46] T. S. Eliot, *The Poems*, vol. 1, 35.
[47] Ibid. 63.
[48] Ibid. 62.
[49] Ibid.
[50] Eliot, *After Strange Gods*, 43.
[51] Empson, 'My God, man, there's bears on it', 197.

social implications, ones associated with themes from his own emotional and sexual life, came what would trouble the senses of *The Waste Land*. Yet how his poem may not be a Keynesian epic, and more than invite the question mark in Paulin's title, emerges in the final section of the two works being compared. 'To Carthage then I came'[52] in *The Waste Land* is a doubly directed allusion in that it draws upon both Augustine's *Confessions* as cited in the poem's own notes, and Keynes's description of the Treaty of Versailles as 'a Carthaginian peace'.[53] The poetic allusion compounds religious beliefs and political policy after a war, just as Keynes does in his prose:

> The policy of reducing Germany to servitude for a generation, of degrading the lives of millions of human beings, and of depriving a whole nation of happiness should be abhorrent and detestable – abhorrent and detestable, even if it were possible, even if it enriched ourselves, even if it did not sow the decay of the whole civilised life of Europe. Some preach it in the name of justice. In the great events of man's history, in the unwinding of the complex fate of nations, justice is not so simple. And if it were, nations are not authorized, by religion or by natural morals, to visit on the children of their enemies the misdoings of parents or of rulers.[54]

As befits an economist writing on the consequences of a peace treaty, in a concluding chapter entitled 'Remedies', Keynes proposes four areas in which the disastrous situation detailed in his book might be mitigated. These are: the revision of the treaty; the settlement of inter-Ally indebtedness; international loans and the reform of the currency; and the relations of Central Europe to Russia.[55] The last section of *The Waste Land* does include the line 'Shall I at least set my lands in order?' But coming as it does immediately before the concluding collage of fragmentary citations, its suggestiveness lies in not referencing any particular lands, let alone the economies of continental Europe that is Keynes's concern. Of course, it doesn't rule out allusion to the material in *The Economic Consequences of the Peace*, but it does not reference the specific remedies that the economist proposes, though the annotated edition of Eliot's poems cites a question from a *Commentary* in *The Criterion* for October 1935: 'until we set in order our own crazy economic and financial systems, to say nothing of our philosophy of life, can we be sure that our helping hand to the barbarian

52 T. S. Eliot, *The Poems*, vol. 1, 66.
53 See ibid. 675, where the editors note the connection with Keynes, who wrote that his purpose was 'to show that the Carthaginian peace is not *practically* right or possible'; J. M. Keynes, *The Economic Consequences of the Peace*, 23.
54 J. M. Keynes, *The Economic Consequences of the Peace*, 142.
55 Ibid. 162.

and the savage will be any more desirable than the embrace of the leper?'[56] It is not difficult to detect the relative tact that Eliot is exercising here, especially in light of what Pound would do with his 1919 readings in ideas for economic reform, for Eliot keeps *The Waste Land* within the space of mental and spiritual well-being, or lack of it, and doesn't employ poetry to promulgate specific policies, as Pound increasingly would attempt to do both in and out of poetry.

There is, perhaps, a final echo of a Keynesian context for the poem in its once mysterious final line: 'Shantih   shantih   shantih'. Eliot's own note tells us: 'Repeated as here, a formal ending to an Upanishad. "The Peace which passeth understanding" is our equivalent to this word.' Is it too much to see the capitalization of the word 'Peace' as making possible an allusion to *The Economic Consequences of the Peace*, to the Treaty of Versailles, a treaty whose terms also 'passeth understanding'? Certainly Keynes's account, despite his manifold and detailed understanding of it and its consequences, suggests that he can't for the life of him understand why such a catastrophically short-sighted peace should have come to pass (though explaining it clearly enough in his portraits of the three main leaders).[57] His book is also prophetic about how the failures of the victorious four Allies would foment desperate measures by resentful persons in the future, as well as seeing exactly why the League of Nations would find itself powerless to prevent it. If Eliot is punning on 'Peace', and there is circumstantial evidence in his contemporaneous letters to suggest that he might have been punning, then his wordplay doesn't so much bring the two senses together, as signal a point where, ever more determinedly, he would, both in and out of poetry, seek for a religious and spiritual peace in the face of, or in spite of, or as a consolation for, the absence of peace in economic or political or indeed personal realms through the inter-war years.

Where Eliot would reach as regards his thinking about money is plainly shown in the penultimate paragraph of the February 1937 broadcast talk that forms the 'Appendix' to *The Idea of a Christian Society* (1939):

> Perhaps the dominant vice of our time, from the point of view of the Church, will be proved to be Avarice. Surely there is something wrong in our attitude towards money. The acquisitive, rather than the creative and the spiritual instincts, are encouraged. The fact that money is always forthcoming for the purpose of making more money, whilst it is so difficult to obtain for purposes of exchange, and for the needs of the most needy, is disturbing to those who

---

[56]   Cited in T. S. Eliot, *The Poems*, vol. 1, 704.
[57]   See J. M. Keynes, 'Mr Lloyd George: A Fragment', *Essays in Biography*, in *The Collected Writings of John Maynard Keynes*, vol. 10, 20–6.

are not economists. I am by no means sure that it is right for me to improve my income by investing in the shares of a company, making I know not what, operating perhaps thousands of miles away, and in the control of which I have no effective voice – but which is recommended as a sound investment. I am still less sure of the morality of my being a moneylender: that is of interest in bonds and debentures. I know that it is wrong for me to speculate: but where the line is to be drawn between speculation and what is called legitimate investment is by no means clear. I seem to be a petty usurer in a world manipulated largely by big usurers. And I know that the Church once condemned these things. And I believe that modern war is chiefly caused by some immorality of competition which is always with us in times of 'peace'; and that until this evil is cured, no leagues or disarmaments or collective security or conferences or conventions or treaties will suffice to prevent it.[58]

Thus Eliot's faith is, after all, not so far from Pound's insight in the 'Usura' Canto 45, and, writing in 1972, Pound would come to align himself with Eliot's word: 're USURY: I was out of focus ... The cause is AVARICE.'[59] But there is no such one cause, and Eliot's 'dominant vice' is not a single explanation, but appears in a prose essay responding with its religious values to the feeling of cultural emptiness produced by the Munich Crisis and the recognition that Anglophone civilization appeared to have nothing better with which to defend itself and its culture against Hitler and National Socialism, with *their* values, than the economic interests of its financial system.

These expressed thoughts of Eliot's inflect a passage that again touches on the stock market and the City of London:

> O dark dark dark. They all go into the dark,
> The vacant interstellar spaces, the vacant into the vacant,
> The captains, merchant bankers, eminent men of letters,
> The generous patrons of art, the statesmen and the rulers,
> Distinguished civil servants, chairmen of many committees,
> Industrial lords and petty contractors, all go into the dark,
> And dark the Sun and Moon, and the Almanach de Gotha
> And the Stock Exchange Gazette, the Directory of Directors,
> And cold the sense and lost the motive of action.

[58] T. S. Eliot, *The Idea of a Christian Society* (London: Faber & Faber, 1939), 97–8. See 'The Hippopotamus', where 'the True Church need never stir / To gather in its dividends' in T. S. Eliot, *The Poems*, vol. 1, 43.

[59] Pound, *Selected Prose 1909–1965*, 6.

And we all go with them, into the silent funeral,
Nobody's funeral, for there is no one to bury.[60]

The move in this passage from 'They all go' to 'And we all go with them' might have been composed with Eliot's criticism of Pound's views of financiers and his view that his fellow poet's 'Hell' is 'for the *other people*' at the front of his mind. But it is curious to read 'for there is no one to bury' in a poem first published in 1940, when there already were plenty to bury. Does this point to a muffling of the apocalyptic strain in Eliot's poetry, so apparently at odds with the sound of his civic prose, and yet not so at odds with the poet's weaker moments of 'other-identifying' in writings for which he would ask forgiveness in 'Little Gidding'? Geoffrey Hill was scathing of Eliot's pronoun use in *Four Quartets*, disliking the gestures of inclusiveness in their 'Everyman' use of 'we', for example.[61]

Yet Eliot's Christian vision of money painfully recognizes that there is nothing else but all of us and our thoughts and feelings, our historically situated and conflicted values; and he then attempts to bolster that realization's vulnerability with institutional traditions of thinking – as when he includes us in his 'we' and remembers that the Church used to condemn usury. The problem as thus characterized remains how any and all of us sustain such values without the support of a religion, if it is, like Christianity, an exclusive one, because, in being that, it only divides 'us' from 'them', they being those with whom 'we' have to act trustingly. And the difficulty here, as I can't help acknowledging, is how thoroughly fragile a position this appears to be, for, to recall Eliot's 1927 comment, it is as if I were asking 'the wall-paper' to 'save us when the walls have crumbled.'[62]

---

[60] T. S. Eliot, *The Poems*, vol. 1, 188.
[61] See Geoffrey Hill, *Collected Critical Writings*, ed. Kenneth Haynes (Oxford: Oxford University Press, 2008), 540–1.
[62] T. S. Eliot, 'Literature, Science and Dogma', *The Dial*, no. 82 (March 1927), 234.

CHAPTER EIGHT

Contracts and prophets

1. *They hear thy words, but they do them not*

D. H. Lawrence's 'Money-Madness' first appeared in the volume *Pansies* (1929), the year of the Wall Street Crash. It is one of the writer's very late, free-verse poems sustained by the urgency and shrill self-assurance of its voice. This assurance takes the form of resorts to persuasive devices as in biblical prophecy and argumentative gesture, devices vulnerable to producing counter-effects in their assertions (inviting other *pensées*), and even more so when isolated in short, aphoristic verse paragraphs:

> Money is our madness, our vast collective madness.
>
> And of course, if the multitude is mad
> the individual carries his own grain of insanity around with him.
>
> I doubt if any man living hands out a pound note without a pang;
> and a real tremor, if he hands out a ten-pound note.
>
> We quail, money makes us quail.
> It has got us down, we grovel before it in strange terror.
> And no wonder, for money has a fearful cruel power among men.[1]

The lines' initial phrases ('And of course', 'I doubt if', and 'And no wonder'), while appearing to buoy up the writer in the confidence of his rightness in what is asserted, helping him on to further statements about what money can do, and not do, simultaneously spread uncertainty and doubt from their very presence and seeming need. These gestures attempt to recruit readers into

---

[1] D. H. Lawrence, *The Complete Poems,* ed. Vivian de Sola Pinto and Warren Roberts (Harmondsworth: Penguin Books, 1980), 486.

support for the writer's assertions, and in this it is important to distinguish between inert gestures towards readers, cajoling them into compliant reading, and the invitation to participate in meaning formation that the use of articles in Pound's 'In a Station of the Metro' enables or that Roy Fisher's revisions to the close of 'Suppose –', explored in Chapter 1, differently invite.

Lawrence confronts what he feels to be the almost unspeakably negative nature of money amongst us – multitudes and individuals, our 'money-madness' – by suggesting that it resembles a perversion, or the breaking of a taboo:

> And if I have no money, they will give me a little bread
> so I do not die,
> but they will make me eat dirt with it.
> I shall have to eat dirt, I shall have to eat dirt
> if I have no money.

The repetitions produce an appropriate air of panic in the voice. Its fear is like that for the prospect of a pauper burial, or being obliged to suffer the means-testing ignominies involved in claiming a benefit payment. The shame of economic humiliation maintains a connection with ritual prophecy by warning against the 'uncleanness' of poverty: 'We must have some money / to save us from eating dirt', the poem continues, and then in a moment of righteous bathos: 'And this is all wrong.'

Yes, it surely is wrong; but merely asserting it does not make for effective poetry or polemic, and such an evaluation returns us to the question of what may be sustaining, and also helplessly failing to sustain, such writing's confidence. This is not intended as a judgment on Lawrence's poetry as a whole. 'On the Balcony', with its decisively plain conclusion ('The boat has gone'), draws upon another source of power altogether in a situated evocation of intimate, collaborative feeling: 'You are near me'.[2] This poet's virtuous hating could exceed its own broad self-permission, and he did not collect an epigram called 'Money', whose revulsion resembles the scatology of passages in Pound's *Cantos*:

> Money is the vast stinking beast
> and men are the lice that creep on it
> and live from its secondary sweat.
>
> All people, like lice
> creep on the vast money-beast
> and feed on it.[3]

---

[2] Lawrence, *Complete Poems*, 208.
[3] Ibid. 843.

Comparing 'Money-Madness' with this late poem on the theme, I notice it uses the pronoun 'we' in an hortatory fashion, calling upon us to behave differently so as to save ourselves from the global catastrophe of the money system; but 'Money' makes it painfully clear that Lawrence could think of us as parasitic upon it, and that we would die were we not to feed on it. This epigram hasn't even a utopian idealism by way of medicine for its diagnosis.

In his essay 'Blessed are the Powerful', published first in *Reflections on the Death of a Porcupine* (1925), Lawrence indicates by means of aphorisms and slogans why 'money has a fearful cruel power among men'. He concludes:

> Power! How can there be power in politics, when politics is money?
> Money is power, they say. Is it? Money is to power what margarine is to butter: a nasty substitute.[4]

Concluding the essay that gave this volume its name, Lawrence states his opposition to money as anti-life. Continuing to be critical of 'Money-Madness', I should underline that the opinion it expresses is far from contemptible, and that his prose rhythms here give the writer's statements a coordinated force and conviction largely absent from the poem:

> Our last wall is the golden wall of money. This is a fatal wall. It cuts us off from life, from vitality, from the alive sun and the alive earth, as *nothing* can. Nothing, not even the most fanatical dogmas of an iron-bound religion, can insulate us from the inrush of life and inspiration, as money can.
> We are losing vitality: losing it rapidly. Unless we seize the torch of inspiration, and drop our moneybags, the moneyless will be kindled by the flame of flames, and they will consume us like old rags.
> We are losing our vitality, owing to money and money-standards. The torch in the hands of the moneyless will set our house on fire, and burn us to death, like sheep in a flaming corral.[5]

For Lawrence both religion and money, as constrainers of human impulse, are equally to be cast aside for the purposes of regaining 'vitality'. 'Money-Madness', though, demonstrates in itself a loss of vitality owing, perhaps, to the infection by taboo-violating revulsion, from money and its ways. Most seriously, as a poem, it has almost nothing to rely on as a

---

[4]   D. H. Lawrence, *Phoenix II: Uncollected, Unpublished and Other Prose Words*, ed. Warren Roberts and Harry T. Moore (London: Heinemann, 1968), 439.

[5]   Ibid. 474.

counteractive force against the money values that it rails against, and this is because Lawrence had previously abandoned any recourse to inherited poetic techniques that call upon a reader's collaborative and fiduciary skills to enable further implications.

Louis MacNeice, writing about Lawrence's late poems on the theme of death, notes that the English writer 'could not disentangle the purposes of poetry and life'.[6] This suggests that he couldn't – and perhaps he wouldn't have wanted to – separate and then attempt to balance the claims of internal structure or aesthetic order and those of external reference, which, according to such a poetic theory, would then be coordinated with it through that very balance. By such means, as I will further explore here, poems about money may simultaneously find themselves under its spell, such a spell as would threaten their 'vitality' in Lawrence's sense, but also capable of offering for their readers a force counteractive of money's ill effects. Lawrence's poem, though, situates itself, by means of its hectoring voice, beyond any context where its authority to speak can be legitimized by a process of collaborative vitality-exchange (whereby the reader, energizing the poem, is revitalized in return), a process coextensive with its reading.

W. H. Auden, also writing of these late poems, saw Lawrence as one who 'had no firsthand knowledge of all those involuntary relationships created by social, economic and political necessity', and, he concludes, it 'was inevitable, therefore, that when he tried to lay down the law about social and political matters, money, machinery etc., he could only be negative and moralistic'.[7] Lawrence's exile from those involuntary relationships (though he still had to deal with agents and publishers) directly influences the style of 'Money-Madness'. It is not 'a very lovely song of one that hath a pleasant voice', as the prophet Ezekiel might have put it.[8] This poem, in its plain assertiveness, which Auden in effect calls laying 'down the law', renounces almost all conventions of poetic form, especially of evoked circumstance, or implied speech-context – as if it were enacting its very detachment from involuntary relationships, as if these were, as a result of the money-madness, equivalents (because ubiquitously infected) of the monetary system that has perverted and maddened everyone.

Lawrence's solution is simple: we must, as a further poem's title has it, 'Kill Money', and in its conclusion it affirms:

> We must have the courage of mutual trust.
> We must have the modesty of simple living.

---

[6] Louis MacNeice, *The Poetry of W. B. Yeats* (London: Faber & Faber, 1941; 1967 reprint), 138.

[7] W. H. Auden, *The Dyer's Hand* (London: Faber & Faber, 1963), 293.

[8] Ezekiel 33: 32.

> And the individual must have his house, food and fire all free
> like a bird.[9]

The paradox in this anaphoric biblical parallelism is that 'the courage of mutual trust' is being unilaterally asserted. Equally, by doing this, the poem requires its utterance to go without support from the formal aspects of poems, formal aspects which have been established and promulgated by just such relationships of 'mutual trust', which are inescapably voluntary, aspects which serve as means by which, during the reading process, the authority to speak is conferred by the invested, and focused, energy of the reader. Lawrence's sincerity is indubitable when he demands that 'Bread', 'shelter', and 'fire should be free / to all and anybody, all and anybody, all over the world'. His 'Money-Madness' concludes:

> We must regain our sanity about money
> before we start killing one another about it.
> It's one thing or the other.

But, unfortunately, 'we' can't do what Lawrence urges, because we would have to be outside those very 'involuntary relationships created by social, economic and political necessity', in a world like an improvised poem where contingencies and necessities are not evoked and registered by the formal checking and constraints such as those which condemn us to 'hope's delusive mine' in Samuel Johnson's elegy for Robert Levet. 'Money-Madness' achieves a status like prophecy by voicing requirements of us which, not being performable, sound in the wilderness which is, in part, of the poem's own making, and, as a consequence, we hear the words, but we do them not – and not because we don't want to, but because the poem doesn't evoke or inhabit any space in which it imagines them as being, or able to be, done.

2. Speech acts and uttering money

While exploring Ezra Pound's obsession with the 'toxicology of money', Peter Nicholls observes that 'the economic thought of the late Cantos is much coloured by the emphasis on state control', and he adds the following to underline the state control the poet had in mind while living in Mussolini's Italy during the Second World War:

> It is clear too in his wartime writings that Pound is thinking of
> money not as the form of social relations but as the symbol of

[9] Lawrence, *Complete Poems*, 487.

effective authority (the other alternative for an idealist theory, money as a sign whose value arises from social consensus, is not a view he would entertain).[10]

In the last chapter we saw a number of reasons why this 'other alternative for an idealist theory' should be closed off to Pound, not least because entertaining ideas could not, by that stage in his career, be squared with his conception of a writer's and a poet's authority as a source of wisdom. It was also because his theory of secured value in language and poetry would not allow him to credit trust-based relations with readers in exchanges of language usage – as distinct, that is, from the reader's being obliged to trust the writer ('in Pound we trust', as Richard Sieburth put it). A clue as to how this unavailable alternative might be conceptualized and understood can be found in a later essay by Nicholls where, building on the insights of his book on the subject, he notes Pound's 'desire, increasingly powerful in these last Cantos, to abolish social complexity in the name of some sovereign act of performative utterance'.[11] While a convincing account of the poet's late poetry, and the state of mind motivating it, as equally true of his desire for assumed authority in his own writings and in the political imagination he favoured, Nicholls's remark is slightly misleading about what might be involved in a 'performative utterance' as outlined by the identifier of such speech acts, the philosopher J. L. Austin.

More fully to characterize the situation required for a 'performative utterance' to take place only increases the contradiction in Pound's thinking between the desire for 'some sovereign act' and the 'social complexity' of the performances that the Oxford philosopher of language introduced. In *How to Do Things with Words*, Austin singles out one requirement for a performative utterance to be 'happy' (for it actually to perform what is to be done), which is that the personnel in the situation must be the right ones:

> it is a necessary *part* of it that, say, the person to be the object of the verb 'I order to …' must, by some previous procedure, tacit or verbal, have first constituted the person who is to do the ordering an authority, e. g. by saying 'I promise to do what you order me to do.' This is, of course, *one* of the uncertainties – and a purely general one really – which underlie the debate when we discuss in political theory whether there is or is not or should be a social contract.[12]

---

10 Peter Nicholls, *Ezra Pound: Politics, Economics, and Writing – A Study of* The Cantos (London and Basingstoke: Macmillan, 1984), 149.

11 Peter Nicholls, '"2 doits to a boodle": Reckoning with *Thrones*', *Textual Practice*, vol. 18, no. 2 (2004), 233–49, 240.

12 J. L. Austin, *How to Do Things with Words*, ed. J. O. Urmson and M. Sbisà (Oxford: Oxford University Press, 1975), 28–9.

Geoffrey Hill touches on the issue of a 'previous procedure' for giving authority to 'the person who is to do the ordering' when considering the justice of charging Pound with treason for his Rome Radio broadcasts during the Second World War: 'The word-monger, word-wielder, is brought to judgement "*by his being the person who does* the uttering ... In written utterances (or "inscriptions"), *by his appending his signature*". Our word is our bond.'[13] Pound's self-created predicament, the consequence of contradictions in his poetic and practice in light of his economic theories presented in the previous chapter, partly came about through his attempting to act out the role of the 'unacknowledged legislator' in the time of the breaking of nations, attempting to speak from a position which could not be so constituted, not least because in the war situation that then pertained, there were at least two conflicting social orders in neither of which, though differently, could he be so constituted as such an authority.

This placed him, if he had not placed himself there through the phases of his exiles, in a position of marginalized extremity, attempting to persuade others of his personally intuited beliefs about the politics and economics of his time. However, he had not been, and could not be, constituted as an authority, and his isolation from both sides in the conflict made him particularly vulnerable. His 'tragedy', differently expressed, was in being taken at his word, and taken as at least attempting to be an authority by the FBI. In this curious sense, his country acknowledged him and his ideas as – in those particular circumstances – not a legislator, but an accused traitor, dangerous to the state's well-being. No official 'previous procedure' had taken place. However, the long history of Pound's publishing career might be considered as precisely such a 'procedure' involving his negotiations with various sources of printed authority. Yet, this is not, I think, how he imagined it, for his sense of authority, as Hill tracks it down, came from the authorizing of his 'judicial sentences',[14] and not from a conception of value as deriving from the acceptance and conferring upon him by others of authority based upon their admiration or respect for those 'sentences'. Nor, as we shall see, was Hill himself un-tempted by ideas of value inhering in a writer's self-validating performances.

Wittgenstein may have been intuiting the existence of performative utterances and institutional facts when he wrote: 'Or suppose we were

---

13   Geoffrey Hill, 'Our Word Is Our Bond', *Collected Critical Writings*, ed. Kenneth Haynes (Oxford: Oxford University Press, 2008), 168, citing Austin, *How to Do Things with Words*, 60.

14   'Pound's error was' to 'fancy that poets' "judicial sentences" are, in mysterious actuality, legislative or executive acts.' Ibid. 169. But Pound did not commit an error or made a mistake; his values were complexly, and contradictorily, of a representative piece.

to speak of a something that distinguishes paper money from mere printed slips of paper and gives it its meaning, its life!'[15] Because both are impersonal, money and language link us together; they are aspects of the life we cannot help but share: we understand them as having power over us and as giving us power because, and only because, we live in the part of the world, the area of human activity, where they operate and hold sway. It is a curiosity worth exploring that the verb used for a bank issuing money is 'to utter', as if the declaring of these pieces of paper as money is a form of speech act where the bank does have the prior authority, from an Act of Parliament for instance, to do such uttering, while Parliament's authority is derived, however imperfectly, from our voting its MPs into office. We have thus, tacitly, acceded to the bank's right to issue the notes, which we reinforce by our treating them as money and thus taking up and confirming the claim.[16] This is then the reason why such political and cultural difficulties arise when there is a 'democratic deficit', as with, for only one example, the relationship of the European Central Bank to the populations of the European Union in the wake of the euro crisis, and the debate over whether the governors of national banks should, or should not, be independent of elected governments and parliaments.

3. Sanctioning continuance

Kathleen Raine's 'Worry about Money' takes more account of the ordinarily humiliating contingencies and obligations that we saw inspiring John Davidson in 'Thirty Bob a Week'. Its title indicates a predicament, and a response to it. For Raine in 'Worry about Money' things appear much the same as they were for Ben Jonson[17] some three hundred years before, when begging alms to relieve his besieged state, even down to her appearing to be writing from her bed – though the person who holds the purse strings is not so high a figure as the Chancellor, but the local manager of a high street bank:

> Wearing worry about money like a hair shirt
> I lie down in my bed and wrestle with my angel.

---

[15] Ludwig Wittgenstein, *Zettel*, 2nd edn. ed. G. E. M. Anscombe and G. H. von Wright, trans. G. E. M. Anscombe (Oxford: Blackwell, 1981), section 143, 25.

[16] For Searle's institutional facts and money, see my *Poetry, Poets, Readers: Making Things Happen* (Oxford: Oxford University Press, 2002), 2, and see Searle, *The Construction of Social Reality* (New York: Free Press, 1995), 54–5 and 87–8.

[17] C. H. Sisson also finds himself in bed with a financial problem in 'Money', *In the Trojan Ditch: Collected Poems and Selected Translations* (Cheadle: Carcanet Press, 1974), 138–9.

> My bank-manager could not sanction my continuance for
>   another day
> But life itself wakes me each morning, and love
>
> Urges me to give although I have no money
> In the bank at this moment, and ought properly
>
> To cease to exist in a world where poverty
> Is a shameful and ridiculous offence.
>
> Having no one to advise me, I open the Bible
> And shut my eyes and put my finger on a text
>
> And read that the widow with the young son
> Must give first to the prophetic genius
> From the little there is in the bin of flour and the cruse of oil.[18]

The poem itself has a distinctly precarious existence. I first came across it in *The Faber Book of Twentieth-Century Verse*, edited by John Heath-Stubbs and David Wright, and published in 1953. The anthology text has variant punctuation and has made three verses out of its five distychs and a tercet. Presumably the poet authorized this variant on its printing four years before. The fact that it exists in these two states might also indicate some anxiety about it on the part of the poet, for it does not appear in *The Collected Poems of Kathleen Raine*, which was first published only three years later, nor in her *Collected Poems 1935–1980*. One conclusion to be drawn from these bibliographical facts might be that she came to think that the poem too 'ought properly / To cease to exist in a world where poverty / Is a shameful and ridiculous offence.' In such a world, after all, it might be as equally shameful and ridiculous to publish the fact that you are in such straits.

'Worry about Money' separates the necessary continuance of life and exchange of love from the continuance sanctioned by financial security, then preferentially advances the value of the former against that of the latter. This may be a version of the prophetic attitude that was seen in Lawrence's 'Money-Madness'. However, in the poem's first four verses, it is itself caught up in the contingencies signalled by 'My bank-manager' and his language that is encrusted onto the shape of her poem: 'sanction my continuance' or 'a shameful and ridiculous offence.' She prefers the values of 'life' and 'love' by varying the pace of her lines, end-stopping or

---

[18] Kathleen Raine, *The Pythoness and Other Poems* (London: Hamish Hamilton, 1949), 24, and see *The Faber Book of Twentieth-Century Verse,* ed. John Heath-Stubbs and David Wright (London: Faber & Faber, 1953), 276.

running on. Line 3 ('My bank-manager could not sanction my continuance for another day') partially withholds its own 'continuance' with the line end, whereas the turn to the next line with 'and love / Urges' leaves us momentarily to dwell on the suspended word 'love', as if it were – to adopt terms of Paul Valéry's which will be further explored in the next chapter – on the edge of or itself 'an enigma, an abyss'.[19] But then the poem moves us through to the full stop at the end of line 8, where a reader can feel distinctly out of breath and money. In hurrying on, it does feel as if even momentarily contemplating that poverty may be 'a shameful and ridiculous offence', or that 'properly' can be taken to mean 'really' as well as 'according with conventions of propriety'. While this running on emphasizes the side of the case that Raine prefers, her poem takes the words at such a speed that they may be felt to tumble in value and grow insipid.

Yet the poem's pace, in effecting a fairly rapid continuance, works equally to pass over those two highly valued words 'life' and 'love'. Its breathless haste suggests that these terms too must be hurried over as quickly as those of the bank-manager and his idiom, lest we pause upon them (taking them out of circulation for a moment) and find a sudden failure of confidence in what they do indicate and mean. These words might then be attacked by the bank-managerial attitude and his idiom, and left, as sentimental assertions, to look for collateral where they can. The fifth and sixth verses find what is intended to be sufficient backing by playing *Sortes Vergilianae* (telling your fortune by random readings from the *Aeneid*), but in this case with scripture, so *Sortes Bibliae*, or the practice of bibliomancy:

> Having no one to advise me, I open the Bible
> And shut my eyes and put my finger on a text
>
> And read that the widow with the young son
> Must give first to the prophetic genius
> From the little there is in the bin of flour and the cruse of oil.

Kathleen Raine's finger fell on 'For thus saith the Lord God of Israel. The barrel of meal shall not waste, neither shall the cruse of oil fail'.[20] This may have been fortunate as far as confidence in the provision by the Christian God is concerned, but not so much for the poem, whose rhythms and lineation grow less definitive. These lines have very little formal life beyond giving a minimal shape to the statements they delineate.

It is as if the assurance of faith and the words of Elijah, the 'prophetic genius', relieve the poet of the need to listen to the support that might be

---

[19] Paul Valéry, 'Poèsie et pensée abstraite', in *The Art of Poetry,* trans. Denis Folliot (Princeton: Princeton University Press, 1958), 55.
[20] İ Kings, 17: 14.

provided by the poem's form. Because this trust in God and the miracle of the widow's cruse takes place elsewhere, beyond the poem, it is as if the work no longer needed to rely upon its techniques, or, for that matter, Hopkins-fashion, to dramatize the embodying of divine action in Creation. In 'Worry about Money' the series of 'and' clauses performs a resistless acceptance of faith in divine providence. The poetic structure's lack of significant shape makes it sound superfluous to that faith beyond the poem. A bohemian unworldliness supported by religious conviction as expressed by a trustingly superstitious recourse to scripture appears to have left both Mammon and poetry, in Keats's senses, somewhere behind.

4. Gambling and nature

John Vernon suggested that 'money becomes an ironic substitute for the discredited spiritual world displaced by matter; it becomes a religion, a god, and it makes one's fortune, in both senses, the way the gods once did.'[21] George Orwell had his fictional poet Gordon Comstock versify along similar lines:

> The lord of all, the money-god,
> Who rules us blood and hand and brain,
> Who gives the roof that stops the wind,
> And, giving, takes away again.[22]

Money appears an all-powerful deity sporting with everyone. For Comstock, money is in direct conflict with poetry, in ways that we have encountered throughout this study. It is, among many other possible sources, William Blake's 'mind-forged manacles' from his 'London' that may be heard rattling again in Orwell's line evoking the money-god who 'binds with chains the poet's wit'.[23] The work of fiction in which this poem appears, *Keep the Aspidistra Flying*, was first published on April 1936, less than seven years after the Wall Street Crash, the same month in which W. H. Auden composed his poem 'Casino', in the middle of a decade in which numerous significant poems about money were composed.

Its final stanza touches on money and divinity with a coolly combative stance:

21 John Vernon, *Money and Fiction: Literary Realism in the Nineteenth and Early Twentieth Centuries* (Ithaca and London: Cornell University Press, 1984), 70.
22 George Orwell, *Keep the Aspidistra Flying: The Complete Works*, vol. 4, ed. Peter Davison (London: Secker & Warburg, 1987), 168.
23 *The Poems of William Blake*, ed. W. H. Stevenson and D. V. Erdman (London: Longmans, 1971), 154, and Orwell, *Keep the Aspidistra Flying*, 168.

As deeper in these hands is grooved their fortune: 'Lucky
Were few, and it is possible that none were loved;
    And what was godlike in this generation
    Was never to be born.'[24]

In 'Casino' fortune's wheel is on the gambling table. Auden's conclusion implies that because we, the gamblers, have made ourselves subject to wheeling and dealing, we cannot begin to shape our destinies. Such a sense of control might be an aspiration to the 'godlike'. Auden's poem suggests that it is not only what strikes the imagination that constitutes poetry, but also what the imagination strikes. It might even harbour the 'godlike' in itself, at least in potential, resisting the mere fluctuations of fortune and fortunes. Thus it might perform a quasi-religious role. Though Matthew Arnold could believe 'More and more mankind will discover that we have to turn to poetry to interpret our life for us, to console us, to sustain us',[25] getting and spending has seemed the natural religion of these times.

As in the case of D. H. Lawrence's late poems about money, a prophet may be one whose relationship to other people in a community is made difficult by his or her assumption of an authority derived either from the prophet's own self, or from a projected source beyond the world – an authority not only unsupported by other speakers and hearers, but which may distinguish itself by being distinct from those others. Ezekiel, who, among many things, attacked the chosen people for practicing usury, has already been cited when he speaks of 'God's judgment upon the mockers of the prophets', then says: 'And, lo, thou *art* unto them as a very lovely song of one that hath a pleasant voice, and can play well on an instrument: for they hear thy words, but they do them not.'[26] Poetry that does not claim the form of prophetic utterance would thus exist in an uncertain position somewhere between 'a very lovely song' and words offered that are to be acted upon, which themselves occasion the performing of actions. For relations between poetry and money bring up, once again, the long-standing difficulty of a poet's role in society and the relation of speech act theory to aesthetic form. In this chapter I have characterized writers who take upon themselves such authority, such self-authorizing performances, as 'prophetic'. Their vocations as 'prophets', ones called to cry in the wilderness, depend upon not being constituted as authorities in advance of their being inspired so to speak.

[24] W. H. Auden, *The English Auden: Poems, Prose, and Dramatic Works, 1927–1939*, ed. Edward Mendelson (London: Faber & Faber, 1977), 165.

[25] Matthew Arnold, 'The Study of Poetry', in *Essays in Criticism*, Second Series (London: Macmillan, 1888), 2.

[26] Ezekiel 33: 32.

W. H. Auden's life had something of the character of Lawrence's as described in his essay from *The Dyer's Hand*. After the age of twenty-six, when he gave up school teaching, Lawrence, a self-employed writer with publishers and an agent, wandered the earth accompanied by his German wife. When Auden wrote 'Casino' in April 1936, he too had – the previous year – given up teaching at Downs School, Colwall, near Malvern. He was travelling and living on earnings derived from his writings. In *Early Auden*, Edward Mendelson makes one passing allusion to this poem. He is discussing 'Certainly our city', which lists eight of Auden's cultural heroes of the moment, two of them relevant to my discussion: there was D. H. Lawrence, who 'revealed the sensations hidden by shame', and Sigmund Freud at his 'candid studies / Of the mind and body of man.' That poem asks 'where are They?',[27] and Mendelson observes:

> The straightforward answer in 1936 would have been: Two out of the eight are alive and at work. But the poem's question is concerned not with the real existence of these men in the world of fact, but with the possibility of heroic healing in the world as Auden understands it. 'Are They dead here?' the last stanza asks. 'Yes,' comes the answer, because for Auden in 1936 redemptive heroism is dead as a possibility, for himself and for everyone else; and, in the words of a poem written at almost the same moment, the only way to be 'godlike in this generation / Was never to be born.'[28]

The critic freely adapts the last lines of 'Casino', making them mean something that, in context, they don't quite say, for Auden's lines indicate that the 'godlike', which was supposed to have existed as a possibility for 'this generation', was never to be born. The critic and editor's sentence, with its illusion of being godlike by deciding not to be born, preserves a sense of will, where Auden's lines, concerned as their title suggests with gambling, suppose its entire loss.

'Casino' is a poem about compulsion, and it comes to further life if read in association with the discussion of gambling in Freud's essay 'Dostoyevsky and Parricide', first published in English translation in *The Realist* (1929). The essay may even be a source for 'Casino' because of the similarity between the opening of Auden's poem ('Only the hands are living; to the wheel attracted') and Freud's description of the story by Stefan Zweig called 'Four-and-Twenty Hours in a Woman's Life':

> In her forty-second year, expecting nothing further of life, she happens, on one of her aimless journeyings, to visit the Rooms at

[27]   W. H. Auden, 'Certainly our city', in *The English Auden*, 165–6.
[28]   Edward Mendelson, *Early Auden* (London: Faber & Faber, 1981), 256.

Monte Carlo. There, among all the remarkable impressions which the place produces, she is soon fascinated by the sight of a pair of hands which seem to betray all the feelings of the unlucky gambler with terrifying sincerity and intensity. The hands belong to a handsome young man – the author, as though intentionally, makes him the same age as the narrator's eldest son – who, after losing everything, leaves the Rooms in the depth of despair, with the evident intentions of ending his hopeless life in the Casino gardens.

The woman seeks to save him, sleeps with him in his hotel, exacts a vow from the young man that he will never play again, and provides him with money to go home. Later, she returns to the Rooms, but she, writes Freud, 'to her horror, sees once more the hands which had first invited her sympathy'. The story ends with her discovery that she has not succeeded in saving the man from suicide. Freud's interpretation, one of his 'candid studies', suggests that the story's invention 'is based fundamentally upon ... a boy's wish that his mother should herself initiate him into sexual life in order to save him from the dreadful injuries of mastur- bation ... The "vice" of masturbation is replaced by the addiction to gambling.'[29]

Auden would also interpret this 'vice', as when in his poem 'Get there if you can ...' from April 1930 he writes in its antepenultimate line: 'Throw the bath-chairs right away, and learn to leave ourselves alone.'[30] Freud's interpretation, that one compulsion replaces another, may account for this association of ideas in Auden's second and third stanzas:

> And as the night takes up the cries of feverish children,
> The cravings of lions in dens, the loves of dons,
>> Gathers them all and remains the night, the
>> Great room is full of their prayers.
>
> To the last feast of isolation, self-invited,
> They flock, and in the rite of disbelief are joined;
>> From numbers all their stars are recreated,
>> The enchanted, the world, the sad.[31]

[29] Sigmund Freud, 'Dostoyevsky and Parricide', in *Art and Literature*, Pelican Library, vol. 14, ed. A. Dickson, trans. James Strachey (Harmondsworth: Penguin Books, 1985), 458–9.

[30] *The English Auden*, 49.

[31] Ibid. 164. For the final version, see W. H. Auden, *Collected Poems,* ed. Edward Mendelson (London: Faber & Faber, 1976, 1991 corrected and reset edn.), 146–7.

The poem's criticism of the gambling compulsion, and its relation to the theme of poetry and money, lies doubly in the conversion of human and spiritual values into 'numbers'. 'From numbers all their stars are recreated' – their fates not in themselves but in their stars, and their stars become the numbers on a roulette wheel. Numbers, too, is a word for versification (Pope, as we saw in 'An Epistle to Dr Arbuthnot', claimed to have 'lisp'd in Numbers, for the Numbers came')[32] – versification being an activity upon which Auden's fortune so largely depended. His poem asserts that the human and spiritual values he defends require a vital relationship with some 'wholly living' other:

> Without, the river flows among the wholly living,
> Quite near their trysts; and the mountains part them; and the bird,
>> Deep in the greens and moistures of summer,
>> Sings towards their work.

These, as 'the wholly living', who must be lovers because they have 'trysts', meet and part in nature, the poem's rivers and mountains, and 'their work' is celebrated by 'the bird, / Deep in the greens and moistures of summer' because this appears to be of a piece with the seasons, landscape, and natural processes. Thus, though Auden, like Lawrence and Pound, seeks to use 'nature' against 'money', in 'Casino' he does it in a form that attempts to engage and enact fiduciary relations with readers, and, by that mean, within the pressures of life's involuntary relations.

In such a light, gambling has two negative aspects: if you win, it involves making money out of nothing, from sheer chance, and not by the sweat of your brow; while, if you lose, it means wasting your resources, not putting your money to use. 'Casino' is thus able to link a sexual diagnosis with an implicit social and political criticism, one made from within the compulsions of 'all those involuntary relationships created by social, economic and political necessity'.[33] The poem represents the frustration of hopes for productive relationship both personally and socially – from a presupposition that social progress depends upon personal psychic health in the reformers. In 'Casino' social and personal states of health are linked by means of money, for, derived from Freud, there is a connection between unprofitable obsession in the form of gambling and a literally life-denying thwarting of sexual relationship: it is precisely because 'To the last feast of isolation, self-invited, / They flock' that 'here no nymph comes naked to the youngest shepherd, / The fountain is deserted, the laurel will not grow'.

---

[32] Alexander Pope, Imitations of Horace *with* An Epistle to Dr Arbuthnot *and* The Epilogue to the Satires, ed. John Butt, Twickenham Edition, vol. 4 (London: Methuen, 1939), 105.

[33] W. H. Auden, *The Dyer's Hand* (London: Faber & Faber, 1963), 293.

At the same time, Auden invites readers to associate the casino with the stock market. This area of human activity and betting is touched upon by poems that bracket Auden's work during the nineteen thirties. 'Consider this and in our time ...' from March 1930 includes:

> Financier, leaving your little room
> Where the money is made but not spent,
> You'll need your typist and your boy no more[34]

In February 1939, composing 'In Memory of W. B. Yeats', he imagined a day 'When the brokers are roaring like beasts on the floor of the Bourse', as the Paris stock market was then called.[35] In 'Casino' the stock market, like the roulette wheel, does not necessarily sustain and enable productive work, such as the bird 'sings towards'. Into this analysis Auden further weaves a religious thread. The casino is full of the gamblers' 'prayers'; they take part in the 'rite of disbelief', praying to win and not believing it when they lose, but also through the very act of secular gambling (in which loss is built in to its structure) they disable Pascal's Wager – and then again in the final stanza:

> As deeper in these hands is grooved their fortune: 'Lucky
> Were few, and it is possible that none were loved;
>   And what was godlike in this generation
>   Was never to be born.'[36]

Luck and fortune figures forms of secular and unreliable providence, because in this context of gambling, self-thwarting, and social frustration, they work as superstitious derelictions of will power and self-determination, of self-regulation. And this free will – in a context inflected with Christian language – is what could be said to make us 'godlike'. Then notice too how the phrase 'it is possible that none were loved' can imply that gamblers were not loved as children, and that they were not able to form love relationships.

Both of these ideas are in Freud's interpretation of the Zweig story. Auden's poem contains many hints and traces of what could be thought a prophetic voice like Lawrence's in 'Money-Madness', but the style of 'Casino' diffuses the persecutory authority of such a voice – a voice clearly audible in earlier works such as 'Consider this and in our time ...' or *The Orators* (the latter being later associated with the authoritarianism of its decade by Auden himself in his foreword to the 1966 reprint). 'Casino'

[34] *The English Auden*, 47.
[35] Ibid. 242.
[36] Ibid. 165.

evokes a tone that is open-eyed, but understanding in a mode derived from psychoanalytic acceptance of human impulses however neurotic, and appears to mourn with them and be tenderly forgiving of the weaknesses it isolates.[37] The quatrain stanza of 'Casino', whose syllabics derive from Horace's *Odes*, does not rhyme strictly, but it has many delicately interlinked sound patterns, which are formed of that fiduciary listening which is an aspect of the imaginative 'contract' whereby readers may find the poet, by a kind of prior arrangement which involves our expectations of poems, in a trustfully constructive relationship with those who are discovering and reaffirming prior arrangements in the reading process.

Each stanza alternates weaker and more strongly stressed syllables at line endings, often producing assonantal chimes on the weak and strong: 'wheel attracted' in line 1 prefigures 'cheek' in line 2. In the second stanza, the last syllable and consonant in line 1's 'children' gives us 'dons', a word also foreshadowed in the internal para-rhyme with 'dens'; in the third stanza 'self-invited' and 'recreated' are almost rhymes themselves, and both prepare for the terminal echo on 'sad'; in the next stanza 'bird' and 'work' share a vowel sound, while 'bird' also part-rhymes with 'shepherd' at the end of the next stanza's first line, a rhyme sound which itself prepares for 'thread'; in the last stanza the penultimate line's 'generation' all but rhymes with the final word 'born'. It is in the following out of such interlinking that a poet establishes the trust required for a reader to move forward in the conviction that these auditory structures are exemplary of the values they promulgate.

'Lucky' and 'loved' have such emblematic presence in the poem because of the familiar saying ('Lucky at cards, unlucky in love', or vice versa). If so, it is a further instance of the art of listening to words in making poetry, which helps bond the poet's activity to the work of communal speech, a bonding which would analogically associate with the complex, ambiguous, and personally involving relationships through money that Auden found absent in Lawrence's writing life, affecting adversely his work, 'those involuntary relationships created by social, economic and political necessity'. Yet in poems such as Auden's 'Casino', the poet's listening and a reader's attention may create a distinctly voluntary relationship of trust out of materials that, in the realm of money, are felt to be damagingly, as well as necessarily, involuntary.

---

[37] On forgiveness in Auden's work, see Lucy McDairmid, *Auden's Apologies for Poetry* (Princeton: Princeton University Press, 1990), 15–45.

5. Inflation and technique

In his elegy for Louis MacNeice called 'The Cave of Making', Auden remembers that basic physical well-being is required to become part of a poet's audience: 'It's heartless to forget about / the under-developed countries, / but a starving ear is as deaf as a suburban optimist's'.[38] While it is hard to contest that the starving are not going to be able to have the leisure to enjoy late Auden, there are many stages of lack which can form steps in the descent from the comfortably off to the destitute, and on those steps there have been, and were, many situations of exile or hardship in which poetry is known to have reassured, revitalized, and comforted. It is also, perhaps, for people in those many stages of struggle or 'just managing', as it is now called, that poetry about money need not be excluded from having some good to offer. In this spirit, Bernard Spencer's poem 'Behaviour of Money',[39] a poem technically and imaginatively embroiled in the economic involuntary, and, by means of poetic rhythm and structure, engaged in the conversion of an emblematic panic into a more positive emotion, offers its distinctive contribution to the subject of this book.

Poetic and reading techniques are forms of recognition for the involuntary conditions of life and, within the space of art, reconfigure them as voluntary relations.[40] The two senses of 'must' in Spencer's 'A Cold Night', the modal for expressing both compulsion and choice, suggest a partial freeing of the will which not only serves to help achieve acceptance of the inevitable, as in elegy, but also encourages and advocates a more humanly fulfilling life 'in' the world, but not merely 'of' its constrictions – such as those senses of humiliation and incapacity that the demands and powers of money may exert. Spencer's 'Behaviour of Money' is imaginatively embroiled in such involuntary constraints, and also in their conversion to a more positive emotion.

First published in *Personal Landscape* in 1943, the poem concerns the rampant inflation that gripped the Egyptian capital's monetary system during the vicissitudes of the Desert campaigns. As a civilian employee at Cairo University, Spencer was paid in the local currency, while military personnel, such as his acquaintance Keith Douglas, were paid in sterling. The poem's form, invented for the occasion, mimics the spiralling instability of the local money. From the suggestion of a personification in the second stanza ('But money changed. Money came jerking roughly alive') Spencer evolves the monstrous figure of the fifth to seventh stanzas. Finally, we

[38] W. H. Auden, *Collected Poems*, 693.
[39] Bernard Spencer, *Complete Poetry, Translations and Selected Prose*, ed. Peter Robinson (Tarset: Bloodaxe Books, 2011), 81–2.
[40] See my *The Sound Sense of Poetry* (Cambridge: Cambridge University Press, 2018), 20–37.

are brought to contemplate 'the sprawled body of Money, dead, stinking, alone!' The second part of the poem is largely composed of questions. Those in stanza 5 to 7 are spoken as the panic of 'the people in bed' who want to know 'What's to become of us?' Yet the final five questions are outside the speech marks, identified with the voice of the poet speaking. They thus inhabit the panicking cries of the people in bed, but turn that voicing into one of curious perplexity:

> Will X contrive to lose the weasel look in his eyes?
> Will the metal go out of the voice of Y? Shall we all turn back
> to men, like Circe's beasts?
> Or die? Or dance in the street the day that the world goes crack?

The poem comes to no conclusions, but is suspended between these proliferating possibilities: one resembling the hopes for human improvement outside corrupted and corrupting monetary systems; another predicting mere anarchy and suffering at the failure of any such structures; and a third, like a revolutionary impulse, dancing at the collapse of an exploitative order. These options economically summarize many of the hopes and fears from the crisis years of the previous decade.

'Behaviour of Money' might be thought to fail to decide between these options out of weakness. Rather, it affirms the possibility of the various outcomes, but to different degrees, and does this with the poem's stanza form, exemplifying what Olivia Manning meant when she affirmed in her 1944 essay that 'his command of technique is obvious':[41]

> Money was once well known, like a townhall or the sky
> or a river East and West, and you lived one side or the other;
> Love and Death dealt shocks,
> but for all the money that passed, the wise man knew his brother.
>
> But money changed. Money came jerking roughly alive;
> went battering round the town with a boozy, zigzag tread.
> A clear case for arrest;
> and the crowds milled and killed for the pound notes that he shed.

The stanza is constructed of three alexandrines (lines 1, 2 and 4), the first pair separated from the final one by a trimeter (making up line 3). The series of short third lines work to upset the order of the first pair, by introducing a surprise, or a contrary force, such as: 'Love and Death dealt shocks' or 'A clear case for arrest'. The natural forces of love and death

[41] Olivia Manning, 'Poets in Exile', *Horizon,* no. 10 (October 1944), 277.

upset the pattern of life grown used to, and, as money starts to run out of control in alexandrines that become 'roughly alive' with a 'zigzag tread', something must be done, so the poet attempts to regulate the circulation with the reigned-in line 3. Yet each quatrain's final line reinforces the state of affairs sketched by the first pair of alexandrines. Thus, despite line 3 of stanza 1, 'the wise man knew his brother', and, despite the need to arrest money's course, 'the crowds milled and killed for the pound notes that he shed.'[42]

This pattern is not maintained pedantically, which would be inept, throughout; rather, it remains as a shadowy series of expectations behind the proliferating disturbances, the hectic circulation, and sudden bouts of panic that occur in stanzas 4 to 7. How does this pattern influence the stanza's conclusion? Its form suggests that lines 1, 2, and 4 will accord with each other, while the third lines will differently resist them. 'Shall we turn back / to men, like Circe's beasts?' singles itself out as a particularly desired hope, but one that is surrounded by unlikelihood. The 'metal' and the 'weasel look' may equally worsen. When the world goes 'crack' (a weak-sounding verb) we may well not dance for joy. In the final stanza, the poet's form endorses the hope of line 3, but hedges it around to attenuate its tenuousness. Here too, at variance with earlier stanzas, there is a slant-rhyme patterning from the 'eyes' in line 1 to the 'Y' in line 2, coming to rest on the 'die' in the poem's final line. If the expectations of line-lengths invite us to hope that we will 'turn back / to men', the concealed rhyming warns us to expect the worst. If the banking system collapsed and died, so too might we.

Spencer was on the lookout for rhymes. In his interview with Peter Orr he noted that 'reading by yourself a poem that is unfamiliar to you, you are in fact, through experience, already looking at the shape of it, and in the first few lines you are observing whether there is a rhyme going on or not.'[43] He offers an illustration of how readers come into a promissory and fiduciary relationship with form when reading a poem, a process which begins with granting its speaker a certain tacit authority, to be ratified, or not, in the subsequent experience of the work. Good rhymes involve both luck and judgment: luck that the word exists, and judgment that, once found, they are aptly kept or dropped. It is in the matrix of verbal luck and judgment that relationship can be shifted from one of involuntary, economic necessity, to more preferable states of desired well-being. From Bernard Spencer's forms, a secularly fiduciary echo, adapted from George

---

[42] Elias Canetti explores inflation as a mass psychology phenomenon in *Crowds and Power* (1960; New York: Farrar, Straus & Giroux, 1984), 90 and 183–8.

[43] See 'Interview with Peter Orr', in Spencer, *Complete Poetry, Translations and Selected Prose*, 298.

Herbert's broken then reformed patterns in 'Deniall', as discussed in an earlier chapter, may be heard beneficially between us.[44]

Though Spencer's forms are never as 'tight' as Herbert's and his trust would appear from his poetry, 'with luck lasting', to resemble something nearer chance than providence, still, his rhyming intelligence draws upon memories of the reassurance in a prayer being answered through the forms of poetry, as explored above in discussing redemption – yet in a poetry of highly circumscribed belief which is not prophetic but meditatively sociable in character. In Spencer's 'Behaviour of Money' there are no answers to the panicky and quizzical interrogatives – no answers, that is, except the rhymes. When you rhyme on 'the world goes crack', your congruence of sounds is attempting to make repairs. Such repairs can't change the painful facts of careering money, and Spencer's rhymes might seem no more than the interior decoration in Eliot's criticism of I. A. Richards's remark that poetry 'is capable of saving us' when he adds: 'it is like saying that the wall-paper will save us when the walls have crumbled'.[45] But in bad times we may be grateful for such small mercies.

---

[44] Spencer also recalled in the interview with Peter Orr that, awarded a school prize, he 'was much laughed at for having chosen George Herbert as the book'. Spencer also praised Herbert's 'sense of a tight pattern' in his University of Madrid lecture. See *Complete Poetry, Translations and Selected Prose*, 292.

[45] T. S. Eliot, 'Literature, Science and Dogma', *The Dial*, no. 82 (March 1927), 243. He is reviewing I. A. Richards, *Science and Poetry* (London: Kegan Paul, 1926).

CHAPTER NINE

Circulatory checks and balances

1. Circulation and rhythm

The first poem in J. H. Prynne's *Kitchen Poems* (1968) is called 'The Numbers', a title that again brings together accountancy and poetics, for, as we saw, Pope 'lisp'd in Numbers',[1] and the intersection of these themes is articulated in the following passage of carefully compacted words:

> The politics, therefore, is for one man,
> a question of skin, that he ask
> of his national point no more, in
> this instance, than brevity. The
> rest follows: so long regardful
> of the rule, the decision
> as knowledge and
> above all, trust.
> All too easy it seems with this slip
> into trust if it weren't that silver
> is another brightness, & we know it.[2]

The passage turns around 'this slip / into trust', the line ending performing a moment of moral hazard which it appears to relieve by the rhythmic

---

[1] Alexander Pope, Imitations of Horace *with* An Epistle to Dr Arbuthnot *and* The Epilogue to the Satires, ed. John Butt, Twickenham Edition, vol. 4 (London: Methuen, 1939), 105.

[2] J. H. Prynne, *Kitchen Poems* (London: Cape Golliard, 1968), unpaginated, [7]. For Prynne's contemporaneous reflections on the emergence of exchange value, see 'A Note on Metal' (1968), in J. H. Prynne, *The White Stones* (New York: New York Review Books, 2016), 125–9.

securing at the start of the next line, partly taken away then by the recall of a precious metal, one from which coins were made – though the final phrase of the passage, referring back to 'decision / as knowledge', suggests that our knowing about the brightness of silver, one of the ways currency value was backed, frees us from its travails and lets us see what is 'above all', namely 'trust'. In 'Die a Millionaire (pronounced "diamonds in the air")' he figures the bifurcation of the word along religious and economic axes as 'the richest tradition / of the trust it is possible to have, to repose / in the mysteries' contrasted with the 'perversions which / thrust it *forward*' into a 'vicious grid of expanding prospects / (profits)'.[3] Inclined but unable to repose, it is loath to be thrust forward.

Kitchen Poems is throughout a wrangling with the language of political economy, its fourth poem, 'Sketch for a Financial Theory of the Self', threaded upon the implications in what it might be 'binds us to our unbroken trust':

> The name of that is of course money, and
> the absurd trust in value is the pattern of
> bond and contract and interest – just where
> the names are exactly equivalent to the trust
> given to them.[4]

Though language and lineation here are flatly essayistic, with little technical or lyric added value, most arresting about the writing in 'The Numbers' above are its methods for slowing down the reading process: how, for instance, phrasal units which might run on are separated out into short comma-separated parts, how the poetic line shortens to increase the number of line-end pauses per number of words, as well as their combinatory use to bring reading almost to a stop, as when, for example, at the end of line 4 a definite article is isolated between a full stop and a line ending. Prynne's vigilance regarding the trust given to words, and a resistance to being thrust forward, is compacted into the reading speed of his poem.

'A New Tax on the Counter-Earth', from the same poet's *Brass* (1971), draws together themes of dreaming, landscape, and the politics of the then Conservative prime minister, whose surname happened to be a word for moorland. It too manages reading attention by combining a more flowing lineation and extended phrase-making with abrupt stop-start arrests and releases, as in 'calm. And' and 'reeds, the' below:

---

[3]   Prynne, *Kitchen Poems*, [16].
[4]   Ibid. [23].

> A dream in sepia and eau-de-nil ascends
> from the ground as a great wish for calm. And
> the wish is green in season, hazy like meadow-sweet,
> downy & soft waving among the reeds, the
> cabinet of Mr Heath.[5]

'A New Tax on the Counter-Earth', in which monetary themes are directly addressed, employs a similarly essayistic and discursive style to that used in *Kitchen Poems*, but further draws attention to difficulty in the processes of communicative exchange through its greater evocation, with sardonic undercurrents, of poetic metaphor, allusion, and unattributed citation. Grocer Heath, as he was called in the popular satire of the time, would eventually take the United Kingdom into the Common Market. Here, in such a state of the economy, patriotic feeling identified with national scenery intersects with balance of trade and financial disturbances to ethical attention:

> and instantly the prospect of
> money is solemnized to the great landscape.
> It actually glows like a stream of evening sun,
> value become coinage fixed in the grass crown.
> The moral drive isn't
> quick enough, the greasy rope-trick
> has made payment an edge of rhetoric;
> the conviction of merely being
> right, that has
> marched into the patter of balance.

Here the counter-mimetic structure of the rapid shift down on 'isn't / quick enough' and the satiric rhyme of 'rope-trick' and 'rhetoric' sardonically mock 'the patter of balance' and exemplify interpretive analogies between poetic and economic management of flow. The poem thus discovers how the economics of its moment alter in consciousness relations to the outside world of landscape and nature. Economic disturbance structures the consciousness of the citizen, numbing relations with experience through sleep and dream, while the 'counter-earth' offers a world over against us, like a countering argument, but also a place of exchange, like the counter in a shop:

> It is cash so distraught
> that the limbic mid-brain system has absorbed
> its reflex massage. We move into sleep portioned
> off in the restored liner, and the drowsy body
> is closer to 'nature', the counter-earth.

[5] J. H. Prynne, *Brass* (Lewes: Ferry Press, 1971), 34–5.

The limbic system is the area of the brain where emotions, behaviour, motivations, and long-term memories are processed. The case Prynne advances is that money in crisis – inflationary spirals, for instance – has effected a contrastive escape reflex; and this, in turn, mutes ethical reflection calling its condition a state of nature or peace, though it is an economically managed slumber, ramified in the poem's lulling cadences that enable 'wayward sentiment' to appear to have 'rightness', as for 'cash' to be taken for 'a principle of nature', which the poem concludes:

> And such affection curdles the effort to be just,
> the absolute perception spreads calm into the air
> and the air works like a sea. The horizon is lit
> with the rightness of wayward sentiment, cash
> as a principle of nature. And cheap at the price.

The two flowing three-line sentences are abruptly broken into by a disjointedly conjoined (the full stop followed by 'And') concluding phrase that equivocates along the axis of a colloquial, a sleep-walking, sense of an opportune bargain, and an insinuated literal taking of the same words as saying that what you get has been cheapened and it comes at a high price. This final insertion underlines in its sardonic double sense the critical and desperately disappointed register in which the poem is composed. Its flexible rhythmic and syntactical performance paces out the significance, allowing the symptomatic senses their forward motion, while in the same process pulling them up with countering-structures to resist, by reader alerting, the tax-cost of ethical numbing at this point of exchange.[6]

Prynne's ethical management of reading speed, with invitations to increase attention to single words and brief phrases as units of meaning-burden, relates to the question of 'trust' in that it involves, at the level of the reading experience, not the politics of that 'one man' in 'The Numbers', but that of at least two people – a poet and a reader. The propositions about poetic language and rhythmic movement to be explored here are illustrated in their plainest forms by a quatrain of Swift's from his poem 'The Run upon the Bankers', written in the South Sea Bubble year of 1720:

> Money, the Life-blood of the Nation,
> Corrupts and stagnates in the Veins,

---

6 Prynne's continuing interest in money appears in *Or Scissel* (Bristol: Shearsman Books, 2018), whose title word 'scissel' refers to waste metal left over after a mechanical operation has been performed, especially that left when a coin is cut out of a blank, which goes to waste if it is not remelted (*OED*).

> Unless a proper Circulation
> Its Motion and its Heat maintains.[7]

The first two lines, with their three commas and strong pause after 'stagnates in the Veins', dramatize the risk of a country's being killed by not enough flow and exchange. The answering pair of lines offers the un-pausing movement to its confirming rhymes. Citing a similar use of this metaphor by Turgot, who wrote that the advance and return of capital ought to be called '*the circulation of money*; that useful and productive circulation which enlivens all the work of society, which maintains movement and life in the body politic, and which has with good reason been compared to the circulation of blood in the animal body', a critic has observed:

> Yet it is not just any circulation that keeps the body politic alive, but the advance and return of capitals: circulation, that is, which yields a surplus. For exchange to be a living exchange, one which animates and enlivens the body politic, 'more' capital must come back than was advanced. But how is it possible that the sums can come out like this? How can fair exchange yield a surplus?[8]

He goes on to relate this product of a surplus to Turgot's defence of usury, and to the categorical separation of gift giving and reciprocal return from exchange value in the then emergent political economy.

By the terms of this analogy, the exchanging of cultural capital in the writing and reading of poetry, by means of the circulation of words through the specific formal system of a poem's rhythms, activated by the work of the poet and that of the engaged reader, produces the surplus value, the life in the body politic, as represented by the significance, but also the usefulness in individual lives, of any particular poem. Swift was capable of behaving like a moneyed man in his private life while articulating the landed interest in his writings.[9] His stanza above expresses the fluctuating metaphorical principles that a poem may articulate in its relationship with a reader, and it is the workings of such principles in the rhythmic and semantic structures of poems that I further explore in this chapter. These metaphors are linked to ideas of rhythm and circulation, by which the formally structured reading speed of the poem is in inverse

---

[7] Jonathan Swift, *Poetical Works,* ed. Herbert Davies (Oxford: Oxford University Press, 1967), 192.

[8] Simon Jarvis, *Wordsworth's Philosophic Song* (Cambridge: Cambridge University Press, 2009), 98.

[9] See Colin Nicholson, *Writing and the Rise of Finance: Capital Satires of the Early Eighteenth Century* (Cambridge: Cambridge University Press, 1994), 70–1.

relationship to the significance-bearing heft of the words. Against this proposal is placed the counter-theory that rhythmic inertia in language, however laden with sense, like an effect of hoarding, will effectively reduce significance yield. Such insight draws attention to variations in styles of poetry with regard to the density of their diction and its fluidity, its liquidity of rhythmic movement.[10]

As was argued in the previous chapter, the ways that monetary systems are maintained by collaborative activities in complex relations of trust has crucial implications for poetry, and poetry about money especially, in that there is always the risk that such trust will be misplaced, as can be seen in the economic realm from credit crunches and bursting bubbles, or in the necessity of anti-trust legislation. Waiting to be brought out is the relationship between the 'social consensus' theory of money and its relationship with the accrual of value in poems. That both of these depend upon judgment in social exchanges, and whether these exchanges are gift-like or interest-bearing-loan-like, brings back attention to the 'numbers', the rhythm and meter in poetry's music. This metering, after all, is a means for managing the delivery of significance, and how such creative activity in poems might relate to what central banks do when they indulge, for instance, in acts of 'quantitative easing' will also be at stake. Building on the implications of observations made about poems looked at so far, poems such as those by John Wilkinson, Kathleen Raine, Bernard Spencer, and J. H. Prynne above, I focus now on poetic rhythm in relation to the circulation of money.

2. Managing economies in poems

Discussing Pound's economic interests in the late *Thrones* Cantos, Peter Nicholls reaches his conclusions by reckoning with ways in which vocabulary such as 'numbers', or 'measure' and 'quantity', for instance, used in referring to poetic music and rhythm have applications for the controlling of monetary value. He notes that these late Cantos work 'in smaller units of rhythm and tend to move at a slower, more emphatic pace, stressing the declarative shape of the line and frequently exploiting a heavily marked caesura as a definitional device', adding that he 'will return to this reformulation of the poem's *measure*, a word which lives a rich double life in the pages of *Thrones*.'[11] Explicatory

---

[10] For more on analogies between the rhythms of life, poetry, music, and money, see Georg Simmel, *The Philosophy of Money*, trans. Tom Bottomore and David Frisby from a first draft by Kathe Mengelberg (London: Routledge, 2004), 527–56.

[11] Peter Nicholls, '"2 doits to a boodle": Reckoning with *Thrones*', *Textual Practice*, vol. 18, no. 2 (2004), 234.

matters are extremely complicated, as they will get with Pound's *Cantos*, when Nicholls makes good on his promise, drawing attention to a passage in Canto 97 that 'explores an idea of "prosody" which might offer an exemplary form of "measure", thus, perhaps, retaining the "truth" of perfect equivalence from the monetary ratio but expanding it into a more clearly aesthetic rhythm.'[12] The bristling scare quotes indicate entry into a metaphorical thicket, and underline the risk of losing critical autonomy in so dark a forest.

Nevertheless, Nicholls voices the aspiration that an epic such as this, approaching its Paradise-aspirant end, might exemplify identified ideals of monetary trust and fidelity by means of analogously faithful poetic measures. He finds, rather, that Pound's 'practice of naming and defining in the opening pages of *Thrones* has so far led not at all to what we might think of as a live and moving verse measure, but has shown instead a certain verbal viscosity which is remote indeed from any songlike "prosody".' Pound's attempts to offer examples of monetary and exchange values which are justly fixed and free of speculative fluctuation through 'formulations of identity and equivalence' are found to be 'fundamentally *anti*-prosodic.' Drawing attention to a further monetary-metrical pun, Nicholls concludes that this lays 'to rest any possibility that "quantity" might be an authentic bridging term between verse scansion and money.'[13]

The reason he offers for this conclusion is that Pound's prosody, and perhaps prosody as such for this critic, being an attuning of differences, does not deal in perfect matches of values between terms, but equivalences of representation in which there are indefinable extents of surplus significance provided by verse musicality in excess of any definitional presentation. The compulsion Pound exemplified to define just value by unchangeable fiat stands in contradiction to what had made the poet's techniques so valuable earlier in *The Cantos* and in his life as a poet:

> 'Measure' is indeed the pivotal term here, disclosing the confluence of conceptual *and* formal contradiction in these late Cantos. For while money is 'exclusively determined by quantity', the prosody to which this 'nummulary grammar' is allegedly 'moving' is one which, as we can see from earlier Cantos, has so far been preoccupied with modes of perception and feeling that *cannot* be simply or absolutely defined. This is why in the famous visionary sequences, such as Canto XVII, objects are presented precisely, but in a curious movement of distantiation are somehow withheld, situated at a certain remove: 'Nor bird-cry, nor any noise of wave

12 Ibid. 242.
13 Ibid. 243.

moving', and in one of Pound's favourite locutions we have the 'sand as of malachite' (but not *of* malachite), 'the turf clear as on hills under light' and 'sound: as of the nightingale too far off to be heard'. Clearly realized as this landscape is, it contains something else, something that seems to lie just out of range, something that complicates and perhaps undermines the kind of clarity at which the writing seems to aim.[14]

Significant, as noted earlier, is the reduction of determiners to a minimum in the phrases Nicholls quotes, one of the strategies simultaneously signalling haiku-like precision, and an indefiniteness of implication – a strategy that exemplifies the desire to shape lines at a remove from syntactic collaboration, yet drawing sharper attention to the role of reader interpretation in the delivery of the 'something else' that Nicholls identifies. He further finds in Pound's musicality at its best a 'remainder which escapes predication', and this remainder turns out to be the 'melopoeia', where, as Pound put it, 'the words are charged, *over and above their plain meaning, with some musical property*, which directs the bearing or trend of that meaning.' It is, he continues, 'a force tending often to lull, or distract the reader from the exact sense of the language.' I have argued at length elsewhere that the 'sound' of poetry need not be interpreted in this intelligence-disabling fashion, even if the disabling is presented as being for some poetic good.[15]

Nevertheless, Nicholls's point is a suggestive one in that it underlines how the meaning in poetic numbers, measures, and quantities does not proceed by near tautological definitions in which the terms on the left are exactly equal, and permanently tied, to the terms on the right, but by means of metaphor-like propositions in which the A and B terms are never the same, but rather overlap to some indeterminate, contextually relevant degree. This is how Pound's 'as of' formulations work, offering affinities but not entailing them. This metaphorical dimension to his representations of utopian landscape allows space for a reader's interpretive imagination, and generates transactional 'value' in reader relations in contradistinction to the supposedly fixed values that the poet was attempting, and failing, to assert and champion. Hence, according to Nicholls, the recurrence in these last Cantos of images that reiterate commitments that it is hoped may remain free from exchange value in reader relations:

Related images of enclosure and mirroring are now associated with peace, silence and the uncontentiousness of self-identity, while

---

[14]   Ibid. 244.
[15]   For intelligence disabling in lyric theory, see *The Sound Sense of Poetry* (Cambridge: Cambridge University Press, 2018), 75–97.

'measure' is increasingly a matter of pregnant fixities expressing absolute value. And such fixities, we should note, are inscribed not only as currency ratios but also as ideograms, and, indeed, as writing itself, for in *Thrones* the rhythmic impulse is under steady pressure from a countervailing tendency towards the visual and the static.[16]

On the basis of contrasts between Pound's theories of the image or ideogrammatic method and the role articles play in 'In a Station of the Metro', I have suggested above that this deep contradiction in his poetics had been present from very early, so that at the heart of Pound's fate as a poet lay his tendency not to understand, or not to retain an understanding of, in appropriately accurate terms, the very things that his skill with little words like the articles or those 'as of' phrasings made possible for his poetry.

Nicholls's discussion of these issues in Pound's late work, and his homing in on terms such as 'measure' and 'quantity', as well as his effective 'laying to rest any possibility that "quantity" might be an authentic bridging term between verse scansion and money', also prompt the question whether what is laid to rest here is also buried for all and any poetry. Underscoring the importance of the word 'moving' in Nicholls's discussion of poetic measure, in what follows I explore the posited relationship dwelt on above between the management of value in a currency, and the numbers, measure, and quantities, the circulation of words in a poem and their variable abilities to evoke meaning and value in reader experience.

3. *Fiduciary symbols and circulation*

In discussing Kathleen Raine's 'Worry about Money', I depended on an analogy implied in the poem between the managed speed of the rhythmic movement activating its words and the circulation of money in an economic system. The analogy exploited in discussions such as those attempted above for Raine's or Wilkinson's poems had been elaborated from a speculation of Donald Davie's in his chapter on 'Syntax in English Poetry and in French' from *Articulate Energy* (1955). There, he cites a discrimination that the French poet St.-John Perse wished to see between the two languages when reporting a conversation with André Gide, who had mentioned 'the attraction that an exhaustive study of the English language was beginning to exert over him':

> I, for my part, deplored the denseness of such a concrete language, the excessive richness of its vocabulary and its pleasure in trying

---

[16] Nicholls, '2 doits to a boodle', 244.

to reincarnate the thing itself, as in ideographic writing; whereas French, a more abstract language, which tries to signify rather than represent the meaning, uses words only as fiduciary symbols like coins as values of monetary exchange. English for me was still at the swapping stage.[17]

This is unlikely to be accurate about the differences between the two languages, just as in the chapter on going off the gold standard we saw that Pound's view of Chinese characters need not be the entire truth of languages that use their writing system. Nevertheless, as a report on writers' imaginative investments in the nature of their medium, it is more than instructive. Davie later explicates the reference to 'fiduciary symbols', noting: '"Fiduciary", says the dictionary, "held or given in trust; relating to a trustee." What is in question plainly is a sort of contract entered into tacitly by speaker and hearer, reader and writer; a convention which both observe.'[18] The slide in Davie's vocabulary here from 'contract' to 'convention' indicates the recurrence of a problem explored in the previous chapter, namely that between the prior conferring of authority, as in a signed contract, and the operation of an unwritten, possibly even unspoken, way of proceeding between people, which might be called a 'convention' and, further, the forms of improvised understanding that might be constructed, *ad hoc* and temporarily, for the purposes of coming to such an understanding.[19]

Thus, when Davie invokes 'a sort of contract entered into tacitly by speaker and hearer, reader and writer; a convention which both observe', he might be trying to calibrate the amount of formality relevant to the situation, though with those four entities 'speaker and hearer, reader and writer' there are a number of conflated situations; but in doing so he may

[17] St.-John Perse, 'André Gide: 1909', cited in Donald Davie, *Articulate Energy: An Inquiry into the Syntax of English Poetry* (London: Routledge & Kegan Paul, 1955), 97. For barter, currency, and language, see Nicky Marsh, 'The Cosmopolitan Coin: What Modernists Make of Money', *Modernism / Modernity*, vol. 24, no. 3 (September 2017), 489–90.

[18] Donald Davie, *Articulate Energy*, 101. See Jean-Joseph Goux, *Les monnayeurs du langage* (Paris: Éditions Galilée, 1984) for Gide's engagement with money, and especially, the chapter called 'La monnaie de Mallarmé' (139–58) for a monetary interpretation of this poet's contribution to the Symbolist theory of poetic language, itself developing Walter Benjamin's suggestion that the poet's '*blanc, absence, silence, vide*' is 'the face of a coin whose other side is by no means insignificant' in *Charles Baudelaire: A Lyric Poet in the Era of High Capitalism* (London: New Left Books, 1973), 106.

[19] For improvised understandings between speakers, see Donald Davidson, 'A Nice Derangement of Epitaphs', in *Truth, Language, and History* (Oxford: Oxford University Press, 2005), 97–8.

be confusing matters focused upon that word 'tacitly', for in such circumstances the tacit-ness of the agreement to a convention is likely to contain
possible future misunderstanding and unhappiness. It hardly counts as a
'contract' if entered into tacitly when the participants were not necessarily
in agreement about how the 'conventions' will function. The individual
character of particular works will be advising sensitive readers about how
they are to be taken, how exactly, and according to what values, they are
attempting in their fashion to be 'good'.

Davie was, at that point in his writing career, arguing for an
understanding that particular types of poetry, ones respectful of syntax,
stanza forms, rhythmic and rhyming conventions, were fulfilling their
side of a 'contract' with regard to their imagined reader. The tacit contract
supposed to have been agreed showed in the conventions that the poet
respected. If there is anything in such tacit agreements, they must be
achieved not through accepting on principle certain formal conventions,
but through processes of acquaintance, learning, and familiarity with
the forms and modes of different writers, processes I sketched in the
earlier chapters in *The Sound Sense of Poetry*.[20] Such ideas regarding the
establishment of contractual relationships recall Austin's requirement for
a performative utterance to be 'happy', namely, that the 'person to be
the object of the verb "I order to …" must, by some previous procedure,
tacit or verbal, have first constituted the person who is to do the ordering
an authority'.[21] The way poets can be constituted as having or being an
authority (but not one to order anybody to do anything) won't happen,
though, through prior decision, aesthetic position, fiat, or diktat; rather –
relevantly related to the picture of prior constituting – the ways a poet can
be so constituted will involve a lengthy social process, one that includes
the forms of the poem, but, decisively, not only those, because necessarily
involving the 'uptake' of appropriately engaged readers.[22]

A second point relating to this question of circulation and value derives
from an observation of Paul Valéry's that Davie cites in his essay 'Syntax
and Music':

> you have surely noticed the curious fact that a certain *word* which
> is perfectly clear when you hear or use it in *everyday* speech, and
> which presents no difficulty when caught up in the rapidity of
> an ordinary sentence, becomes mysteriously cumbersome, offers a
> strange resistance, defeats all efforts at definition, the moment you

[20] See *The Sound Sense of Poetry*, 164–87.
[21] J. L. Austin, *How to Do Things with Words*, ed. J. O. Urmson and M. Sbisà
(Oxford: Oxford University Press, 1975), 28–9.
[22] See *The Sound Sense of Poetry*, 1–74.

withdraw it from circulation for separate study and try to find its meaning after taking away its temporary function.

Valéry later gives as example the word *Time* and says that, in isolation, it becomes 'an enigma, an abyss, a sense of mental torment of thought … It is the same with the word *Life* and all the rest.'[23] This observation might be supported by Wittgenstein's noting in *Philosophical Investigations* that for 'a *large* class of cases – though not for all – in which we employ the word "meaning" it can be defined thus: the meaning of a word is its use in the language.'[24] The innumerable sentences that could include the words 'time' and 'life', and what they may be used for, and so mean, will each have its speech rhythm and pitch contour, for a word's use in a language requires it to be stressed and integrated rhythmically, as it will be if articulated by a poet into the more closely focused shapes of a verse structure – and it is this indissoluble connection between a word's contextually determined sound and its meaning that lies behind the analogy of rhythmic movement and currency circulation explored here.

Davie's idea, derived from the French poet, is that the contract, the presupposed trust in reading and writing, involves taking the words 'in the rapidity of an ordinary sentence' and not 'withdrawing them from circulation' – words in which the metaphor guiding this chapter is audible. In poems of a fiduciary or contractual imagination, as we might see it, 'the rapidity of an ordinary sentence', and especially in poetry, is not merely like a cartoon character who can keep running on air if he doesn't look down, where the 'rapidity' is, precisely, a not thinking about what grounds there are for belief in the meaning of this or that word; but it is subject to a continuously monitored variation in pace, placing the appropriate amount of emphasis on words for them to perform fully in the rhythmic, conceptual, and ethical economy of the lines. This fluctuating speed of movement through the words as they are read alters, however infinitesimally, the degree of emphasis being put on the individual word alone, and so on the degree to which it is being taken out of circulation, as, for instance, in the rhyming positions at the end of lines. From this follows the degree to which such words become, in an image that is remarkably

---

23 Donald Davie, *The Poet in the Imaginary Museum*, ed. Barry Alpert (Manchester: Carcanet Press, 1977), 101–2, citing Paul Valéry, 'Poésie et pensée abstraite', in *The Art of Poetry*, trans. Denis Folliot (Princeton: Princeton University Press, 1958), 55.

24 Ludwig Wittgenstein, *Philosophical Investigations*, 3rd edn., trans. G. E. M. Anscombe (Oxford: Blackwell, 2001), 18e. See also J. L. Austin, 'The Meaning of a Word', *Philosophical Papers*, 3rd edn., ed. J. O. Urmson and G. J. Warnock (Oxford: Oxford University Press, 1979), 53–75.

like Baudelaire's for a cliché, 'an enigma, an abyss'. Therefrom, too, emerge the contrary ways in which words can empty of meaning: either by being taken out of circulation, through a fetishized hoarding of dictionary definitions, for instance, or through being passed too quickly, like toxic debt bundles, between mouths, eyes, and ears without memory of historically accrued implications.[25]

The general rule – if there is one – derived from analogies between the words in a sentence and the circulation of money in a system might be this: fall in value is proportional to increase in speed of circulation; but it is inflected by a counter-proposition, that slowness, like the stagnation and corruption in Swift's poem, will also reduce the functioning of language, as money, when hoarded or, as Valéry imagined, taken out of circulation. Thus there are dangers in both poem and economy when its currency is hurried over too quickly, and when dwelt on too slowly. If this is so, it further qualifies the idea of rhythmic 'trust', because the memory of Baudelaire on clichés plays its part too: the more the words are thoughtlessly used, the more they run the risk of descending into spendthrift abysses of meaning loss. The role of the poet is not to write sentences that have the rapidity of ordinary usage, so that we can hurry over them with not a thought for what might be meant by 'time' or 'life', but to modulate the words so that they neither lose meaning through merely assuming that they are understood, nor attempt to take meaning out of circulation in a form of avarice – the equivalent of assuming that value-retention is independent of use. Thus the poet is engaged in a task of adjusting a poem's rhythm so as to negotiate a path between inflationary rapidity and miserly stagnation.

4. Linguistic density, savings, and stagnation

Adrian Stokes's poem 'Weathering' composes on the effects of time upon its 'rich deposits'. Towards its reading, here is a remark Stokes made on the language of poetry:

> It was in fact poets who first of our time employed a bared dualism. Since many words have numerous overtones, it became important to allow to them their varied actuality even while they were pressed into the service of a narrow theme; a consideration that has led to an employment of images forged from juxtaposed, previously

---

[25] For a discussion of money's pace in relation to value, and its effects on the pace of life, see Simmel, *Philosophy of Money*, 453–4.

dissociated parts, of metaphor divorced from simile, an interplay of matter-of-factness with a poetic intent.[26]

Stokes's sense of poetic language attempts to comprehend both the history and the psychopathology of words. In 'Listening to Clichés and Individual Words', he cites many examples of monetary idiom which figure an anal fixation:

> It is similarly unpleasant 'to be cleaned out' of money, very different from being 'hard up' whereby a constipated hold is largely maintained on what we have: when retention becomes impossible, the situation may 'cost a pretty penny'. We spend money at other times 'like water' or 'make a pile', a 'pot of money'. At a nearby target we 'take a pot-shot'. Among the vulgar names for money are 'filthy lucre', 'filthy pelf'.[27]

He concludes that though none of his suggestions about the psychoanalytical significance of clichés is conclusive, nonetheless 'we might welcome in no very distant future a dictionary of some thousands of words and phrases and grammatical mistakes viewed psycho-analytically.'[28] Unlike the conception of language criticized at the opening of Wittgenstein's *Philosophical Investigations*, one based on the idea of words linked securely to things, language's varied actuality includes the sense of words tarnished by use, as if worn flat and grimed when passed from hand to hand. It includes within its alertness to what may be rich ambiguities an awareness of social usage, the effect of time on currency, which can both condense senses in communal speech and hollow them out in forgettings of innumerable kinds.

In 'Weathering', words with numerous overtones cluster around the language of accountancy and the description of the inner world:

> Gorging on the pointed brick
> – Spaces fattening plenteous time –
> Seasons picnic stretched full length.
> Rains are spreading capes.
>
> The years are crumbling vivid stone
> Revetment with their feet.

---

[26] Adrian Stokes, *Reflections on the Nude,* in *The Critical Writings,* 3 vols. (London: Thames & Hudson, 1978), vol. 3, 315.

[27] Adrian Stokes, 'Listening to Clichés and Individual Words', in *A Game That Must Be Lost: Collected Papers* (Cheadle: Carcanet Press, 1973), 17–18.

[28] Ibid. 21.

Why roseate? The Bank dome hoards
All poaching thrusting fingers.

The figures of the balance show
Rich deposits, swollen greed;
While the hours are nosing paint
Silently as fungi feed.[29]

The 'figures' and 'balance' in the third stanza are ones derived from Melanie Klein's internalized parent figures combined with those of financial statements. Accounting for mental states by exploring an assemblage of images modelled upon an infant's relations with a mother is associated with what accountants do when weighing up debits and credits. The integration as whole objects of these figures, again in Kleinian psychoanalytic theory, coincides with the stabilizing, the balancing, of the infant's ego. This process, which Klein called the reparative phase, becomes a form of breaking even, able to detach from both greed and envy, the word 'balance' suggesting an evening out of inequalities in psychic debit and credit, of an infant's developmental losses and gains.

For Stokes, the preliminary attack in making art, the aggressive first stage in creation, is imagined as the infant's gnawing at the nipple, and its destruction of the mother in fantasy: this complex of ideas is then brought into play with the poem's description of the seasons 'gorging', a devouring of the Bank's stone, the architectural 'dome' figuring as an image of the breast. It is certainly not far-fetched in the context of Stokes's thinking to find an overtone in the 'pointed' brickwork, and the question 'Why roseate?', for he wrote of 'the smooth and rough motif that is native to architectural composition, that is perennial for all styles, for every type of building however modest, in terms of the breast and nipple, a theme of contrasting textures that characterizes music also, particularly concerted music.'[30] Music for Stokes was a form of involving that embraced the auditor, a relationship of unity physically reminiscent of infantile identification with the breast-source of Freud's 'oceanic feeling.'

What Stokes came to appreciate in music as such, he also found true of the music of poetry: 'The poem, the sum-total, has the articulation of a physical object, whereas the incantatory element of poetry ranges beyond, ready to interpenetrate, to hypnotize.'[31] This interpenetrating and hypnotic effect is encouraged in poetry by the unequal power of elements

[29] Adrian Stokes, *With All the Views: The Collected Poems* ed. Peter Robinson (Manchester: Carcanet Press, 1981), 94.
[30] Adrian Stokes, *The Invitation in Art*, in *Critical Writings*, vol. 3, 285.
[31] Adrian Stokes, *Michelangelo: A Study in the Nature of Art*, in *Critical Writings*, vol. 3, 11.

in a work, and it may be felt in local invitations to register a loaded complexity: 'The years are crumbling vivid stone / Revetment with their feet.' The first line is a completed semantic unit, and could be closed with a full stop. However, the turn of the enjambment ('stone / Revetment'), aggravated by the capitalization of the first letter of the new line, blurs that momentarily offered prior completeness, the object 'stone revetment' being split across the line-ending, and this draws a reader into the work of delayed comprehension. Likewise the words' varied actualities aid in the process of involvement, so that the metaphorical use in art appreciation of the term 'vivid' allows the unexceptional sense 'lively', while the theme of infantile object-relations projected onto architecture is promoted by 'alive'. This theme is reinforced by 'Revetment' – in English a word whose sense is confined to civil and military engineering, with its architectural sense being 'a facing of stone or other hard material over a less durable substance'. However, it derives this meaning from the French verb 'revêtir' (to clothe, dress), a meaning that distantly suggests the underlying motif of the maternal body. Further, the curious notion of the 'years' having 'feet' (a word that also evokes the largely iambic tread of the poem's lines) recalls a description of the Tempio's carved infants in *Stones of Rimini,* where Stokes writes that the 'putti have a swollen vigour' and 'are never separated from their mother whom they ride and trample, each upon his block.'[32] Such acts of teasing out that readers perform in responding to the poem are engaged by its rhythm and lineation drawing them into it and on.

'Similarly a poem, like a picture, properly appreciated, stands away from us as an object on its own'.[33] Rhyme as a frame for clinching formulation, a having-the-last-word, a closing-off of sense, like Donne's coining hammer-blow, serves to promote the wholeness in a poem, suggesting the internal consistency of a free-standing artwork. The only rhyme in 'Weathering' occurs in the poem's final quatrain:

> The figures of the balance show
> Rich deposits, swollen greed;
> While the hours are nosing paint
> Silently as fungi feed.

Yet 'Weathering' doesn't only act formally; it bears sense, and what Stokes called a 'narrow theme'. In *Smooth and Rough,* he notes that 'it is at first disquieting to concede paramount importance to the issue from the balancing of forces present in infancy.'[34] The ideal of balanced inner figures

---

[32] Adrian Stokes, *Critical Writings,* vol. 1, 271.
[33] Adrian Stokes, *The Invitation in Art,* in *Critical Writings,* vol. 3, 272.
[34] Stokes, *Critical Writings,* vol. 2, 215.

presented in 'Weathering' suggests a relationship to the world at odds with the notion that a healthy bank balance is one as much in credit as possible. The suffered losses and reparative gains of the developing self take as their model economy, as I have suggested, a breaking even. This is because stability is characterized by the recognition of limits – unending loss being as debilitating as omnipotent, unbounded gain. Thus, in line 2 of the stanza quoted above, 'Rich deposits' are matched by 'swollen greed'.

So the equanimity and the evenness of tone in 'Weathering' suggest a limit established and accepted. 'For a moment luxury may satisfy greed and provide the riches that separate us from loneliness'.[35] This sentence from 'The Luxury and Necessity of Painting' in *Three Essays on the Painting of our Time* (1961) shows a distrustful understanding of surfeit, echoing the baby's attack, but it also indicates (by the phrase 'for a moment') the action of weather in conjunction with time. The opening line of 'Weathering' describes the seasons as 'gorging'. By the last stanza this has become a process of 'nosing' and 'feeding'. In that same essay on contemporary painting, Stokes describes the role of the gallery director: 'we are not interested in his business acumen but in his nose.'[36] So the hours nose paint and the fungi feed to give the surfaces they weather a low relief of flaking, cracking, and encrustation. These offer the eye a purchase on the wall, as it were on 'Leonardo's homogeneous wall with adventitious marks',[37] enabling the viewer to be nourished by its presence – both to be involved, and to have otherness reaffirmed. So the poem balances its books, its view of weathering developed from greedy incorporation to coexistence. Matter-of-factness and poetic intent, the Bank of England and a baby at the breast: the ambition of Adrian Stokes's poetry was to enrich with associations the ways in which the everyday world is viewed and understood, while retaining the recognizable lineaments, the familiarity of where we live. Formulating in the detail of everyday life a psychologically founded sense of the human mind in responding to texture and space does strain his bared dualism, but that strain comes in inviting a reader to respond to the suggestion that our earliest developmental needs are embroiled in the management of the national economy, which is to say, the Bank of England's task of maintaining conditions in which a vast debt is serviced on the basis of a trust that it will, at some ever-receding date, eventually be repaid.

[35] Stokes, *Critical Writings*, vol. 3, 145.
[36] Ibid. 153.
[37] Ibid. 148.

5. *Commerce, society, syntax, and rhythm*

Geoffrey Hill's *Mercian Hymns* (1971) figures its involvement with Offa's kingdom in a number of sections through a weighing of his currency, as here in XI: 'Coins handsome as Nero's; of good substance and weight. *Offa Rex* resonant in silver, and the names of the moneyers. They struck with accountable tact.'[38] Donne's idea that 'the whole frame of the Poem is a beating out of a piece of gold, but the last clause is as the impression of the stamp, and that is it that makes it currant'[39] may be behind this analogy in Hill's prose poem between the 'accountable tact' of Offa's coin-minters and that of his own composition, behind which lies a manifestation of power and its wielding: 'Exactness of design was to deter imitation; mutilation if that failed.' The poems too will maintain their uniqueness by exactness of design, and woe betide any imitators or critics who attempt to devalue then by chipping away at their edges or mimicking their strategies. These poems too are 'Exemplary metal, ripe for commerce.' The quality of the manufacture and the precious material from which they are made will render these poems appropriate and ready for circulation within a culture and community, enabling its wealth-creating exchanges: 'Value from a sparse people, scrapers of salt-pans and byres', a phrase in which can be heard the sound of them 'scraping by' and being 'buyers'. Thus what Stokes called the words' 'varied actuality' is brought to bear, often also in 'the service of a narrow theme', and this polysemy contributes through its density of possible reference to the value of the currency, and thus to the poem.

'Of Commerce and Society: Variations on a Theme', from Hill's first collection *For the Unfallen* (1959), 'originally bore an epigraph from [Allen] Tate', as Steven Matthews reminds us, going on to note that for this poet,

> as (depressingly) for Pound, and for Tate, notions of poetic 'value' are never detached from 'intrinsic monetary value'. Tate had associated the invasion of the South from the East of the United States, and New England in particular, with a rampant plutocracy: 'The "message" of modern art at present is that social man is living, without religion, morality or art (without the high form that concentrates all in an organic whole), in a system of money references through which neither artist nor plutocrat can perform as an entire person.' For Hill, this has been the source of a particular fellow-feeling for Tate.[40]

[38] Geoffrey Hill, *Broken Hierarchies: Poems 1952–2012*, ed. Kenneth Haynes (Oxford: Oxford University Press, 2013), 93. The Offa's coins sections are XI–XIII.

[39] *The Sermons of John Donne*, 10 vols., ed. George R. Potter and Evelyn Simpson (Berkeley and Los Angeles: University of California Press, 1953–62), vol. 6, 41.

[40] Steven Matthews, 'Geoffrey Hill's Complex Affinities with American Agrarian

Yet while there appears to have never been such 'intrinsic monetary value', there has evidently been a great desire for stabilities in currency that may adopt such a concept as its ideal. In Pound's poetic theory, as we saw, the fantasy of fixed relations between words, definitions, and things, idealized in his view of how Chinese characters 'retain their value' as images of the world and not symbols for it, stood in a contradictory relationship with his belief that governments could and should issue 'fiat' money for the benefit of natural productivity.

Matthews's parenthetical word 'depressingly' – applied to Pound, but kept away from Hill and Tate – passes delicately over, without effacing, the possibility that the errors of Pound's monetary campaigns, with their related damage to his poetry and life, are not a consequence of his personal illusions about Mussolini, or the authority of poetic facture, but connected to the very illusion of 'intrinsic monetary value'. Yet the implications of Matthews's move from that phrase to 'plutocratic anarchy', words of William Morris's that Hill adopted to discuss post-2008 conditions, indicates another either/or structure, one common to much of the writing we have encountered, namely that the alternative to secured and stabilized values in currency and its relations with other things is a value free-for-all, one in which all values are perpetually shifting and under no control.

Yet while there may be no 'intrinsic monetary value', the abandonment of such an illusory 'good' does not necessarily lead to 'plutocratic anarchy'. It is, after all, fatal to build your resistance to a manifest state of affairs on a conceptualization that does not, and cannot, exist. This is part of what made Pound's project 'depressingly' what it was; and Tate himself, as Matthews shows, was capable of proposing his Southern Agrarian programme as exactly the sort of 'value-in-defeat' that would associate the Confederacy, for Tate and Ransom, with the Royalists in the Civil War, for T. S. Eliot. Poets are particularly prone to using fictionally emblematic politics as a way of promoting their versions of human history. Being thoughtful and useful about poetry and money requires the establishment of some intermediate locations between these all or nothing-at-all options. Accessing and exploring them, I have been looking at how instabilities of value in both words and money may be managed and regulated within the circulating systems upon which in the economies of a poetry and a currency area they depend for their value.

'Of Commerce and Society' focuses both the complex density and depth of individual items of diction, and the role of rhythmic and formal structure and constraint.[41] Hill's writings on poetry and poetic technique

---

Poetry', *The Cambridge Quarterly*, vol. 44, no. 4 (2015), 340. The epigraph was the sestet from the second poem in Allen Tate, 'More Sonnets at Christmas', in Geoffrey Hill, *For the Unfallen: Poems 1952–1958* (London: André Deutsch, 1959), 48.

[41] For the role played by words and their etymologies, see Matthew Sperling, *Visionary Philology: Geoffrey Hill and the Study of Words* (Oxford: Oxford University Press, 2014).

show how his views on value in poetry are linked to formal ethics in the poetic vocation. The first poem, entitled 'The Apostles: Versailles, 1919', takes us back to Keynes and *The Economic Consequences of the Peace*:

> They sat. They stood about.
> They were estranged. The air,
> As water curdles from clear,
> Fleshed the silence. They sat.
>
> They were appalled. The bells
> In hollowed Europe split
> To the gods of coin and salt.
> The sea creaked with worked vessels.[42]

Called 'The Apostles' perhaps because the Great War is figured as an epochal 'sacrifice', analogous with Christ's, so the Big Three at the Paris Peace Conference are disciples in the immediate aftermath of the crucifixion. They knew not what they did. One possible reason can be found in Keynes's treatise, where, in the war's aftermath, the flow and exchange, which depended so on international trade by sea – the commerce and society – had broken down. Keynes was also a member of the Cambridge Apostles, and certainly 'appalled' by the treaty. There is near stasis in the relation of the syntax (very brief, fully stopped sentences) to its three-stress rhythm and near inaudible rhymes.

The deity here, though, may not only be the Christian one, but the polytheism of 'coin and salt' ('salary' derived from the latter). The pun on salt, also employed in *Mercian Hymns* XI, occasions the metaphorical motif upon which these variations are played, namely the sea, deriving from that unstated pun as deployed in Swift's 'The Run upon the Bankers':

> The bold Encroachers on the Deep,
> Gain by Degrees huge Tracts of Land,
> 'Till Neptune with a Gen'ral Sweep
> Turns all again to barren Strand.
>
> The Multitude's Capricious Pranks
> Are said to represent the Seas,
> Breaking the Bankers and the Banks,
> Resume their own when e'er they please.[43]

---

[42] Hill, *Broken Hierarchies*, 28–30 for this and subsequent references to the sequence.
[43] Jonathan Swift, *Poetical Works,* ed. Herbert Davies (Oxford: Oxford University Press, 1967), 192.

The 'banks' pun indicates both dykes against the sea and those speculative 'bold Encroachers on the Deep'. Hill takes up this wordplay more discreetly in the second section, where the European theme of the sequence is sharply focused. In 'The Lowlands of Holland' he associates the Dutch land management and their financial innovation, a connection formulated long before by Andrew Marvell, who also makes that 'banks' pun in 'The Character of Holland': 'To make a bank was a great plot of state; / Invent a shovel and be magistrate.'[44] He notes how religious sectarianism and toleration coincided with the rise of credit systems for a mercantile economy:

> Hence Amsterdam, Turk-Christian-Pagan-Jew,
> Staple of sects and mint of schism grew;
> That bank of conscience, where not one so strange
> Opinion but finds credit, and exchange.[45]

Freedom of conscience provided a context in which the inventions and developments of credit instruments could thrive, and this, in turn, depended on the creating and maintaining of the country's banks – in both senses of that word.

Hill combines such embedded contexts with his awareness that the Dutch, when invaded, would protect themselves and their banking system, by breaking their banks, their dykes against the sea:

> Europe, the much-scarred, much-scoured terrain,
> Its attested liberties, home-produce,
> Labelled and looking up, invites use,
> Stuffed with artistry and substantial gain:
>
> Shrunken, magnified (nest, holocaust)
> Not half innocent and not half undone;
> Profiting from custom: its replete strewn
> Cities such ample monuments to lost
>
> Nations and generations: its cultural
> Or trade skeletons such hand-picked bone:
> Flaws in the best, revised science marks down:
> Witness many devices; the few natural
>
> Corruptions, graftings; witness classic falls
> (The dead subtracted; the greatest resigned);

---

[44] Nigel Smith (ed.), *The Poems of Andrew Marvell* (London: Longmans, 2007), 252.
[45] Ibid. 253.

> Witness earth fertilized, decently drained,
> The sea decent again behind walls.

The rhythmical movement of 'The Lowlands of Holland' is quite other than the stasis noted in the Versailles section. Its sixteen lines form a single sentence made up of incomplete phrases, often further separated by commas, and held together by semicolons and colons. It is also rhymed in the ABBA form, which serves to dramatize a reiterative returning upon itself in slowed evolutions of accreted sense. Criticizing some of Hill's then more recent poems, ones that were to appear in *King Log* (1968), Christopher Ricks pointed to the poetic danger, not of over-rapid circulation and loss of semantic complexity, but stagnation of signification in rhythmic immobility, which he signals with a passing allusion to Keats's urging Shelley in his 16 August 1820 letter to serve Mammon: 'His recent work seems to me too obdurately to have abandoned fluency in its determination to contract, to load every rift'; and Ricks adds that the 'intricacy of syntax, or bullying of it, is becoming an entanglement, and the poems, though they still have force, no longer have so much momentum.'[46]

'The Lowlands of Holland' slows the verse movement down by insistent end-stopping and rhymes – and by jamming together phrases in apposition within a line, where the unfolding of the sense is slower than the unfolding of the verse, very much slower – the movement from one word to the next hesitating to near stoppage, and yet pointedly ordered: 'Shrunken, magnified (nest, Holocaust)'. One anthologist had lamented the obduracy of Hill's condensed style, part of which may be explained and justified by suggesting that it was only by drastically slowing down the verse and dwelling on each individual word and phrase that the words could gain their compacted value.[47] But just as Kathleen Raine's poem in effect asks how rapidly a poem can run on before it damages its own linguistic continuance, just so Hill's must raise a question about how slowly a poem can move before it begins to stagnate.

In *Queen Mab*, Shelley had articulated his views on commerce and society in fluidly lofty blank verse, where it is not the stopping, but the liquidity that is the threatening state of affairs: 'Hence commerce springs, the venal interchange / Of all that human art and nature yield', so that 'natural kindness' and 'boundless love' are for ever 'stifled, drained,

---

[46] Christopher Ricks, review of *Preghiere*, *The New Statesman*, vol. 68, no. 1741 (24 July 1964), 123–4. For his sense of this poem's compacted language and punctuation, see 'Geoffrey Hill 1: "The Tongue's Atrocities"', *Force of Poetry* (Oxford: Oxford University Press, 1984), 317.

[47] See the headnote to Hill's poems in Kenneth Allott (ed.), *The Penguin Book of Contemporary Verse 1918–1960* (Harmondsworth: Penguin Books, 1962), 390–3.

and tainted now'.[48] Hill's adoption of Shelley word 'drained' in 'The Lowlands of Holland' figures a similarity and difference in address, for while the earlier poet uses the word to characterize the choked fountain of 'boundless love', for Hill it points, paradoxically, to the fertility to be achieved by flooding, then draining, putting the sea to use behind banks. In the next part, 'The Death of Shelley', again the fragmentary syntax draws unusual attention to individual words by means of disjunctive punctuation: 'Slime; the residues of refined tears; / And, salt-bristled, blown on a drying sea, / The sunned and risen faces.' Hill then suggests the disabling of Shelley's legitimate protests with a mythological analogy: 'Through poisonous baked sea-things Perseus / Goes – clogged sword, clear, aimless mirror – / With nothing to strike at or blind'; and in the second part the relevance to his sequence's theme is reiterated with an architectural-ornament image of money and trade, one such as Stokes would later use in 'Weathering': 'Over the statues, unchanging features / Of commerce and quaint love, soot lies.'

From this poem's 'clogged' density, its flurry of mythological figures, we move to an untitled section that further evokes Hill's lifelong concern with the fate of the Jews in Europe, whose relation to the theme of commerce and society he does not need to spell out in the wake of their role in the poetry and cultural criticism of his predecessors, T. S. Eliot and Ezra Pound. Hill's poem is strangely mute on this prejudicial connection with its theme. Even though, in the words of this section's final line 'At times it seems not common to explain', explanation is what Hill, showing not telling, effectively reserves.[49] The next section, a terse 'Ode on the Loss of the "Titanic"', comparable in its criticism of wealth, opulence, and hubris to Hardy's 'The Convergence of the Twain', alludes too to the biblical account of the money changers in the Temple:

> Thriving against façades the ignorant sea
> Souses our public baths, statues, waste ground:
> Archaic earth-shaker, fresh enemy
> ('The tables of exchange being overturned');
>
> Drowns Babel in upheaval and display;
> Unswerving, as were the admired multitudes
> Silenced from time to time under its sway.
> By all means let us appease the terse gods.

---

[48] Geoffrey Matthews and Kelvin Everest (eds.), *The Poems of Shelley 1804–1817*, vol. 1 (London and New York: Longman, 1989), 312–13.

[49] For a reading, see Ricks, 'Geoffrey Hill 1', *The Force of Poetry*, 288–90.

The relative liquidity of these lines' cadences, the three sentences threaded over their line ends within eight lines, plays its oceanic part in the continuing theme of human hubris by enacting Christ's fatal but also fortunate (for the Christian redemption) loss of temper in the Temple at Jerusalem.

The sequence concludes with 'Homage to Henry James', called 'The Martyrdom of Saint Sebastian', which, as the poem notes, is a 'grotesque situation, / But priceless, and harmless to the nation.' Reflecting on the Marshall Plan and the rebuilding of Europe with American economic help, it performs a return from destruction similar to that evoked in 'The Lowlands of Holland', but one Hill had lived through himself. Although 'Well-stocked with foods, / Enlarged and deep-oiled, America / Detects music', the American dream, as it had in 1919, is compromised in the specificities of the old continent's historical conflicts: 'Europe muddles her dreaming, is loud / And critical beneath the varied domes / Resonant with tribute and with commerce.' Hill's compacting conclusion combines echoes from 'la musique avant toute chose' of Verlaine's 'Art poétique' with his 'Parsifal' where 'ces voix d'enfants' are 'chantant dans la coupole',[50] the latter phrase connected to the City of London through its citation as line 202 of 'The Fire Sermon' in *The Waste Land*, and thus to financial architecture in such domes as the Bank of England's that focused the economic and psychoanalytic themes in Stokes's poem.

Matthews further notes that the poet's early affinity with the Southern Agrarians 'may have prompted Hill's effort to reassert the importance of Tate and Ransom through the Oxford lectures, at a time when he has felt responsibility to comment both in prose and poetry upon the 2008 world crisis in the banking system.'[51] His concern with poetry and money extends over sixty years, from *For the Unfallen* (1959) to his posthumous volume *The Book of Baruch by the Gnostic Justin* (2019). There Hill employs a form of internally rhymed prose line to combine a fluidity of movement with gravely laden diction: 'What is a "fiduciary symbol" to make us tremble?' he asks, or 'When you say "old solid money", what exactly do you mean?' 'I mean intrinsic value coin,' he replies, 'such as the cartwheel tuppence of seventeen ninety-seven'. Hill reiterates his faith in 'Intrinsic value'[52] which 'is as tenuous and wiry as a bit of great verse', and says that the 'discourtesy of history is like the debasement of money' or that '"Turbo-capitalism" encourages fatalism' and 'Futures' is 'a term of

---

50 Paul Verlaine, 'Art poétique' and 'Parsifal', *Oeuvres poétiques*, ed. Jacques Robichez (Paris: Garnier, 1969), 261 and 381.

51 Matthews, 'Geoffrey Hill's Complex Affinities', 340.

52 For an account of Hill's struggle with 'intrinsic value' and its consequences for his aesthetics and his poetry, see my 'Contemporary Poetry and Value', in *The Oxford Handbook of Contemporary British & Irish Poetry*, ed. Peter Robinson (Oxford: Oxford University Press, 2013), 727–47.

hypothetical values, cash-sutures.'[53] The rhymes haver between sound and hollow on their tenuously beaten syntactic wires.

The adjustment of a poem's rapidity in relation to the variable values of its words' senses is an accommodation into the poetic texture of the contingent truth that our money is not fixed in value, is not absolutely or intrinsically reliable, and that what we imagine it to be worth may turn out to be worthless, like Confederate money, or worth less, when it is devalued, or floats downwards in the currency markets. Yet at the same time, this system of fluctuating values is all we have to furnish our continuance. To make such an accommodation, it is necessary to accept that poetic language too is not stabilized entirely viz-à-viz an object or a dictionary definition, but maintains and sustains its meaningfulness and value in the exchanges of collaborative fiduciary usage.

Yet, at the same time, adjusting the speed of the verse in relation to the quandaries of sense that a naturally ambiguous language bears gives to words such value as notes not unbacked by trust, and yet not so loaded as to be hoarded – for words which circulate too quickly lose value, and words which circulate too slowly do as well, in the one case because they don't mean enough, and in the other because they mean, insufficiently directed, too much. The poem's regulated circulation provides an experience of language to be dwelt on and to be lived on. In such ways, both poetry and money support life. Yet, once again, the metaphor reveals itself and underlines that if these poems are admired for their ability to incorporate and yet resist or counteract involuntary economic forces, then this is to assert that there is a value within economic exchanges that is other than them, and it is to the isolation and definition of this value, to the evaluation of literary value, that I now finally turn.

[53]   Geoffrey Hill, *The Book of Baruch by the Gnostic Justin* (Oxford: Oxford University Press, 2019), 23, 31, 87, 136, 141, and 144.

CHAPTER TEN

Getting value out of money

1. *Money and friendship*

William Matthews's 'Money' includes a number of aphoristic lines, such as his assertion that 'Friendship, too, is a species of money'.[1] Friendships require mutual trust and investments of both time and money, and in so investing people will expect returns, and there may thus be an economy of friendship.[2] Once again, you could think money and economics have penetrated everything. But the consequences I have been following out here underline poetry's similarity not with aureate analogies of the *Golden Treasury* variety, but with the much suspected paper money, with how, like friendship, it is based upon our trust in it, and how, in this respect, it can be considered a prime example of what Searle called an institutional fact. His crucial difference between formal and informal institutional facts might be illustrated by a marriage contract, with its legal and economic consequences, and an agreement to meet made between friends.[3] A great difference between poetry and money, underlined by paper or, now, digital money is that where the officially issued and supported currency is a formal institutional fact, both poetry and friendship are informal ones. This further implies that money *can* and must have a worth other than its face value, and getting that value out of money is the matter for this final chapter.

Barnabe Googe's 'Of Money' reflects upon the reliability of early modern gold-coined money and the fickleness of 'fair weather friends':

---

[1] William Matthews, *Time & Money* (Boston: Houghton Mifflin, 1995), 54.
[2] For an account of Hume's influence on *The Wealth of Nations* in light of his friendship with its author, see Dennis C. Rasmussen, *The Infidel and the Professor: David Hume, Adam Smith, and the Friendship that Shaped Modern Thought* (Princeton: Princeton University Press, 2017), 160–85.
[3] For this distinction's relevance in Christina Rossetti's 'Promises Like Pie-Crust', see *The Sound Sense of Poetry* (Cambridge: Cambridge University Press, 2018), 140–63.

Give money me, take friendship whoso list,
For friends are gone, come once adversity,
When money yet remaineth safe in chest,
That quickly can thee bring from misery.
Fair face show friends, when riches do abound,
Come time of proof, farewell, they must away;
Believe me well, they are not to be found,
If God but send thee once a louring day.
Gold never starts aside, but in distress
Finds ways enough to ease thine heaviness.[4]

By what his editor calls a 'clever reversal of expectation',[5] Googe's emblem poem challenges Matthews's idea that 'Friendship, too, is a species of money', an idea that has to be tacitly entertained (you can rely on your good friends to come to your aid in hard times) for it to be rhymed away. For Googe's are 'fair weather friends' ('If God but send thee once a louring day'), and his poem aligns 'God' and 'Gold' at the beginnings of its antepenultimate and penultimate lines. Its worldliness has the behaviour of friends parallel the actions of a God who sends, as a test of faith *à la* Job, that 'louring day' and then, as in the Parable of the Prodigal Son, the friends reinforce the test and allow the allegory of the return to the father to occur. But in this case, the poet contrastingly recommends keeping money about you so as to obviate the need to return home.

Nor would Robert Frost appear to have agreed with Matthews, for he too made a point of more hard-mindedly recommending that there is a virtue in financial independence. In 'Provide, Provide' it is neither wise nor good to think of relying on others, especially when past our prime:

The witch that came (the withered hag)
To wash the steps with pail and rag,
Was once the beauty Abishag,

The picture pride of Hollywood.
Too many fall from great and good
For you to doubt the likelihood.

If friends are fickle, then so is the one-way projective fantasy-friendship of fame. Frost's triplet rhymes underline that there are no grounds here 'to doubt the likelihood' of what he is asserting in this poem:

[4] Barnabe Googe, *Eclogues, Epitaphs, and Sonnets,* ed. Judith M. Kennedy (Toronto: University of Toronto Press, 1989), 100.
[5] Ibid. 22.

> Die early and avoid the fate.
> Or if predestined to die late,
> Make up your mind to die in state.
>
> Make the whole stock exchange your own!
> If need be occupy a throne,
> Where nobody can call *you* crone.
>
> Some have relied on what they knew;
> Others on being simply true.
> What worked for them might work for you.
>
> No memory of having starred
> Atones for later disregard,
> Or keeps the end from being hard.
>
> Better to go down dignified
> With boughten friendship at your side
> Than none at all. Provide, provide![6]

This might also be an answer to Googe's problem, or the Prodigal Son's: make sure you don't run out of money and, in effect, bribe your friends to stick by your bedside. The degree of irony, the extent to which Frost is voicing a position that he only partially holds, is left open. The fifth stanza promises a glimpse of other possibilities: 'Some have relied on what they knew; / Others on being simply true. / What worked for them might work for you.' However, as Frost famously asserted in 'The Figure a Poem Makes':

> The figure is the same as for love. No one can really hold that the ecstasy should be static and stand still in one place. It begins in delight, it inclines to the impulse, it assumes direction with the first line laid down, it runs a course of lucky events, and ends in a clarification of life – not necessarily a great clarification, such as sects and cults are founded on, but in a momentary stay against confusion.[7]

To put the edge of irony on this, the figure a poem makes *provides* 'a momentary stay against confusion'. Doubtless, Frost provided for himself by earning money from his writings, and spectacularly managed not to end his life in literary oblivion. He read a poem at J. F. Kennedy's inauguration in

---

[6] Robert Frost, *Collected Poems, Prose, and Plays,* ed. Richard Poirier and Mark Richardson (New York: Library of America, 1995), 280.

[7] Ibid. 777.

1961.[8] But in his theory of poetry, which accounts thoroughly and neatly for the shape, structure, direction, and conclusion of 'Provide, Provide', it does appear that if the figure 'is the same as love', then the poet in this poem is peddling values that are not in complete integration.

In this, 'Provide, Provide' might illustrate the opening comments in Marcel Mauss's conclusions to *The Gift*. Having explored the implications of his theme in 'archaic societies', he extends his 'observations to the present day', and notes:

> Much of our everyday morality is concerned with the question of obligation and spontaneity in the gift. It is our good fortune that all is not yet couched in terms of purchase and sale. Things have value which are emotional as well as material; indeed in some cases the values are entirely emotional. Our morality is not solely commercial. We still have people and classes who uphold past customs and we bow to them on special occasions and at certain times of year.[9]

Perhaps what's not quite right about this is its derivation from the anthropology of remote cultures, allowing Katharine Maus to note that the 'alternative to a debased commodity culture seems, in Marx, in Mauss, and in Miss Manners [...] always-already gone'.[10] Its having gone is what Matthews is inclined to emphasize: 'What's wrong with money is what's wrong with love', he notes, and explains: 'it spurns those who need it most for someone / already rolling in it.' What's more, his poem continues:

> If you're rich enough you can be haunted
> by all the dross you ever wanted,
> and if you're poor enough you itch
>
> for money all the time and scratch yourself
> with anger, or, worse, hope.[11]

---

[8] For Frost's inauguration poem 'The Gift Outright' and 'The Paradox of Patronage', see Marjorie Garber, *Patronizing the Arts* (Princeton: Princeton University Press, 2008), 23–31.

[9] Marcel Mauss, *The Gift: Forms and Functions of Exchange in Archaic Societies,* ed. Ian Cunnison (London: Cohen & West, 1969), 63.

[10] Katharine Eisaman Maus, 'Fetish and Poem: Ben Jonson's Dilemma', in Linda Woodbridge (ed.), *Money in the Age of Shakespeare* (New York and Basingstoke: Palgrave Macmillan, 2003), 262. Miss Manners was a *Washington Post* columnist who criticized couples that demand expensive wedding presents or charge admission to their receptions as breaches of etiquette.

[11] Matthews, *Time & Money*, 55.

Yet what this indicates, and *The Gift* can help us think about it, is that we can still get value out of money, in one of that phrase's senses, by identifying what Mauss describes in his conclusion to the book not as 'always-already gone', but as structures still present in contemporary societies that are not monolithically modernized, but heterogeneously made up of conflicting values, survivals felt as presently active, and among them the implications of the 'anger' and 'hope' that Matthews mentions – for these are, surely, the signs that ideas about justice and fairness, which cannot be monetary in origin, are still motivating sensations. So can the values Mauss recognizes in his present day be identified in poetry, and in the ways that this form of life is sustained by values indicated in poetic addresses and dedications? My chapter title, 'Getting value out of money', equivocates between 'making sure that you get value for your money' and 'demonetizing the data'. The proposition it tacitly articulates, and which I explore, is that you can only do the former by, in some sense or to some degree at least, doing the latter.

2. Value in activity

One double-faced value of poems, which we have encountered in various forms throughout this book, has been characterized in conflicts between patronage contexts and those of the marketplace. Discussing Ben Jonson's 'An Elegy', a poem that includes a voyeuristic fetishism among its tacit analogies for the reader-poet relationship, Katharine Maus notes that by 1624, when it was composed, Jonson's 'career as a patronage poet, which had been thriving in the first two decades of the seventeenth century, was seriously endangered by changing court tastes', obliging the poet and playwright to re-enter 'the frankly commercial world of the public playhouse', only to find that 'he had lost his ability to please the multitude', and she concludes:

> The oblique, even tortuous progress of 'An Elegy' records Jonson's simultaneous recoil from, and sense of immersion in, a social universe degraded by commerce but also unthinkable apart from mercantile analogies. The poem's aggression suggests the desperation of a poet who understands that his immediate fortunes, and eventually his literary immortality, depends precariously upon the interpretive kindness of strangers.[12]

---

[12] Katharine Eisaman Maus, 'Fetish and Poem: Ben Jonson's Dilemma', in Linda Woodbridge (ed.), *Money in the Age of Shakespeare* (New York and Basingstoke: Palgrave Macmillan, 2003), 263.

Jonson again finds himself caught between evaluations based upon status claims underwritten by recognition from Maecenas-figures ('An Elegy' begins by comparing himself with Virgil, Horace, and Anacreon) and the fickly fluctuating tastes and favours of courts and marketplaces. Maus had noted that the 'distinction between gift and commodity is as valid, and as unstable, in the twenty-first as it was in the seventeenth century.' It may be true, as she indicates, that the 'alternative to a debased commodity culture seems, in Marx, in Mauss, and in Miss Manners as in Jonson, always-already gone',[13] but the continuing practice of attaching epigraphs and dedications to poems, of addressing friends or lovers, and inscribing books at launches to individual purchasers, suggests that poetry has remained unusually tied to value guarantees promulgated by friendships, coteries, and social support structures, and that these are a likely consequence of its precarious relationship with exchange value, markets, and multitudes.

So if 'the love of money is the root of all evil', what is the love of poetry? This not-very-answerable question returns me, in this final chapter, to contestations of value. Nietzsche in *The Genealogy of Morals* (1887) mocks Kant's idea of the disinterested contemplation of autonomous and function-free art objects by asserting that the earlier philosopher's conception of beauty is centred not in the artist's activity but in the viewer's: '"That which pleases *without interest*", Kant has said, "is beautiful." Without interest! Compare this definition with that offered by a genuine "spectator" and artist – Stendhal, who once described the beautiful as *une promesse de bonheur*.'[14] Value accrues to works of art because we are interested by and in them, because they keep the promise of happiness that they make at first acquaintance. Yet it is rather as if what the poem has been used for cannot be determined until it has been so used, and that its use will inevitably vary with the occasions upon which it is returned to and reread.

This value is, I argue, neither 'intrinsic' nor 'instrumental', not least because each of these much-canvassed possibilities is weakened by the fact that it attempts to give a justification for activity which is other than the actor, other than the values expressed in the acting, that's to say, not in what is done, *its* supposedly intrinsic value, or in the ulterior motive, the intention behind doing it, its purpose in some larger scheme, but in the value expressed in the actual *doing* of it. Consider Frank O'Hara's dilemma about the value of his poetry:

> It is 12:10 in New York and I am wondering
> if I will finish this in time to meet Norman for lunch

---

[13]   Ibid. 262.
[14]   Friedrich Nietzsche, *On the Genealogy of Morals: A Polemic,* trans. Douglas Smith (Oxford: Oxford University Press, 1996), 83.

> ah lunch! I think I am going crazy
> what with my terrible hangover and the weekend coming up
> at excitement-prone Kenneth Koch's
> I wish I were staying in town and working on my poems
> at Joan's studio for a new book by Grove Press
> which they will probably not print
> but it is good to be seven floors up in the dead of night
> wondering whether you are any good or not
> and the only decision you can make is that you did it[15]

But what decision, exactly, is he making, and in what context (and I don't mean 'seven floors up / in the dead of night')? The social obligations of a weekend house party are played off against being able to work at your art, and the costs of that sociality are set against the idea of value, as a social matter – whether Grove Press will publish it or not – and against being evaluated and attempting to internalize those evaluations, prefiguring them, or guarding against them, and then recognizing that you can't, you can only decide that you did it; but then, is it that you did this thing independently of its value, or is that value in the activity a part of the value in your doing it now? Put differently, does the idea of doing it have to have value before you try? Surely it does. This is one of the ways in which an artist is in Stendhal's sense an interested party, and that this interest in poetry sufficient to try and write some already manifests a value.

When 'the only decision you can make is that you did it', you are underlining the idea that in poetry, as in many other human projects, you find yourself in a situation that Empson describes, in a review of John Laird's *Inquiry into Moral Notions,* 'whether or not the values open to us are measurable, we cannot measure them, and it is of much value merely to stand up between the forces to which we are exposed'.[16] This is cited by John Haffenden to explicate 'Value is in Activity':

> Celestial sphere, an acid green canvas hollow,
> His circus that exhibits him, the juggler
> Tosses, an apple that four others follow,
> Nor heeds, not eating it, the central smuggler.
>
> Nor heeds if the core be brown with maggots' raven,
> Dwarf seeds unnavelled a last frost has scolded,

15 'Adieu to Norman, Bon Jour to Joan and Jean-Paul', *The Collected Poems of Frank O'Hara,* ed. Donald Allen (Berkeley and Los Angeles: University of California Press, 1995), 328.
16 Cited in William Empson, *The Complete Poems,* ed. John Haffenden (London: Allen Lane, 2000), 158.

218

Mites that their high narrow echoing cavern
Invites forward, or with close brown pips, green folded.

Some beetles (the tupped females can worm out)
Massed in their halls of knowingly chewed splinter
Eat faster than the treasured fungi sprout
And stave off suffocation until winter.[17]

The circus juggler's performance at the beginning ignores the state of goodness or badness of the apple (symbol of sin, after all) because not eating it. What's the value implied in this activity? Is it merely doing it? Probably not: the juggling entertains in the circus and that depends upon the transactional relationship with the circus audience. Inside the apple you have the maggots working to fulfill the purposes of their own continued existence, and the natural cycle, which is why the seeds and the pips come in. Then the third verse switches to another instance concerning eating, procreation, and so survival. But is he saying that you do the right thing (as it were) even though you don't know what it is, or you do know what it is, but can't measure its goodness?

Because you can't do the latter, you can't be an instrumentalist, a utilitarian, and because the exact quality of the object produced is not the issue but the fact that you can juggle with it, then the intrinsic is not there either. What is left is the value demonstrated in the doing of it, in the activity. I am therefore arguing that the trouble with both the 'intrinsic' and the 'instrumental' is that they alienate the value from the actor. In the judgment of a work of art (as I have been asserting with Richard Wollheim, and not only here),[18] it is the decisions regarding continuing to work and stopping that are primarily with the actor, though they contain the internalized values of the society, its culture and tradition (which are evolving and conflicted, of course) within which the work is done, and they require a response to the made object, which is not the same as the identification of a value, but the finding of value in a process of evaluation.

But, then, how does money come into this 'intrinsic' and 'instrumental' value debate? Can poetry be distinguished from money at precisely this point? No, it can't. The point about this 'value in activity' is that it can be facilitated by money – in fact in our society it needs to be – but money can only prepare the conditions, and you can't use it to buy the result. To

---

[17] Ibid. 11.
[18] See Richard Wollheim, *Art and Its Objects,* 2nd edn. (Cambridge: Cambridge University Press, 1980), 229; and, for its application to the writing and revising of poetry, see my 'Wittgenstein's Aesthetics and Revision', in *Inspiration and Technique: Ancient and Modern Views on Beauty and Art,* ed. John Roe and Michele Stanco (Oxford: Peter Lang, 2007), 261–76.

see this may require distinguishing between artworks in which speculation can take place because they trade on their rarity, and poems, as opposed to rare editions of their printing, that are almost entirely spared from this particular fetish value. The difference with money can then perhaps be defined by precisely the ways in which poetry can't be used, how it has so little to do with the world, although, again, it has to exist *in* the world, as can be seen by its marginal, but real, involvement with the book trade, and the prize circuit. But then think of why 'prizes' for poetry seem so beside the point. It's because the relationship between the value of the prize and the work of producing the poetry seems so relation-less, and this is because prizes require an arbitrary, though 'adjudged', picking out of one thing. Poetry competitions are not a Caucus Race. The prize-giving is given value precisely by the fact that not everyone shall have prizes, and that thinking these awards are an expression of real value is as hollow as thinking that the paintings, whose value evidently fluctuates over time, are 'worth' what they can get at auction on a particular day.

We can see the inescapability of the value issue by reflecting a moment on ways we can use the word 'poetry'. The song called 'Poetry in Motion' in praise of a girl 'walking by my side', or of a football player's abilities as 'poetry' suggests that the word-in-use can function as an indicator of value. But applied descriptively to actual or mere poetry, the two senses are never entirely separated, for you might find yourself having to say 'this *is* poetry, but not very good poetry', because the word on its own is ambiguous between the descriptive and the evaluative, implying, though not always meaning, that if you are calling it poetry, you are in effect saying that it is good poetry. There is a parallel here with use of the word 'art' and the way it can't be used value-neutrally.

The word 'poem', though not as sharply marked as 'poetry' with a combination of description and evaluation, is nevertheless likely to need 'good' or 'bad' added to it in use, for perhaps the slightly different reason that merely to identify something as a poem, so as to ask for it to be read with appropriate kinds of attention, for instance, is already to be engaged in a tacit evaluation of it as a poem worthy of such mental and emotional focus and eliciting of meaning-and-affect as in Marianne Moore's 'To a Stream Roller' where she asserts that 'Were not "impersonal judgment in aesthetic / matters, a metaphysical impossibility," you / might fairly achieve / it.'[19] Lawrence Gilman (1878–1939) is the source of the quotation, attributed in Moore's own notes. So I can't help preferring some poems to others, but this can be misleading, because I value poetry too.

---

[19] Marianne Moore, *New Collected Poems,* ed. Heather Cass White (New York: Farrar, Straus & Giroux, 2017), 17.

3. Neither intrinsic nor extrinsic value

'Good criticism', Ivan Gaskell writes, 'is not the discovery of a quality intrinsic to the object that had not previously been noted, but rather an ascription of a quality to the object that is radically extrinsic to it, but which might plausibly be thought to be intrinsic.'[20] A problem with this formulation is suggested by Bernard Williams when discussing the idea that 'keeping one's word … has an *intrinsic value*':

> This immediately raises a very important question: how intrinsic is intrinsic? There is a danger that if trustworthiness (or anything else) is regarded as having an intrinsic value, it will be supposed that there is nothing else to be said about its valuableness – it is good because it is good, and that is all there is to be said about it. If, on the contrary, one gives an account of how its value might relate to other, perhaps more primitive, values and needs, such as securing co-operative activity which is in everyone's interests, one seems to be giving a reductive and instrumentalist account of the value – which shows (it will be said) that it is not really an intrinsic value at all.[21]

Williams understandably wants to resist such a knock-down reductive argument and suggests that, rather, we want 'some insight into these values, some account of their relations to other things which we know that we need and value, but an insight' that 'does not reduce them to the merely instrumental.'[22] I have already suggested the difference between something being of use and having instrumental value. Now there are three factors to intrinsic value in relation to appreciation of art objects such as poems: the first is whether these values are strictly intrinsic to the objects, the second is whether the intrinsic value is compromised at all if perceived by an interested perceiver, and the third is the added value, self-protective by being non-relational, claimed by asserting that a value is intrinsic.

Williams's comments above appear to dismantle the extreme purity in each of these, even while intending to preserve what is felt to be valuable in the intrinsic claim: they point out how unhelpfully tautological it is to assert that something is good because it's good; they assume that a subject will be making evaluative judgments (about whether something is intrinsic, for instance); and he proposes to protect the intrinsic worth of something

[20] Ivan Gaskell, *Vermeer's Wager: Speculations on Art History, Theory and Art Museums* (London Reaktion Books, 2000), 218.
[21] Bernard Williams, *Truth and Truthfulness: An Essay in Genealogy* (Princeton: Princeton University Press, 2002), 90.
[22] Ibid.

by relationally supportive explanations connecting it to other more basic values. All three resist monetary value in that money is an abstract measure, it proposes an equivalence in a price, and this makes possible economic comparison with other priced things, such as the relationship between the cost of buying a poetry book or a hamburger. So the question is – and it is at the heart of what this book has found itself concerned with – whether the loss of an intrinsic claim for poetry and any other non-commercial cultural objects or activities means they must sink or swim in a marketplace context where, given the terms of competition, sink looks the more likely outcome.

Gaskell's provocative observation concerning the relationship in art between the characteristics of the work and those brought to it by, in the case of poems, a reader, leaves these three terms undecided or begged.[23] The language being used to articulate his formulation produces a conventional binary structure: the qualities intrinsic to the work, and those extrinsic to it. Yet are there intrinsic 'qualities', as distinct, for instance, from facts about it that can be listed? It might after all be that 'qualities' (which sound, as in the expression 'quality control', as if evaluation has already taken place) are by their nature, like values, extrinsic in that they have to be brought to bear relevantly on the object of reading or study. Gaskell makes the further point that these 'qualities', which, I am going to take it, have to be, strictly if not radically, extrinsic, can nonetheless 'plausibly be thought to be intrinsic'. What does this plausibility consist in, and is it a more or less benign illusion? And, if an illusion, is it worth having? Perhaps a way forward, and one in line with Williams's suggestions, would be to see if it is possible to do without the idea of values or qualities as either intrinsic or extrinsic. After all, if, with me, you feel inclined to say that no values or qualities can be, strictly speaking, intrinsic (in that they have to be thought to be there), then it is not that the values and qualities can then continue to be called 'extrinsic' – because the other term is not available to make the contrast. Attributed values and qualities, as all must be in this account, may then be judged to be 'appropriate' or 'relevant' and can match their objects 'accurately', 'faithfully', or 'convincingly'. In such a light, I will be enabled, then, to see what you mean, even if, for me, your attributions of value are not, finally, decisive.

Gaskell's comment is helpful, though, in identifying a theory of value that accepts value as inescapably 'extrinsic' to the object to which it is applied,

---

[23] Gaskell's observation and my reflections on it are irreducibly contentious. For accounts of 'intrinsic' or 'essentialist' positions left to one side here, see Malcolm Budd, *Values in Art: Pictures, Poetry and Music* (London: Allen Lane, 1995), 4–8, and Peter Lamarque, *Work and Object: Explorations in the Metaphysics of Art* (Oxford: Oxford University Press, 2010), 99–121. For intrinsic value and doing something 'for its own sake', see Helen Small, *The Value of the Humanities* (Oxford: Oxford University Press, 2013), Chapter 5, 151–73.

and which nonetheless has a sense of how this said-to-be-extrinsic value can be felt appropriately to adhere to the object. Yet if we wonder about the content of 'appropriately' here, we can sense that Gaskell's formula would fail to discriminate between being deluded into thinking that the values are there in the object, and feeling that the values are fitting to the object and its uses. The values need not be thought or felt to be intrinsic, as if you were trying to trick another reader into seeing them there, but as appropriate to the object, fitting with it. The problem with this, again, is that such ideas of 'fit' require a sense of the object without the value to which it can be added. But what is the object without the value? In art there doesn't seem to be such a thing. Rather there are objects with contested added values, the contests beginning with those values and judgments engaged in the processes of the work's making. Yet again, this appears to say that there are objects that can be perceived without values, to which the values may then be attached; but art objects can't be seen in a value-free state, for if there's no 'value' then no 'art' is being identified.

Rather, what Gaskell calls 'qualities' might be thought of as perceived phenomena which can only be seen because given a certain evaluation (a quality being then a description with value), and in order to see a work of art aright, the evaluation itself has to be contested, or, at the least, contestable. This is to suggest that you can't point something out in an artwork unless you are also, implicitly or explicitly, saying that it's important to note this feature, and that this 'importance' is the minimal evaluation. So even if you want to say that a work of art has 'intrinsic' qualities, you might also be saying that they can only be expressed extrinsically. By means of the ascription of value by a separate agent, characteristics of an art object then become relevantly visible, even if this implies, perhaps incorrectly, that they were already potentially there.

One approach might be to notice that you need to have an extrinsic evaluation to make a salient description, but those other readers who see a poem in the light of the description do not have to accept that evaluation, even if they allow the existence of the salient characteristics picked out by its means. We cannot get a value-free description of an art object, but we can dispute the value imputed to its characteristics in such a description (implying that there are characteristics that can be separated from the evaluation) except that, once again, they can only be separated by an act of counter-evaluation, which is able to make those characteristics differently salient in the alternative description. The 'intrinsic or extrinsic value' debate might then be further clarified by showing how the fact that we can't get descriptions of aesthetic objects without evaluations, and yet that we can contest the values which come with the descriptions, seeming to separate the one from the other, might go to explain the various versions of these conundrums as attempts to fix in a permanent state of affairs, as a correct explanation (value as extrinsic, or as intrinsic or seeming-intrinsic), one of the many and various interdependent stages in a never completed process of communal describing and counter-describing that is the valuing of art objects in a culture.[24]

4. *Value in evaluation*

I began here with interrelations between money and friendship, a theme that had already been encountered in the employment of the Parable of the Talents in Samuel Johnson's poem on his household friend's demise. 'On the Death of Dr Robert Levet' uses, as we saw, its poetic regularity, with those minimal variations, to exemplify the life of what some North American readers might call 'a regular guy', and the poem includes a subtext that concerns what it feels like simultaneously not to fit, or, better, simultaneously to fit (in being a human being), but not in being a fitting sort of person. Johnson had experienced this through the various tics from which he suffered, which are now associated with Tourette syndrome. This is how 'Nor made a pause, nor left a void' serves to express an unusual range of implied thoughts and feelings about the fate of an ordinary life and its value. Yet the value of the poem depends, as I suggested, upon its effecting of a double portrait. Thomas Tyers's *A Biographical Sketch of Dr. Samuel Johnson* (1785) includes the following observations upon the composition of the Levet poem:

> His dependent Levet died suddenly under his roof. He preserved his name from oblivion, by writing an elegiac epitaph for him, which shews that his poetical fire was not extinguished, and is so appropriate, that it could belong to no other person in the world. Johnson said, that the mark of appropriation, was just criticism: his friend was induced to pronounce, that he would not have so good an epitaph written for himself.[25]

The friend is complimenting Johnson on having written a far better epitaph for Levet than he could expect to receive. As Geoffrey Hill put it in another context: 'I have made / an elegy for myself it / is true'.[26] What

[24] For an analysis of Geoffrey Hill's attachment to 'intrinsic value', see my 'Contemporary Poetry and Value', in *The Oxford Handbook of Contemporary British and Irish Poetry,* ed. Peter Robinson (Oxford: Oxford University Press, 2013), 727–47, and for value as neither 'intrinsic' nor 'instrumental', 739–40.
[25] *The Early Biographies of Samuel Johnson*, ed. O. M. Brack, Jr. and Robert E. Kelley (Iowa City: University of Iowa Press, 1974), 84.
[26] Geoffrey Hill, 'September Song', in *Broken Hierarchies: Poems 1952–2012* (Oxford: Oxford University Press, 2013), 44.

Hill concedes, Johnson doesn't even mention. He illustrates a virtuous lack of show in this omission too. This can be illustrated by comparing 'On the Death of Dr Robert Levet' with a work that appears, probably not unconsciously, to echo its opening stanza, a work which is also an exercise in double portraiture, but where the balance between the two portrayals has been disturbed. The result is a poem that, for all its celebrity, does not begin to match the 'just criticism' which makes 'On the Death of Dr Robert Levet' so appropriate a tribute to Johnson's household friend and social comfort.

Here is the quatrain from that very different poem, 'Fare Thee Well', written in March 1816, and in which Lord Byron echoes Johnson's elegy:

> Yet – oh, yet – thyself deceive not –
>   Love may sink by slow decay,
> But by sudden wrench, believe not
>   Hearts can thus be torn away:[27]

Johnson's 'By sudden blasts, or slow decline, / Our social comforts drop away', an observation about the death of those near, is called upon to express attitudes related to changes in conjugal love, contrasting the decline of such feeling in marriage with the precipitate and public crisis in his marital relations. The later poet is also engaging in some complex double portraiture, and thinking about death, too, as his final line indicates: 'More than this I scarce can die'. Yet just as the portrait of his wife, Arabella Millbanke, is so much less a model of appropriateness in Byron's exasperated calculating, so too is the implicit portrait of its author, and the extremity of contrast attempted almost inevitably misfires, not so much dyeing the poet's hand in his material as tarring himself with the brush of his wife's portrayal. This greater extremity in the doubled portraiture is also effected in the greater disturbance of the octosyllabic iambic tetrameter quatrains, a disturbance produced above by the hectic exclamatory insertions of an address to a single living person ('Yet – oh, yet – thyself deceive not'), which intends to be heard by an implicit audience of interested parties. Byron sent the poem to his wife: 'Dearest Bell – I send you the first verses that ever I attempted to write upon you, and perhaps the last that I may ever write at all.'[28] 'Fare Thee Well' is again quite different from Johnson's poem, for 'On

---

[27] Lord Byron, *The Complete Poetical Works*, vol. 3, ed. Jerome J. McGann (Oxford: Oxford University Press, 1981), 381.

[28] This text, with allusion to 'the lover, the lunatic, and the poet' in *A Midsummer Night's Dream*, is described as the 'substance' of the note sent with the poem, as Hobhouse recollected it. See *'So late into the night': Byron's Letters and Journals*, ed. Leslie A. Marchand, vol. 5, 1816–1817 (London: John Murray, 1976), 51–2.

the Death of Dr Robert Levet' has no intimate second-person address, and the portraiture of its subject is only momentarily troubled by that passing inclination to address and rebuke the abstract personification of 'letter'd arrogance', or those other kinds of doctor who illustrate 'chill delay' and 'pride'.

The speed and mode of publication for the two poems may be contrasted. Johnson's was read to friends and acquaintances less than three months after Levet's death. It did not appear in *The Gentleman's Magazine* until some eighteen months later. Byron's poem, also prompted by an event of life, was privately printed by Murray within weeks of its composition, and it was published in newspapers, apparently without the poet's knowledge, at almost the same time as the signing of the marital separation on 21 April 1816.[29] Whatever its addressee Annabella Milbanke thought of the poem, William Wordsworth was not impressed, and wrote to the editor John Scott on 18 April:

> You yourself, appear to me to labour under some delusion as to the merits of Lord B's Poetry, and treat those wretched verses, The farewell, with far too much respect. They are disgusting in sentiment, and in execution contemptible. 'Though my many faults defaced me' etc. Can worse doggrel be written than such a stanza? One verse is commendable, 'All my madness none can know', 'Sine dementia nullus Phoebus'; but what a difference between the amabilis insania of inspiration, and the fiend-like exasperation of these wretched productions.[30]

Here a practitioner engages in describing a poem and a poet in an arena of highly contested value, value which spills over from a poetic performance into an evaluation of the person, one branded with that 'mad, bad, and dangerous to know' tag, taking upon himself the first of these in the lines Wordsworth quotes. Byron is reproved by the more senior poet for mistaking the authentic 'madness' of poetic inspiration for the fiendish madness of what Wordsworth believes is instanced in wretchedly inappropriate verbal behaviour – for 'Fare Thee Well' in being published at the very moment in which the matters it addresses were crossing boundaries between public and private that foreshadow the private life in public of celebrities in contemporary media culture.

---

[29] Fiona MacCarthy comments on the aggravation of public feeling produced by its publication in *Byron: Life and Legend* (London: John Murray, 2002), 273–4; and for financial details of the marriage and divorce settlements, see 230 and 278.

[30] Ernest de Selincourt (ed.), *The Letters of William and Dorothy Wordsworth*, vol. 3, part 2 (1812–1820), 2nd edn. rev. Mary Moorman and Alan G. Gill (Oxford: Oxford University Press, 1970), 304–5.

Wordsworth's letter usefully exemplifies how it is in the nature of art works' evaluations that they be contestable and contested, for the poet challenges Scott's view of Lord B's work; that they depend upon attributing value to performance ('wretched ... disgusting ... contemptible'); and that it is assumed these extremely expressed views do coincide with their object, as, again, in Gaskell's terms above, the radically extrinsic is offered as intrinsic to the work under debate. Yet, at the same time, the intemperateness of Wordsworth's letter underlines the disjunction between evaluative description and object, emphasized by an alternative, implied, positive view of the same 'Fare Thee Well' that Wordsworth is so exasperatedly contesting. Even his concession that one verse is 'commendable' is alighted on only further to damn with praise for its symptomatic concession of 'madness' in the author. What Gaskell describes, then, in his idea of good criticism as an attempt to make the radically extrinsic qualities be taken as intrinsic is the wish to have attributed values manifested in the artwork. Yet for these values to be appreciated, or contested, they need to be distinguishable from the work – so that the reasons for accepting evaluation are themselves appreciated. The illusion of intrinsic values manifested in works is indeed an illusion, a means for discouraging further reflection and activity in defence of what we differently and variously value. Wordsworth's letter is illustrative of how such evaluation simultaneously claims appropriateness in judgment and indicates the distinction between object and value upon which any ascription of quality must take its stand.

The later critic was right to remind us that 'As Johnson says in his prologue to Oliver Goldsmith's *The Good Natured Man* (1768), "social sorrow loses half its pain".'[31] This is a far better comment on the desire to compose poetry about losses than it is about the losses themselves, for if our social comforts have dropped away, how can we lose half the pain by making our sorrows social? We can write about them and share them in art, and the subsequent evaluation of the works will be calibrated in part upon the purposes behind that making public of pain – as Wordsworth's comments on Byron's poem also indicate. Johnson's 'On the Death of Dr Robert Levet' was brought into being and made public for distinctly different reasons to Byron's 'Fare Thee Well'. Yet both Robert Levet and Annabella Millbanke were granted their degrees of poetic immortality, because their behaviour in life and that of their poets in writing was caught up into an arena of self- and other-evaluation that inevitably encounters the projective and introjective applications of values that we experience

---

[31] Cited by Howard D. Weinbrot in 'Johnson's Poetry', *The Cambridge Companion to Samuel Johnson*, ed. Greg Clingham (Cambridge: Cambridge University Press, 1997), 39.

in both these poems. As readers and writers of and on poetry, we are similarly exercised by such a double application of qualities, qualities which are neither intrinsic nor extrinsic, either to the objects of our study and work, or to ourselves in studying and working. Rather, living and working involves a perpetual process of stabilizing and sustaining value in circumstances where there can be no definitive or final establishment of them. Whatever the rights and wrongs of his separation from his wife and baby daughter, Byron may not have been wholly wrong in thinking that – in a way quite unlike that of Johnson's elegy for his domestic friend to which Byron places 'Fare Thee Well' in comparative evaluation by allusion – he too would soon see those 'social comforts drop away' forever.

5. The gift of attention exchanged

That painfully memorably moment in a teaching situation with which I began *Poetry & Money* is relevant again, because, as you'll recall, it was precipitated by my inviting the students to evaluate a short story and, instead of commenting on or describing it to attribute value in relation to qualities in its representation of human relationships, gender, sexual and cultural differences, all these as expressed through a literary style (it was 'Cat in the Rain' by Ernest Hemingway), we went straight to its dismissal on the basis of how much it might cost to buy, and whether the time and energy required to read it would be worth that imagined amount of money – a reductive assessment which then prompted the more drastic pricing of our very existence in that room when talking about such things as a short story. What that first and the subsequent chapters have shown, shown in their pursuit of ways in which poetry has found itself inextricably bound up with money, is that while the art cannot continue without an involvement with its economic conditions, however resistant to them or not, nevertheless it has remained an example of a human implement and activity (one among a great many) that manifests values other than money into which its numbers would have to be converted, into rhythmical numbers, to recall that pun, in order to instance or manifest wealth.

Having begun with a teaching situation in which the financial underpinnings of what was making our activity both possible, and then momentarily not possible, were being brought painfully home, I conclude now by pointing towards what might be required for such an occasion to work well, and how, in light of Marcel Mauss's *The Gift*, it might be possible to see a form of gift exchange continuing to enliven our own money-suffused culture. This is not so much the situation in which we look at a story or a poem by an already distinguished practitioner who is, almost always, not present at the occasion. This is the workshop itself, and requires at least one of the participants to come forward with an example of work – a proto-work of art, as it were – to be presented to the group for evaluation. This, I believe, is an example of such a 'gift' in that it involves a spiritual risk, for the presenter doesn't know in advance how the group will evaluate it, and it is not a 'free gift' because its being presented to the group incurs the implicit (when not explicitly solicited by the teacher) need for a return gift.

This return gift is the assembled students' attention to the work presented. The objection that the requirement of gift exchange nullifies the 'gift' concept is an equivalent of thinking that aesthetic engagement requires a pure disinterestedness.[32] But the students' attention, if appropriately focused and intentioned, is not a tit-for-tat; it does not nullify the original offering unless literally 'returned' by being rejected, because the attention adds further spirit to the original offering. This is a return gift only by constructive criticism, because damning is in effect gift rejection, just as bland praise is its passive acceptance. Because the purpose of this occasion is precisely the enhancement of the student's offering, the other students, whose task it is kindly to report their responses, have to be discouraged from merely liking the piece of would-be art. The reason for this, aside from its near uselessness as regards the eventual self-improvement aimed at, is that it exemplifies the others present as failing sufficiently to risk a valuable – because truly helpful – spiritual gift of their own. For the well-intentioned criticism of the presenting writer's work is, in the risked negativity, an equivalent giving which matches and, as it were, exchanges its gift, as coordinated descriptively with the original offering. Given, then, the risk of spiritual damage on both sides, the establishing of a trusting environment with the good will all round acknowledged and credited is essential, both for the risks to be taken, and the benefits of attending to be received. This reciprocal exchange, in expenses of spiritual energy, is, if properly intentioned, a sharing of kindness.

Such, then, is how a creative writing workshop might best work. The person presenting the work offers a gift to the assembled group, risking self-esteem and spirit in that social situation. They are asking to have the work evaluated, and be given advice about how to improve it. The others in the group are then required in effect to reciprocate with their energy, engagement, and spirit, evaluating, yes, but only with the idea of improving the work, and so, to that extent, adding their spirit to it. The benefit to be drawn from these exchanges calls upon other values, including sincerity, authenticity, honesty, and truthfulness, as well as tempering these values with still others, such as respect for the person whose work is the focus of

---

[32] For whether the existence of 'return gifts' means the term 'gift' is nullified, see Matthew Rowlinson, *Real Money and Romanticism* (Cambridge: Cambridge University Press, 2010), 16–22.

attention. Such free exchanges of values in evaluation during a workshop depend upon the building up of trust between all the practitioners present. So it is not a Shakespearean 'expense of spirit in a waste of shame', though it is situated within earshot of such humiliations and interpersonal disasters; but it is an exchange of spirit and value, in a context where the very transfer of these is one of the qualities to be monitored and enhanced by its practice. And the result, not merely ideally, but ordinarily, is a virtuous circle of mutual improvement not only in the work done, but also in the qualities displayed by the doers of the work.

Now the current term for this response is 'feedback', and to note one use of this term in the distortion of an overloaded amplifier need not necessarily denigrate or damage the reciprocal exchanges I am identifying here. The word 'feedback', sometimes meaning distortion, suggests, in the context of a series of individual responses to a piece of candidate art, that if you go into such a workshop expecting to receive but what you give, then you will always be mistaken, and likely disappointed. What you receive from such a reciprocal exchange is always different, probably sometimes more and sometimes less, than you initially gave. If the original giver responds positively to the reciprocated gifts of the well-intentioned criticism, as I say, this produces a virtuous circle of beneficial call-and-response behaviour. It has the collateral benefit of helping to bond the group, and particularly when, the following week, for two of the contributors these roles will be reversed, since now we have a different person offering the initial gift and last week's receiver of criticism must now offer the like to a fellow student.

In his book on Wordsworth, Simon Jarvis proffers a criticism of Coleridge's 'we receive but what we give' proposal, which Wordsworth naturally associated with 'dejection' because he had encountered it in Coleridge's Ode. The critic then asserts that life cannot be 'a simple shuttling back and forth between mind and nature of the same spiritual capital'.[33] He's right. Yet matters are further complicated in cases involving the relative value of particular poems or oeuvres in the larger economies of literary and poetic traditions. We are far beyond the early-stage decisions about whether candidate workshop writings are poems or not (which is frequently the form that processes of early reception take), and find ourselves accustomed to their acceptance as poetry, but then discover that they do not command secured or timeless values, values which, in any case, may not have other than an ideal existence. Instancing this likely predicament for once highly valued works is a monetary analogy employed to invite what appears a necessary revaluing of Wordsworth's poetic sublimities:

---

[33] Simon Jarvis, *Wordsworth's Philosophic Song* (Cambridge: Cambridge University Press, 2009), 155.

Where do we stand with respect to the infinities, the endlessnesses, the illimitabilities with which Wordsworth is so often concerned? Are they, for us, merely so much devalued currency? Or is it possible that, by trying to distinguish among the precise tenors and weights of their various occurrences – in the city as well as at the summit – we might arrive at a sense of their real value?[34]

Yet their 'real value' may be a further bid to insinuate the intrinsic where contested evaluation is evidently the issue. We are being asked to reconsider this aspect of Wordsworth's legacy. Revaluing such work is a form of what I have been describing as happens in the writing workshop, for to do such revaluing, new qualities, or new ways of seeing familiar qualities, have to be 'brought to the table', as Michael Thompson's *Rubbish Theory* envisaged. The reason why receiving but what we give might be dejecting is that it promises a cycle of depleted capital and declining response (which is what Coleridge's poem is about, as, differently, is his later 'Work without Hope'). Nevertheless, even there, dejection such as this 'would not exert the fascination it does, did it not, however hopelessly, shelter all those hopes which a cost-accountancy of meaning would delete.'[35] The new qualities brought by those investing their time and attention are the reciprocal return gift that can then lift their exchanges beyond receiving what we give into a virtuous circle of surplus towards which we can trustingly work but not speculatively gamble.

Yet if I tried to assert such values as strictly extra-monetary, this would be to attempt to live outside the social structures of exchange, as we saw Auden and MacNeice suggesting that Lawrence had done, ending up with non-transactional fetishes of one kind or another – providing no escape from the vicious circle there. However, Mauss's *The Gift* does suggest how monetary circulations that must underlie educational and other collaboratively creative activities may produce a virtuous circle of human energy exchange, and engage purposeful and socially sanctioned values that are not defined in the diminishing-return *mise-en-abîme* of a money value only. Thus the required monetary component may neither hamper nor hinder those differently valued purposes.

As *Poetry & Money* has acknowledged throughout, this art, and its teaching, cannot exclude money from its exchanges; but it can get value out of money by doing things with it that are beyond any monetary value. The Zurich-based Italian poet Pietro De Marchi, like many others we have encountered here, alights, in his 'Lisbona, Rua Garret', upon a moment in experience where behaviours symbolically confirming the value of a poet,

---

34 Ibid. 133.
35 Ibid. 155.

in this case Fernando Pessoa (who earned a living by managing international correspondence in an import-export company), are associated, most
probably via coffee production and consumption (*A Brasileira* is a café
frequented by Pessoa near the commercial district of Lisbon), with, at its
unexpected close, the price of a book:

> *A Brasileira* is in all of the guidebooks
> and so everybody goes there.
> The poet's statue awaits them
> for the ritual photo.
> There are those who sit beside him, on the bronze seat,
> those who climb onto his crossed legs
> crossing their own legs,
> those who touch his hands, the brim of his hat,
> who throw an arm about his neck.
> There's even one finally who doesn't stop,
> but going by gives him
> three pats on the back.
>
> I read on my flight the next day
> how a paperback book in Brazil
> costs a sixth of the minimum monthly pay.[36]

This final chapter has been grappling with an issue present from the start,
that poetry and money are both ways of attributing value to the world, but
that the kinds of attribution and value, as illustrated by the actions of the
tourists and passersby in De Marchi's poem, are inevitably different, and
themselves differently valued.

Poetry, if it is to exist and continue to exist (for it is not unimaginable,
as Thomas Love Peacock suggest in 'The Four Ages of Poetry', that a state
of society could develop in which it had died out), has to adapt itself,
however independently motivated or produced, to whatever economic
conditions befall. Despite its dependence upon material and labour costs,
upon 'consumer' confidence and market conditions, poetry can be seen to
have benefitted from its minimal material base and consequent smallness of
up-front economic investment. Thus, down the years covered by *Poetry &
Money*, this particular cultural activity has managed, as best it can, to live

---

[36] Pietro De Marchi, *Parabole smorzate e altri versi 1990–1999* (Bellinzona: Edizioni
Casalgrande, 1999), 43. The translation is mine. For discussion of Giorgio
Caproni's observation that 'a perfect restitution' in translating poetry is 'a chimera',
not least 'because of the inevitable usury that the words, like money, suffer in
the exchange', see my *Poetry & Translation: The Art of the Impossible* (Liverpool:
Liverpool University Press, 2010), 61.

with the necessity of money, and has attempted to survive despite countervailing, or amidst unsympathetic, market and monetizing forces, and has thus found ways of existing in all the varied and fluctuating economic conditions that have thus far supervened.

In 'Courage Means Running', responding perhaps to the introduction of uncertainty into conceptualizing supply-and-demand balances through the work on probability in Keynes's *The General Theory of Employment, Interest, and Money* (1936), Empson evoked how now 'the economists raise / Bafflement to a boast we all take as guard'.[37] The Keynesian and Cambridge economist Joan Robinson candidly admitted:

> The economist has to proceed by interpreting the events which happen to be thrown up in the course of history, and there is no generally accepted code of rules for interpreting history. Economics therefore consists of a tangled mass of imperfectly tested hypotheses – about how an economy works, why one economy differs from another, what consequences are to be expected from particular events or particular policies, and so forth.[38]

Yet the mysterious ambiguities and unpredictable happenings of economics are not despaired of in 'Courage Means Running'. They might even be something to make grim jests about – ones such as the joke about a literature professor and an economist discussing the annual chore of preparing examination papers. The former is lamenting having each year to think up a new question on Virginia Woolf's *Three Guineas*, as it might be, to get the same old answers, when the economist interrupts: 'Oh, I don't have that problem: each year I ask the same question, but each year the answer is different.' It is in such economic and monetary realms where the question of what we ought and ought not to do remains unclear, where confidence and trust may have to be credited, and where to act well is to act in the awareness of uncertainty, with all its consequences for others and ourselves, that poetry may yet have some 'essential, / though menial' work still to do.[39]

---

[37] William Empson, *The Complete Poems,* ed. John Haffenden (London: Penguin Books, 2000), 76. Haffenden notes that Keynes's book appeared two months before Empson's poem was first published in May 1936 (339–40).

[38] Joan Robinson, *Exercises in Economic Analysis* (London: Macmillan, 1960), xv–xvi.

[39] Roy Fisher, *Matrix* (London: Fulcrum Press, 1971), 64.

Bibliography

Allott, Kenneth (ed.), *The Penguin Book of Contemporary Verse 1918–1960* (Harmondsworth: Penguin Books, 1962)

Amis, Martin, *Money: A Suicide Note* (London: Jonathan Cape, 1984)

Amis, Martin, *The War against Cliché: Essays and Reviews, 1971–2000* (London: Jonathan Cape, 2001)

Andrewes, Lancelot, *Selected Sermons and Lectures,* ed. Peter McCullough (Oxford: Oxford University Press, 2003)

Arnold, Matthew, *Essays in Criticism*, Second Series (London: Macmillan, 1888)

Auden, W. H., *The Dyer's Hand* (London: Faber & Faber, 1963)

Auden, W. H., *The English Auden: Poems, Essays, and Dramatic Writings, 1927–1939,* ed. Edward Mendelson (London: Faber & Faber, 1977)

Auden, W. H., *Collected Poems,* ed. Edward Mendelson (London: Faber & Faber, 1976, 1991 corrected and reset edn.)

Austin, J. L., *How to Do Things with Words*, ed. J. O. Urmson and M. Sbisà (Oxford: Oxford University Press, 1975)

Austin, J. L., *Philosophical Papers*, 3rd edn., ed. J. O. Urmson and G. J. Warnock (Oxford: Oxford University Press, 1979)

Bacon, Sir Francis, *The Essayes or Counsels, Civill and Morall,* ed. Michael Kiernan (Oxford: Oxford University Press, 1985)

Bagehot, Walter, *Lombard Street: A Description of the Money Market* (1873; Kitchener, Ontario: Batoche Books, 2001)

Bate, Walter Jackson, *Samuel Johnson* (London: Chatto & Windus, 1978)

Bates, Catherine, *On Not Defending Poetry: Defence and Indefensibility in Sidney's Defence of Poetry* (Oxford: Oxford University Press, 2017)

Baudelaire, Charles, *Oeuvres complètes*, 2 vols., ed. Claude Pichois (Paris: Gallimard, 1975)

Bellow, Saul, *Humboldt's Gift* (New York: Viking Press, 1975)

Benjamin, Walter, *Charles Baudelaire: A Lyric Poet in the Era of High Capitalism* (London: New Left Books, 1973)

Bishop, Elizabeth, *One Art: The Selected Letters,* ed. Robert Giroux (New York: Farrar, Straus & Giroux, 1994)

Bishop, Elizabeth, *Edgar Allan Poe & the Juke-box,* ed. Alice Quinn (New York: Farrar, Straus & Giroux, 2006)

Bishop, Elizabeth, *Poems, Prose, and Letters,* ed. Robert Giroux and Lloyd Schwartz (New York: Library of America, 2008)

Biswas, Robindra Kumar, *Arthur Hugh Cloughs: Towards a Reconsideration* (Oxford: Oxford University Press, 1972)

Blocksidge, Martin, *The Banker Poet: The Rise and Fall of Samuel Rogers* (Brighton, Chicago, and Toronto: Sussex Academic Press, 2013)

Bourdieu, Pierre, 'The Forms of Capital', in *Handbook of Theory and Research for the Sociology of Education*, ed. John Richardson (Westport, CT: Greenwood, 1986)

Brack, Jr., O. M., and Kelley, Robert E. (eds.), *The Early Biographies of Samuel Johnson* (Iowa City: University of Iowa Press, 1974)

Brett-Smith, H. F. B., and Jones, C. E. (eds.), *The Works of Thomas Love Peacock,* vol. 7 (London: Constable, 1931)

Brooks, Gwendolyn, *Selected Poems* (New York: Perennial Classics, 1999)

Browning, Robert, *The Poems,* 2 vols., ed. John Pettigrew and Thomas J. Collins (Harmondsworth: Penguin Books, 1981)

Budd, Malcolm, *Values in Art: Pictures, Poetry and Music* (London: Allen Lane, 1995)

Byron, Lord, *The Complete Poetical Works,* 7 vols., ed. Jerome McGann (Oxford: Oxford University Press, 1980–93)

Canetti, Elias, *Crowds and Power* (1960; New York: Farrar, Straus & Giroux, 1984)

Carswell, John, *The South Sea Bubble* (London: Cresset Press, 1961)

Chapin, Chester F., *The Religious Thought of Samuel Johnson* (Ann Arbor: University of Michigan Press, 1968)

Chaucer, Geoffrey, *The Minor Poems,* ed. George B. Pace and Alfred David (Norman: University of Oklahoma Press, 1982)

Cheyette, Bryan, 'Eliot and "Race": Jews, Irish and Blacks', in *A Companion to T. S. Eliot,* ed. David E. Chinitz (Oxford: Wiley-Blackwell, 2009)

Clubbe, John, *Victorian Forerunner: The Later Career of Thomas Hood* (Durham, NC: Duke University Press, 1968)

Clubbe, John (ed.), *Selected Poems of Thomas Hood* (Cambridge, MA: Harvard University Press, 1970)

Connell, Philip, *Romanticism, Economics and the Question of 'Culture'* (Oxford: Oxford University Press, 2005)

Cowper, William, *Poetical Works,* ed. H. S. Milford, 4th edn. with corrections and additions by Norma Russell (London: Oxford University Press, 1967)

Coyle, Beverly, and Filreis, Alan (eds.), *Secretaries of the Moon: The Letters of Wallace Stevens and José Rodríguez Feo* (Durham: Duke University Press, 1986)

Cox, Jeffrey N., *Poetry and Politics in the Cockney School: Keats, Shelley, Hunt and Their Circle* (Cambridge: Cambridge University Press, 1998)

Crosthwaite, Paul, Knight, Peter, and Marsh, Nicky (eds.), *Show Me the Money: The Image of Finance, 1700 to the Present* (Manchester: Manchester University Press, 2014)

Cruickshanks, Eveline, and Erskine-Hill, Howard, *The Atterbury Plot* (Basingstoke: Palgrave Macmillan, 2004)

Davidson, Donald, 'A Nice Derangement of Epitaphs', in *Truth, Language, and History* (Oxford: Oxford University Press, 2005)

Davidson, John, *The Man Forbid and Other Essays*, introduction by Edward J. O'Brien (Boston: Ball Publishing Company, 1910)

Davie, Donald, *Articulate Energy: An Inquiry into the Syntax of English Poetry* (London: Routledge & Kegan Paul, 1955)

Davie, Donald, *The Poet in the Imaginary Museum*, ed. Barry Alpert (Manchester: Carcanet Press, 1977)

De Marchi, Pietro, *Parabole smorzate e altri versi 1990–1999* (Bellinzona: Edizioni Casalgrande, 1999)

De Selincourt, Ernest (ed.), *The Letters of William and Dorothy Wordsworth*, vol. 3, part 2 (1812–20), 2nd edn., rev. Mary Moorman and Alan G. Gill (Oxford: Oxford University Press, 1970)

De Vane, William Clyde, *A Browning Handbook* (New York: Appleton-Century-Crofts, 1955)

Dick, Alexander, *Romanticism and the Gold Standard: Money, Literature, and Economic Debate in Britain 1790–1830* (Basingstoke and New York: Palgrave Macmillan, 2013)

Donaldson, Ian, *Ben Jonson: A Life* (Oxford: Oxford University Press, 2011)

Donne, John, *The Complete English Poems*, ed. A. J. Smith (Harmondsworth: Penguin Books, 1973)

Donovan, Jack, et al. (eds.), *The Poems of Shelley 1819–20*, vol. 3 (London: Longman, 2011)

Douglas, Mary, 'Conclusion: The Prestige of the Games', in *Pindar's Poetry, Patrons and Festivals: From Archaic Greece to the Roman Empire*, ed. Simon Hornblower and Catherine Morgan (Oxford: Oxford University Press, 2007)

Drury, John, *Music at Midnight: The Life and Poetry of George Herbert* (London: Penguin Books, 2014)

Duggan, Christopher, *Fascist Voices: An Intimate History of Mussolini's Italy* (Oxford: Oxford University Press, 2013)

Duncan-Jones, Katherine (ed.), *Shakespeare's Sonnets* (London: Thomas Nelson and Sons, 1997)

Dylan, Bob, 'It's Alright, Ma (I'm Only Bleeding)', track 10 on *Bringing It All Back Home* (CBS, 1965)

Edwards, John Hamilton, and Vasse, William W., *Annotated Index to The Cantos of Ezra Pound* (Berkeley and Los Angeles: University of California Press, 1975)

Eliot, T. S., 'Literature, Science and Dogma', *The Dial*, no. 82 (March 1927)

Eliot, T. S., *After Strange Gods* (London: Faber & Faber, 1934)

Eliot, T. S., *The Idea of a Christian Society* (London: Faber & Faber, 1939)

Eliot, T. S., *Selected Essays*, 3rd edn. (London: Faber & Faber, 1951)

Eliot, T. S., Preface to *John Davidson: A Selection of his Poems*, ed. Maurice Linday (London: Hutchinson, 1961)

Eliot, T. S., *The Waste Land: A Facsimile & Transcript of the Original Drafts Including the Annotations of Ezra Pound*, ed. Valerie Eliot (London: Faber & Faber, 1971)

Eliot, T. S., *Selected Prose,* ed. Frank Kermode (London: Faber & Faber, 1975)

Eliot, T. S., *The Letters,* vol. 1, *1898–1922,* ed. Valerie Eliot (London: Faber & Faber, 1988)

Eliot, T. S., *The Poems,* 2 vols, ed. Christopher Ricks and Jim McCue (London: Faber & Faber, 2015)

Empson, William, *The Structure of Complex Words* (1951; London: Penguin Books, 1995 edn.)

Empson, William, *Using Biography* (London: Chatto & Windus, 1984)

Empson, William, *Argufying: Essays on Literature and Culture,* ed. John Haffenden (London: Chatto & Windus, 1987)

Empson, William, *The Complete Poems,* ed. John Haffenden (London: Allen Lane, 2000)

Erskine-Hill, Howard, *The Social Milieu of Alexander Pope: Lives, Example and the Poetic Response* (New Haven and London: Yale University Press, 1975)

Faber, Toby, *Faber & Faber: The Untold Story* (London: Faber & Faber, 2019)

Ferguson, Margaret, et al. (eds.), *The Norton Anthology of Poetry*, 5th edn. (New York: Norton, 2005)

Filreis, Alan, *Wallace Stevens and the Actual World* (Princeton: Princeton University Press, 1991)

Finch, Anne, Countess of Winchilsea, *Selected Poems,* ed. Denys Thompson (New York: Routledge, 2003)

Finnel, Andrew J., 'The Poet as Sunday Man: "The Complaint of Chaucer to His Purse"', *The Chaucer Review* (Autumn 1973)

Fisher, Roy, No. 25 Workbook 11/xi/66–12/i/69

Fisher, Roy, *Matrix* (London: Fulcrum Press, 1971)

Fisher, Roy, *Interviews through Time,* ed. Tony Frazer (Bristol: Shearsman Books, 2013)

Ford, Mark (ed.), *London: A History in Verse* (Cambridge: Harvard University Press, 2012)

Freud, Sigmond, 'Dostoyevsky and Parricide', *Art and Literature*, Pelican Library, vol. 14, ed. A. Dickson, trans. James Strachey (Harmondsworth: Penguin Books, 1985)

Frost, Robert, *Collected Poems, Prose and Plays,* ed. Richard Poirier and Mark Richardson (New York: Library of Congress, 1995)

Galbraith, John Kenneth, *Money: Whence It Came, Where It Went,* rev. edn. (Boston: Haughton Mifflin, 1995)

Garber, Marjorie, *Patronizing the Arts* (Princeton: Princeton University Press, 2008)

Gaskell, Ivan, *Vermeer's Wager: Speculations on Art History, Theory and Art Museums* (London Reaktion Books, 2000)

Gay, John, *Poetry and Prose,* 2 vols., ed. Vinton A. Dearing and Charles E. Beckwith (Oxford: Oxford University Press, 1974)

Gill, Stephen, *William Wordsworth: A Life* (Oxford: Oxford University Press, 1989)

Gioia, Dana, *The Gods of Winter* (Calstock: Peterloo Poets, 1991)

Godley, A. D. (ed.), *The Poetical Works of Thomas Moore* (London: Oxford University Press, 1910)

Goldgar, Anne, *Tulipmania: Money, Honor, and Knowledge in the Dutch Golden Age* (Chicago: University of Chicago Press, 2007)

Googe, Barnabe, *Eclogues, Epitaphs, and Sonnets,* ed. Judith M. Kennedy (Toronto: University of Toronto Press, 1989)

Goux, Jean-Joseph, *Les monnayeurs du langage* (Paris: Éditions Galilée, 1984)

Graham, W. S., *New Collected Poems,* ed. Matthew Francis (London: Faber & Faber, 2004)

Graves, Robert, *The Complete Poems,* ed. Beryl Graves and Dunstan Ward (London: Penguin Books, 2003)

Heath-Stubbs, John, and Wright, David (eds.), *The Faber Book of Twentieth-Century Verse* (London: Faber & Faber, 1953)

Heinzelman, Kurt, *The Economics of the Imagination* (Amherst: University of Massachusetts Press, 1980)

Hill, Alan, *In Pursuit of Publishing* (London: John Murray, 1988)

Hill, Geoffrey, *For the Unfallen: Poems 1952–1958* (London: André Deutsch, 1959)

Hill, Geoffrey, *Collected Critical Writings,* ed. Kenneth Haynes (Oxford: Oxford University Press, 2008)

Hill, Geoffrey, *Broken Hierarchies: Poems 1952–2012,* ed. Kenneth Haynes (Oxford: Oxford University Press, 2013)

Hill, Geoffrey, *The Book of Baruch by the Gnostic Justin* (Oxford: Oxford University Press, 2019)

Holmes, Sarah C. (ed.), *The Correspondence of Ezra Pound and Senator William Borah* (Urbana and Chicago: University of Illinois Press, 2001)

Hood, Thomas, *The Complete Poetical Works,* ed. Walter Jerrold (London: Oxford University Press, 1911)

Hoppit, Julian, 'The Myths of the South Sea Bubble', *Transactions of the Royal Historical Society,* vol. 12 (2002)

Hume, David, *Essays: Moral, Political, and Literary,* ed. Eugene F. Miller (Indianapolis: Liberty Classics, 1985)

Hynes, Samuel (ed.), *The Complete Poetical Works of Thomas Hardy*, 5 vols. (Oxford: Oxford University Press, 1982–95)

Jackson, Kevin (ed.), *The Oxford Book of Money* (Oxford: Oxford University Press, 1995).

Jackson, Virginia, *Dickinson's Misery: A Theory of Lyric Reading* (Princeton and Oxford: Princeton University Press, 2005)

Jarrell, Randall, *The Complete Poems* (New York: Farrar, Straus & Giroux, 1969)

Jarvis, Simon, *Wordsworth's Philosophic Song* (Cambridge: Cambridge University Press, 2009)

Jarvis, Simon, 'Why Rhyme Pleases', in *Lyric Theory Reader: A Critical Anthology,* ed. Virginia Jackson and Yopie Prins (Baltimore: Johns Hopkins University Press, 2014)

Jenkins, Alan, *Paper-Money Lyrics* (London: Grey Suit Editions, 2014)

Johnson, Samuel, *Diaries, Prayers, and Annals,* ed. E. L. McAdam, Jr. with Donald and Mary Hyde (New Haven: Yale University Press, 1958)

Johnson, Samuel, *Poems,* ed. E. L. McAdam, Jr. with George Milne (New Haven: Yale University Press, 1964)

Johnson, Samuel, *The Complete English Poems,* ed. J. D. Fleeman (Harmondsworth: Penguin Books, 1971)

Johnson, Samuel, *Rasselas and Other Tales,* ed. Gwin J. Kolb (New Haven: Yale University Press, 1990)

Johnson, Samuel, *Letters,* 5 vols., ed. Bruce Redford (Oxford: Oxford University Press, 1994)

Johnson, Samuel, *A Commentary on Mr. Pope's Principles of Morality, Or Essay on Man,* ed. O. M. Brack, Jr. (New Haven: Yale University Press, 2004)

Johnson, Samuel, *The Lives of the Poets,* 3 vols., ed. John H. Middendorf (New Haven: Yale University Press, 2010)

Jones, Fredrick L. (ed.), *The Letters of Percy Bysshe Shelley,* 2 vols. (Oxford: Oxford University Press, 1964)

Jonson, Ben, *The Complete Poems,* ed. George Parfitt (London: Penguin Books, 1996)

Joyce, James, *Dubliners,* ed. Terence Brown (London: Penguin Books, 1992)

Julius, Anthony, *T. S. Eliot, Anti-Semitism and Literary Form* (Cambridge: Cambridge University Press, 1995)

Karlin, Daniel, *The Courtship of Robert Browning and Elizabeth Barrett* (Oxford: Oxford University Press, 1985)

Keats, John, *The Complete Poems,* ed. John Barnard, 3rd edn. (London: Penguin Books, 1988)

Kerrigan, John, and Robinson, Peter (eds.), *The Thing about Roy Fisher: Critical Studies* (Liverpool: Liverpool University Press, 2000)

Kersnowski, Frank L. (ed.), *Conversations with Robert Graves* (Jackson: University of Mississippi Press, 1989)

Keynes, John Maynard, *The Economic Consequences of the Peace* in *The Collected Writings of John Maynard Keynes,* vol. 2 (London and Basingstoke: Macmillan, 1971)

Keynes, John Maynard, 'Mr Lloyd George: A Fragment', *Essays in Biography* in *The Collected Writings of John Maynard Keynes,* vol. 10 (London and Basingstoke: Macmillan, 1972)

Keynes, John Maynard, *The Collected Writings of John Maynard Keynes,* vol. 19, *Activities 1922–1929: The Return to Gold and Industrial Policy,* 2 vols., ed. Donald Moggridge (London: Macmillan, 1981)

Kintner, Elvan (ed.), *Letters of Robert Browning and Elizabeth Barrett Barrett 1845–1846,* 2 vols. (Cambridge, MA: Harvard University Press, 1969)

Lakoff, George, and Johnson, Mark, *Metaphors We Live By* (Chicago and London: University of Chicago Press, 1980; rev. edn. 2003)

Lamarque, Peter, *Work and Object: Explorations in the Metaphysics of Art* (Oxford: Oxford University Press, 2010)

Larkin, Philip, *Required Writing: Miscellaneous Pieces 1955–1982* (London: Faber & Faber, 1983)

Larkin, Philip, *The Complete Poems,* ed. Archie Burnett (New York: Farrar, Straus & Giroux, 2012)

Lawrence, D. H., *Phoenix II: Uncollected, Unpublished and Other Prose Words,* ed. Warren Roberts and Harry T. Moore (London: Heinemann, 1968)

Lawrence, D. H., *The Complete Poems,* ed. Vivian de Sola Pinto and Warren Roberts (Harmondsworth: Penguin Books, 1980)

Leader, Zachary, and O'Neill, Michael (eds.), *Percy Bysshe Shelley: The Major Works* (Oxford: Oxford University Press, 2003)

Le Gallienne, Richard, *The Romantic '90s* (London and New York: G. P. Putnam's Sons, 1926)

Lerner, Ben, *The Hatred of Poetry* (London: Fitzcarraldo Editions, 2016)

Lonsdale, Roger (ed.), *Eighteenth-Century Women Poets: An Oxford Anthology* (Oxford: Oxford University Press, 1989)

Loy, Mina, *The Lost Lunar Baedeker: Poems,* ed. Roger L. Conover (New York: Farrar, Straus & Giroux, 1996)

MacCarthy, Fiona, *Byron: Life and Legend* (London: John Murray, 2002)

Mack, Maynard, *Alexander Pope: A Biography* (New Haven: Yale University Press, 1985)

MacNeice, Louis, *The Poetry of W. B. Yeats* (London: Faber & Faber, 1941; 1967 reprint)

MacNeice, Louis, *Varieties of Parable* (Cambridge: Cambridge University Press, 1965)

MacNeice, Louis, *Collected Poems,* ed. Peter McDonald (London: Faber & Faber, 2007)

Makin, Peter, *Pound's Cantos* (London: George Allen & Unwin, 1985)

Manning, Olivia, 'Poets in Exile', *Horizon,* no. 10 (October 1944)

Marchand, Leslie A. (ed.), *'So late into the night': Byron's Letters and Journals,* vol. 5, 1816–17 (London: John Murray, 1976)

Marsh, Nicky, *Money, Speculation and Finance in Contemporary British Fiction* (London: Continuum, 2007)

Marsh, Nicky, 'The Cosmopolitan Coin: What Modernists Make of Money', *Modernism / Modernity,* vol. 24, no. 3 (September 2017)

Matthews, Geoffrey, and Everest, Kelvin (eds.), *The Poems of Shelley 1804–1817,* vol. 1 (London and New York: Longman, 1989)

Matthews, Steven, 'Geoffrey Hill's Complex Affinities with American Agrarian Poetry', *Cambridge Quarterly,* vol. 44, no. 4 (2015)

Matthews, William, *Time & Money* (Boston: Houghton Mifflin, 1995)

Mauss, Marcel, *The Gift: Forms and Functions of Exchange in Archaic Societies,* ed. Ian Cunnison (London: Cohen & West, 1969)

May, Will (ed.), *Reading F. T. Prince* (Liverpool: Liverpool University Press, 2017)

McDairmid, Lucy, *Auden's Apologies for Poetry* (Princeton: Princeton University Press, 1990)

McGann, Jerome (ed.), *The Complete Poetical Works of Lord Byron,* vol. 5 (Oxford: Oxford University Press, 1986)

Melchiori, Barbara, *Browning's Poetry of Reticence* (Edinburgh and London: Oliver & Boyd, 1968)

Mendelson, Edward, *Early Auden* (London: Faber & Faber, 1981)

Merrill, Linda, *A Pot of Paint: Aesthetics on Trial in Whistler v Ruskin* (Washington and London: Smithsonian Institute Press, 1992)

Miller, Christanne (ed.), *Emily Dickinson's Poems: As She Preserved Them* (Cambridge MA and London: Harvard University Press, 2016)

Moody, A. David, *Ezra Pound: Poet. A Portrait of the Man & his Work,* vol. 1: *The Young Genius 1885–1920* (Oxford: Oxford University Press, 2007)

Moody, A. David, *Ezra Pound: Poet. A Portrait of the Man and His Work,* vol. 2: *The Epic Years 1921–1939* (Oxford: Oxford University Press, 2014)

Moore, Doris Langley, *Lord Byron: Accounts Rendered* (London: John Murray, 1974)

Moore, Marianne, *New Collected Poems,* ed. Heather Cass White (New York: Farrar, Straus & Giroux, 2017)

Mordini, Maura, 'Pound e l'Archivio di Stato di Siena: Note sulle storia del Monte dei Paschi', in Ezra Pound, *The Fifth Decad of Cantos: Siena, The Leopoldine Reforms* (Rimini: Raffaelli Editore, 2006)

Morgan, Peter F. (ed.), *The Letters of Thomas Hood* (Edinburgh: Oliver and Boyd, 1973)

Mulhauser, F. L. (ed.), *The Correspondence of Arthur Hugh Clough,* 2 vols. (Oxford: Oxford University Press, 1957)

Mulhauser, F. L. (ed.), *The Poems of Arthur Hugh Clough,* 2nd edn. (Oxford: Oxford University Press, 1974)

Nemerov, Howard, *The Collected Poems* (Chicago: University of Chicago Press, 1977)

Nicholls, Peter, *Ezra Pound: Politics, Economics, and Writing – A Study of* The Cantos (London and Basingstoke: Macmillan, 1984)

Nicholls, Peter, '"2 doits to a boodle": Reckoning with *Thrones*', *Textual Practice,* vol. 18, no. 2 (2004)

Nicholson, Colin, *Writing and the Rise of Finance: Capital Satires of the Early Eighteenth Century* (Cambridge: Cambridge University Press, 1994)

Nietzsche, Friedrich, *On the Genealogy of Morals: A Polemic,* trans. Douglas Smith (Oxford: Oxford University Press, 1996)

Nokes, David, *Jonathan Swift, a Hypocrite Reversed: A Critical Biography* (Oxford: Oxford University Press, 1985)

O'Gorman, Francis (ed.), *Victorian Literature and Finance* (Oxford: Oxford University Press, 2007)

O'Hara, Frank, *The Collected Poems,* ed. Donald Allen (Berkeley and Los Angeles: University of California Press, 1995)

Orwell, George, *Keep the Aspidistra Flying: The Complete Works,* vol. 4, ed. Peter Davison (London: Secker & Warburg, 1987)

Parks, Tim, 'Does Copyright Matter?', *The New York Review of Books*' NYRDaily: http://www.nybooks.com/daily/2012/08/14/does-copyright-matter/

Paulin, Tom, *Crusoe's Secret: The Aesthetics of Dissent* (London: Faber & Faber, 2005)

Peacock, Thomas Love, *Paper Money Lyrics and Other Poems* (London: C. and W. Reynell, 1837)

Pearson, Roger, *Unacknowledged Legislators: The Poet as Lawgiver in Post-Revolutionary France* (Oxford: Oxford University Press, 2016)

Poovey, Mary, *Genres of the Credit Economy: Mediating Value in Eighteenth-Century and Nineteenth-Century Britain* (Chicago: Chicago University Press, 2008)

Pope, Alexander, *Imitations of Horace with An Epistle to Dr Arbuthnot and The Epilogue to the Satires,* ed. John Butt, Twickenham Edition, vol. 4 (London: Methuen, 1939)

Pope, Alexander, *Epistles to Several Persons (Moral Essays),* ed. F. W. Bateson, Twickenham Edition, vol. 3, 2nd vol. (London: Methuen, 1951)

Potter, George R., and Simpson, Evelyn (eds.), *The Sermons of John Donne,* 10 vols. (Berkeley and Los Angeles: University of California Press, 1953–62)

Pound, Ezra, *ABC of Reading* (London: Faber & Faber, 1951)

Pound, Ezra, *Literary Essays,* ed. T. S. Eliot (London: Faber & Faber, 1954)

Pound, Ezra, *Guide to Kultur* (1938; New York: New Directions, 1970)

Pound, Ezra, *Selected Prose 1909–1965,* ed. William Cookson (London: Faber & Faber, 1973)

Pound, Ezra, *Collected Early Poems* (London: Faber & Faber, 1977)

Pound, Ezra, *'Ezra Pound Speaking': Radio Speeches of World War II,* ed. Leonard W. Doob (Westport, CT: Greenwood Press, 1978)

Pound, Ezra, *Collected Shorter Poems* (London: Faber & Faber, 1984)

Pound, Ezra, *The Cantos,* 4th collected edn. (London: Faber & Faber, 1987)

Pound, Ezra, *The Pisan Cantos,* ed. Richard Sieburth (New York: New Directions, 2003)

Pound, Ezra, *Early Writings: Poems and Prose,* ed. Ira B. Nadel (New York: Penguin Books, 2005)

Prince, F. T., *Collected Poems 1935–1992* (Manchester: Carcanet Press, 1993)

Prynne, J. H., *Brass* (Lewes: Ferry Press, 1971)

Prynne, J. H., *George Herbert, 'Love (III)': A Discursive Commentary* (Cambridge: privately printed, 2011)

Prynne, J. H., *Poems* (Hexham: Bloodaxe Books, 2015)

Prynne, J. H., *The White Stones* (New York: New York Review Books, 2016)

Pyman, Avril, *The Life of Alexandr Blok,* 2 vols.: *The Distant Thunder 1880–1908* and *The Release of Harmony 1908–1921* (Oxford: Oxford University Press, 1979 and 1980)

Raine, Kathleen, *The Pythoness and Other Poems* (London: Hamish Hamilton, 1949)

Rainey, Lawrence, *Institutions of Modernism: Literary Elites and Public Culture* (New Haven: Yale University Press, 1998)

Rainey, Lawrence, *Revisiting* The Waste Land (New Haven: Yale University Press, 2004)

Rasmussen, Dennis C., *The Infidel and the Professor: David Hume, Adam Smith, and the Friendship that Shaped Modern Thought* (Princeton: Princeton University Press, 2017)

Rawlinson, Matthew, *Real Money and Romanticism* (Cambridge: Cambridge University Press, 2010)

Reynolds, Myra (ed.), *The Poems of Anne Countess of Winchilsea* (Chicago: University of Chicago Press, 1903)

Richards, I. A., *Science and Poetry* (London: Kegan Paul, 1926)

Ricks, Christopher, review of *Preghiere, The New Statesman,* vol. 68, no. 1741 (24 July 1964)

Ricks, Christopher, *Tennyson* (London: Macmillan, 1972)

Ricks, Christopher, *Force of Poetry* (Oxford: Oxford University Press, 1984)

Ricks, Christopher (ed.), *The Poems of Tennyson*, 3 vols. (London: Longmans, 1987)

Ricks, Christopher, *T. S. Eliot and Prejudice* (London: Faber & Faber, 1988)

Ricks, Christopher, *Essays in Appreciation* (Oxford: Oxford University Press, 1996)

Robinson, Peter, 'Ezra Pound and Italian Art', *Pound's Artists: Ezra Pound and the Visual Arts in London, Paris and Italy*, ed. Richard Humphries (London: Tate Gallery, 1985)

Robinson, Peter, *In the Circumstances: About Poetry and Poets* (Oxford: Oxford University Press, 1992)

Robinson, Peter, *Poetry, Poets, Readers: Making Things Happen* (Oxford: Oxford University Press, 2002)

Robinson, Peter, *Twentieth Century Poetry: Selves and Situations* (Oxford University Press, 2005)

Robinson, Peter, 'Wittgenstein's Aesthetics and Revision', in *Inspiration and Technique: Ancient and Modern Views on Beauty and Art*, ed. John Roe and Michele Stanco (Oxford: Peter Lang, 2007)

Robinson, Peter, *Poetry & Translation: The Art of the Impossible* (Liverpool: Liverpool University Press, 2010)

Robinson, Peter, '"Written at least as well as prose": Ford, Pound and Poetry', in *Ford Madox Ford: Modernist Magazines and Editing*, ed. Jason Harding (Amsterdam and New York: Rodopi, 2010)

Robinson, Peter (ed.), *The Oxford Handbook of Contemporary British & Irish Poetry* (Oxford: Oxford University Press, 2013)

Robinson, Peter, 'The Poetry of Modern Life', in *The Oxford Handbook of Victorian Poetry*, ed. Matthew Bevis (Oxford: Oxford University Press, 2013)

Robinson, Peter, 'Truth in Style', in *Reading F. T. Prince*, ed. Will May (Liverpool: Liverpool University Press, 2017)

Robinson, Peter, *The Sound Sense of Poetry* (Cambridge and New York: Cambridge University Press, 2018)

Robinson, Peter, 'The Edge of Satire: Post-Mortem and Other Effects', in *The Oxford Handbook of Eighteenth-Century Satire*, ed. Paddy Bullard (Oxford: Oxford University Press, 2019)

Robinson, Peter, '"I like the Spanish title": William Carlos Williams's *Al Que Quiere!*', in *Modernism and Non-Translation*, ed. Jason Harding and John Nash (Oxford: Oxford University Press, 2019)

Robinson, Peter, '"On the Power of Sound": The *"Moral* Music" of Wordsworth at Work in Later Life', in *Poetry in the Making*, ed. Daniel Tyler (Oxford: Oxford University Press, 2020)

Rogers, Pat, 'South Sea Bubble Myths', *The Times Literary Supplement*, 9 April 2014

Rogers, Samuel, *Table-Talk & Recollections*, ed. Christopher Ricks (London: Notting Hill Editions, 2011)

Rollins, Hyder Edward (ed.), *The Letters of John Keats 1814–1821*, 2 vols. (Cambridge: Harvard University Press, 1958)

Rowlinson, Matthew, *Real Money and Romanticism* (Cambridge: Cambridge University Press, 2010

Rumrich, John P., and Chaplin, Gregory (ed.), *Seventeenth-Century British Poetry 1603–1660* (New York and London: Norton, 2006)

Ruskin, John, *The Library Edition of the Works*, 39 vols., ed. E. T. Cook and Alexander Wedderburn (London: George Allen, 1903–12)

Rylance, Rick, *Literature and the Public Good* (Oxford: Oxford University Press, 2016)

St Clair, William, *The Reading Nation in the Romantic Period* (Cambridge: Cambridge University Press, 2004)

St John, John, *William Heinemann: A Century of Publishing 1890–1990* (London: Heinemann, 1990)

Scattergood, John, 'London and Money: Chaucer's *Complaint to his Purse*', in *Chaucer and the City*, ed. Ardis Butterfield (Woodbridge and Rochester, NY: D. S. Brewer, 2006)

Searle, John, *The Construction of Social Reality* (New York: Free Press, 1995)

Seidel, Frederick, *Widening Income Inequality* (New York: Farrar, Straus & Giroux, 2016)

Share, Don (ed.), *The Poem of Basil Bunting* (London: Faber & Faber, 2016)

Shell, Marc, *The Economy of Literature* (Baltimore: Johns Hopkins University Press, 1978)

Sidney, Philip, *A Defence of Poetry*, ed. J. A. Van Dorsten (Oxford: Oxford University Press, 1966)

Sieburth, Richard, 'In Pound We Trust: The Economy of Poetry/The Poetry of Economics', *Critical Inquiry*. vol. 14, no. 1 (Autumn 1987)

Simmel, Georg, *The Philosophy of Money*, trans. Tom Bottomore and David Frisby from a first draft by Kathe Mengelberg (London: Routledge, 2004)

Simic, Charles, 'Poets and Money', *The New York Review of Books*' NYRDaily: http://www.nybooks.com/daily/2012/08/21/poets-and-money/

Sisson, C. H., *In the Trojan Ditch: Collected Poems and Selected Translations* (Cheadle: Carcanet Press, 1974)

Sloan, John, *John Davidson, First of the Moderns: A Literary Biography* (Oxford: Oxford University Press, 1995)

Small, Helen, *The Value of the Humanities* (Oxford: Oxford University Press, 2013)

Smith, Adam, *The Wealth of Nations,* ed. Edwin Cannan (New York: Modern Library, 2000)

Smith, Nigel (ed.), *The Poems of Andrew Marvell* (London: Longmans, 2007)

Spencer, Bernard, *Complete Poetry, Translations and Selected Prose,* ed. Peter Robinson (Tarset: Bloodaxe Books, 2011)

Spenser, Edmund, *The Faerie Queene,* ed. Thomas P. Roche, Jr. and C. Patrick O'Donnell, Jr. (Harmondsworth: Penguin Books, 1978)

Sperling, Matthew, *Visionary Philology: Geoffrey Hill and the Study of Words* (Oxford: Oxford University Press, 2014)

Stevens, Wallace, *Collected Poetry and Prose,* ed. Frank Kermode and Joan Richardson (New York: Library of America, 1997)

Stokes, Adrian, *A Game that Must be Lost: Collected Papers* (Cheadle: Carcanet Press, 1973)

Stokes, Adrian, *The Critical Writings*, 3 vols. (London: Thames & Hudson, 1978)

Stokes, Adrian, *With All the Views: The Collected Poems,* ed. Peter Robinson (Manchester: Carcanet Press, 1981)

Surette, Leon, *Pound in Purgatory: From Economic Radicalism to Anti-Semitism* (Urbana and Chicago: University of Illinois Press, 2001)

Sutherland, Daniel E., *Whistler: A Life for Art's Sake* (New Haven and London: Yale University Press, 2014)

Swaab, Peter, 'Wordsworth's Elegies for John Wordsworth', *Wordsworth Circle,* vol. 45, no. 1 (Winter 2014)

Swift, Jonathan, *Poetical Works,* ed. Herbert Davies (Oxford: Oxford University Press, 1967)

Symons, Arthur, *The Romantic Movement in English Poetry* (New York: E. P. Dutton, 1909)

Thompson, Michael, *Rubbish Theory: The Creation and Destruction of Value* (Oxford: Oxford University Press, 1979)

Thornton, R. K. R. (ed.), *Poetry of the 'Nineties* (Harmondsworth: Penguin Books, 1970)

Thwaite, Anthony (ed.), *The Selected Letters of Philip Larkin 1950–1985* (London: Faber & Faber, 1992)

Tomlinson, Charles, *The Way In* (Oxford: Oxford University Press, 1974)

Trotter, David, *The Poetry of Abraham Cowley* (London and Basingstoke: Macmillan, 1979)

Turnbull, Andrew (ed.), *The Poems of John Davidson*, 2 vols. (Edinburgh and London: Scottish Academic Press, 1973)

Valéry, Paul, *The Art of Poetry,* trans. Denis Folliot (Princeton: Princeton University Press, 1958)

Verlaine, Paul, *Oeuvres poétiques,* ed. Jacques Robichez (Paris: Garnier, 1969)

Vernon, John, *Money and Fiction: Literary Realism in the Nineteenth and Early Twentieth Centuries* (Ithaca and London: Cornell University Press, 1984)

Walker, Keith (ed.), *The Oxford Authors John Dryden* (Oxford: Oxford University Press, 1987)

Walkiewicz, E. P., and Witemeyer, Hugh (eds.), *Ezra Pound and Senator Bronson Cutting: A Political Correspondence 1930–1935* (Albuquerque: University of New Mexico Press, 1995)

Weinbrot, Howard D., 'Johnson's Poetry', in *The Cambridge Companion to Samuel Johnson,* ed. Greg Clingham (Cambridge: Cambridge University Press, 1997)

Wilcox, Helen (ed.), *The English Poems of George Herbert* (Cambridge: Cambridge University Press, 2007)

Wilkinson, John, *Useful Reforms* (Richmond, Surrey, Arnica Press, 1975)

Williams, Bernard, *Truth and Truthfulness: An Essay in Genealogy* (Princeton: Princeton University Press, 2002)

Wittgenstein, Ludwig, *Zettel*, 2nd edn., ed. G. E. M. Anscombe and G. H. von Wright, trans. G. E. M. Anscombe (Oxford: Blackwell, 1981)

Wittgenstein, Ludwig, *Philosophical Investigations*, 3rd edn., trans. G. E. M. Anscombe (Oxford: Blackwell, 2001)

Wollheim, Richard, *Art and Its Objects*, 2nd edn. (Cambridge: Cambridge University Press, 1980)

Woodbridge, Linda (ed.), *Money and the Age of Shakespeare: Essays in the New Economic Criticism* (New York and Basingstoke: Palgrave Macmillan, 2003)

Wordsworth, William, *Poems, in Two Volumes, and Other Poems, 1800–1807*, ed. Jared Curtis (Ithaca: Cornell University Press, 1983)

Wordsworth, William, *Shorter Poems, 1807–1820*, ed. Carl H. Ketcham (Ithaca: Cornell University Press, 1989)

Wordsworth, William, *Lyrical Ballads, and Other Poems, 1797–1800*, ed. James Butler and Karen Green (Ithaca: Cornell University Press, 1992)

Index